My Life in Full

Indra K. Nooyi served as CEO and chairman of PepsiCo from 2006 to 2019. Her prescient strategic thinking, insight into consumer behavior, and wisdom in managing a vast, global workforce make her one of the world's most sought-after advisors to entrepreneurs, executives, and governments. She is also revered as a role model for women and immigrants, and celebrated for her empowering messages on inclusivity. She is also the first female independent director of the International Cricket Council. Nooyi has been awarded the Padma Bhushan, India's third-highest civilian honor, and the Outstanding American by Choice by the U.S. Department of Homeland Security, and has received 15 honorary degrees, including an honorary doctorate of humane letters from Yale University in 2019. She is married to Raj Nooyi and has two daughters, Preetha and Tara.

My Life in Full

Work, Family, and Our Future

INDRA K. NOOYI

hachette
INDIA

First published in India in hardcover in 2021 by Hachette India
Registered name: Hachette Book Publishing India Pvt. Ltd
An Hachette UK Company
www.hachetteindia.com

This edition published in 2023

1

Hardback edition ISBN 978-93-89253-81-8
Paperback edition ISBN 978-93-89253-83-2
Ebook edition ISBN 978-93-89253-82-5

Book design by Jessica Shatan Heslin/Studio Shatan, Inc.

For sale in the Indian Subcontinent only

Hachette Book Publishing India Pvt. Ltd
4th/5th Floors, Corporate Centre,
Plot No. 94, Sector 44, Gurugram 122003, India

Typeset in Bembo Std 11/15.5
by InoSoft Systems, Noida

Printed and bound in India by
Manipal Technologies Limited

FSC www.fsc.org
MIX
Paper from
responsible sources
FSC™ C043100

For my husband, Raj,

My children, Preetha and Tara,

My parents,

My thatha

CONTENTS

INTRODUCTION

One foggy Tuesday in November 2009, after hours of meetings in Washington, DC, with two dozen top US and Indian business executives, I found myself standing between the president of the United States and the prime minister of India.

Barack Obama and Manmohan Singh had entered the room for an update on our group's progress, and President Obama began introducing the American team to his Indian counterpart. When he got to me—Indra Nooyi, CEO of PepsiCo—Prime Minister Singh exclaimed, "Oh! But she is one of us!"

And the president, with a big smile and without missing a beat, responded, "Ah, but she is one of us, too!"

It's a moment I never forget—spontaneous kindness from the leaders of the two great countries that have given me so much. I am still the girl who grew up in a close family in Madras, in the South of India, and I am deeply connected to the lessons and culture of my youth. I am also the woman who arrived in the US at age twenty-three to study and work and, somehow, rose to lead an iconic company, a journey that I believe is possible only in America. I belong in both worlds.

Looking back, I see how my life is full of this kind of duality—competing forces that have pushed and pulled me from

one chapter to another. And I see how this is true of everyone. We are all balancing, juggling, compromising, doing our best to find our place, move ahead, and manage our relationships and responsibilities. It's not easy in a society that changes very fast yet sticks to some age-old habits and rules of behavior that feel out of our control.

The twin demands that define me have always been my family and my work. I joined PepsiCo, in 1994, in part because the company's headquarters were close to my house. I had two daughters, ages ten and one-and-a-half at the time, and a husband whose office was nearby. PepsiCo's job offer made sense, we thought, because the commute was short. I'd be able to drive to the school or home to the baby in fifteen minutes. Of course, this is not the only reason I chose PepsiCo, an exuberant, optimistic company that I wholeheartedly enjoyed from the moment I walked in. I also felt that Pepsi-Co was a place that was open to changing with the times.

That was important. I was female, an immigrant, and a person of color entering an executive floor where I was different from everyone else. My career had started when the dynamics between women and men at work were not the same as they are now. In fourteen years as a consultant and corporate strategist, I had never had a woman boss. I had no female mentors. I wasn't upset when I was excluded from the customs of male power; I was just happy to be included at all. But by the time I got to PepsiCo, waves of educated, ambitious women were pouring into the workforce, and I could sense the atmosphere changing. The competition between men and women was becoming more acute, and, in the subsequent decades, women have altered the game in ways that would have been unthinkable to me early

on. As a business leader, I always tried to anticipate and respond to the shifting culture. As a woman and the mother of girls, I wanted to do everything possible to encourage it.

As my career progressed, and my children grew up, I wrestled with the ever-present conflicts of working motherhood. For fifteen years, I kept a whiteboard in my office that only my daughters could write on or erase. Over time, that board was a comforting kaleidoscope of doodles and messages, a constant reminder of the people closest to me. When I moved out of my office, I kept a canvas replica of its last iteration: "Hey Mom, I love you very, very much. XOXOXOX." "Hang in there. Never forget that you have people that love you!" "Have a great day!" "Hey Mom, you are the absolute best! Keep doing what you are doing!" the image exclaims, with cartoon characters and pictures of suns and clouds, all in green and blue dry-erase marker.

As a high-profile female CEO, I was asked over and over to discuss work and family conflicts in front of large audiences. I once commented that I wasn't sure my daughters thought I was a good mother—don't all moms feel that way sometimes?—and an Indian TV network produced a full-hour prime-time discussion program, without me, on what Indra Nooyi said about working women.

Over the years, I met thousands of people worried about how to be true to their families, their jobs, and their ambitions to be good citizens. This engagement had a great impact on me; I learned and absorbed the details at a visceral level. I thought about how family is such a powerful source of human strength but realized that creating and nurturing families is a source of stress for so many.

At the same time, I was among a vaunted group of global CEOs regularly invited into rooms with the most influential leaders on the planet. And I came to notice that the painful stories about how people—especially women—struggle to blend their lives and livelihoods were entirely absent in those rooms. The titans of industry, politics, and economics talked about advancing the world through finance, technology, and flying to Mars. Family—the actual messy, delightful, difficult, and treasured core of how most of us live—was fringe.

This disconnect has profound consequences. Our failure to address work and family pressures in the senior reaches of global decision-making restrains hundreds of millions of women every day, not only from rising and leading, but also from blending a satisfying career with a healthy partnership and motherhood. In a prosperous marketplace, we need all women to have the choice to work in paid jobs outside the home and for our social and economic infrastructure to entirely support that choice. Women's financial independence and security, so central to their equality, are at stake.

More broadly, ignoring the fact that the work world is still largely skewed toward the "ideal worker" of yore—an unencumbered male breadwinner—depletes us all. Men, too. Companies lose out because productivity, innovation, and profit suffer when so many employees feel they can't bring their whole selves to work. Families lose out because they spend so much energy coping with old systems, from short school hours to a lack of parental leave or elder care, that don't mesh with their reality.

And, of course, the entire global community suffers. Many young people, worried about how they will manage it all,

are choosing not to have children. This could not only have dire economic consequences in the decades to come, but, on a very personal note, I find this detail sad. With everything I have accomplished, my greatest joy was having children, and I wouldn't want anyone to miss the experience if they want it.

I believe that we must address the work and family conundrum by focusing on our infrastructure around "care" with an energy and ingenuity like never before. We should consider this a moonshot, starting with ensuring that every worker has access to paid leave, flexibility, and predictability to help them handle the ebb and flow of work and family life, and then moving fast to develop the most innovative and comprehensive childcare and eldercare solutions that our greatest minds can devise.

This mission will require leadership that we don't often see. I think the fundamental role of a leader is to look for ways to shape the decades ahead, not just react to the present, and to help others accept the discomfort of disruptions to the status quo. We need the wisdom of business leaders, policy makers, and all women and men passionate about easing the work and family burden to come together here. With a can-do sense of optimism and a must-do sense of responsibility, we can transform our society.

Transformation is difficult, but I have learned that with courage and persistence—and the inevitable give-and-take—it can happen. When I became PepsiCo's CEO, in 2006, I laid out an extremely ambitious plan to address the underlying tensions in a company still rooted in selling soda and chips. I knew we had to balance supporting our prized Pepsi-Cola and Doritos brands with a full-throttle effort to make and market more healthy products. We had to keep stocking stores and pantries

with convenient, delicious snacks and beverages but account for the environmental impact of that growth. We had to attract and retain the very best thinkers in their fields but ensure that PepsiCo was also a terrific place to work for a quarter of a million people. I called this mission Performance with Purpose, and, for a dozen years, I weighed every decision against these measures, making constant trade-offs to achieve a more sustainable, contemporary organization.

In the months before I left PepsiCo, in 2018, I thought about how I would contribute in the years ahead, knowing that I am one in a chain of woman leaders who can help move us forward for generations to come. I set out to write a book and insisted to all around me that it would not be a memoir. Instead, I thought, I would devote every ounce of my experience and intellect to a manual for fixing how we mix work and family.

The book you hold is not that book.

First, I soon found that the research on work and family has been done. From every angle, in every corner of the world, the arguments and ideas for supporting families—from maternity leave to early childhood education to multi-generational living—have been compiled, analyzed, scored, and debated by brilliant minds. I didn't need to repeat all that.

Second, everything I bring to this issue, I know now, comes from my own life in full.

Part I

Growing Up

1

The women's living room in my childhood home had a single piece of furniture—a huge rosewood swing with four long chains that were anchored into the ceiling when my grandfather built the house, on a leafy road in Madras, India, in 1939.

That swing, with its gentle glide back and forth in the South Indian heat, set the stage for a million stories. My mother, her sisters, and her cousins—wearing simple saris in fuchsia, blue, or yellow—rocked on it in the late afternoon with cups of sweet, milky coffee, their bare feet stretched to the floor to keep it moving. They planned meals, compared their children's grades, and pored over Indian horoscopes to find suitable matches for their daughters or the other young people in their extensive family networks. They discussed politics, food, local gossip, clothes, religion, music, and books. They were loud, talked over one another, and moved the conversation along.

From my earliest days, I played on the swing with my older sister, Chandrika, and my younger brother, Nandu. We swayed

and sang our school songs: "The Teddy Bears' Picnic," "The Woodpecker Song," "My Grandfather's Clock," or the Beatles, Cliff Richard, or Beach Boys tunes we'd heard on the radio: "Eight Days a Week," "Bachelor Boy," "Barbara Ann." We snoozed; we tussled. We read British children's novels by Enid Blyton, Richmal Crompton, and Frank Richards. We fell onto the shiny red-tiled floor and scrambled back on.

Ours was the big, airy house where a dozen cousins would gather for festivals and holidays. The swing was a set piece for elaborate plays we wrote and performed, based on anything that caught our fancy. Parents, grandparents, aunts, and uncles gathered to watch, holding bits of torn newspaper with the words *one ticket* scrawled on them. Our relatives felt free to critique our shows or to start chatting or simply walk away. My childhood was not a world of "Great job!" It was more like "That was so-so" or "Is this the best you can do?" We were accustomed to honesty, not false encouragement.

The reviews didn't matter on those busy, happy days. We felt important. We were in motion, laughing and carrying on to our next game. We played hide-and-seek, we climbed trees, and picked the mangoes and guavas that grew in the garden surrounding the house. We ate on the floor, sitting cross-legged in a circle, with our mothers in the center ladling sambar sadam and thayir sadam—lentil stew and curds mixed with rice—from clay tureens and dishing out Indian pickles onto banana leaves that served as plates.

In the evenings when the cousins were visiting, the swing was dismantled—the great, shiny-wood plank unhitched from the silver-colored chains and carried to the back porch to be stored overnight. Then we'd line up in the same space to sleep, boys and girls in a row on a large, colorful mat, each with our

own pillow and cotton sheet. Sometimes, we'd be under a mosquito net. If the power was on, a fan turned lazily overhead, pretending to break the heat when the overnight temperature was 85 degrees Fahrenheit (29.5 degrees Celsius). We'd sprinkle water on the floor around us, hoping its evaporation would cool the place.

Like many houses in India at the time, Lakshmi Nilayam, as our house was named, also had a men's living room—a vast hall with big square windows directly off the entry portico, where it was easy to keep an eye on who came and went.

My paternal grandfather, a retired district judge, had used all his savings to design and construct this grand, two-story residence, with its terrace and balconies. But he spent all his time in the men's living room, reading newspapers and books and lounging in a large easy chair with a canvas seat. He slept on a carved-wood divan with deep-blue upholstery.

He warmly welcomed visitors, who almost always dropped by unannounced. The men would gather on the room's two large sofas and talk about world affairs, local politics, or current issues. They had strong points of view about what government or companies should be doing to help citizens. They spoke in Tamil or in English, often alternating between the two. Children came and went—hanging out, reading, or working on homework. I never saw a woman sit in that room in front of my grandfather, whom I called Thatha. My mother was always in and out of the room, serving coffee and snacks to visitors or tidying up.

The *Oxford English Dictionary* and the *Cambridge Dictionary*, both bound in burgundy leather, lay on a wooden side table. Thatha once had my sister and me read *Nicholas Nickleby*, the almost one-thousand-page novel by Charles Dickens. Every few

chapters he'd take the book, point to a page, and ask, "What's the meaning of this word?" If I didn't know, he'd say, "But you said you'd read these pages." Then I'd have to look up the word and write two sentences to show I understood it.

I adored and revered Thatha, whose full name was A. Narayana Sarma. He was born in 1883 in Palghat, in the state of Kerala, which, under the British, was part of the Madras Presidency. He was already in his late seventies when I was a schoolgirl, a slight man of five feet seven or so with thick bifocal glasses, regal, very firm, and very kind. He dressed in a perfectly pressed white dhoti and a light-colored half-sleeve shirt. When he talked, no one else did. He had studied math and law and, for decades, had presided over both civil and criminal cases. His marriage was puzzling to me. My grandparents had eight kids, but when I knew my grandmother before she died, they never seemed to speak. They lived in different parts of the house. He was entirely dedicated to his young grandchildren, introducing us to ever more sophisticated books and ideas, explaining geometry theorems, and pressing for detail and clarity on our school efforts.

I was never in doubt that the head of the household—and of the family—resided in the men's living room.

But the heart and soul of our lively existence was down the hall, in the open space with the red-tiled floor and the gigantic rosewood swing. That's where my mother kept the household running, with the help of Shakuntala, a young woman who did the dishes at the outdoor sink and mopped the floors.

My mother was always in motion—cooking, cleaning, loudly barking out orders, feeding others, and singing along with the radio. The house was eerily quiet when she wasn't home. None of us liked that at all.

My father, an unusual man for the times, was around, too, assisting with the chores and helping care for the children. He had a master's degree in mathematics and worked in a bank. He shopped for essentials, helped make beds, and he loved to compliment my mother when she made his favorite foods. He often allowed me to tag along with him. He was a quiet man, filled with wisdom and a wicked sense of humor. I often refer to the Greek philosopher Epictetus's saying: "We have two ears and one mouth, so that we can listen twice as much as we speak." My father was a living example of this. He was adept at walking away from any tense situation without exacerbating it.

Every month, my father handed his paycheck to my mother, who handled the everyday expenses. She documented all the transactions on a paper "cash register" and balanced the accounts each week. It's a bookkeeping system that she set up intuitively, and it's still amazing to me that she developed it with no training at all in accounting.

Madras in the 1950s and '60s was a huge but fairly simple place for children like us. It was a city of roughly 1.5 million people, a sleepy, nerdy, safe town that came to life at 4 a.m., when morning prayer songs and bicycle bells began to fill the air. The lights went out promptly at 8 p.m., when everything—stores, restaurants, entertainment places—shut down. The young people went home to study. The day was over.

The British East India Company landed on this shore in 1639, and, more than three hundred years later, we lived in a mix of ancient Indian temples and nineteenth-century colonial offices, courthouses, schools, and churches. Broad tree-lined streets were full of buses, motorbikes, rickshaws, bikes, and a

few cars—little Fiats or Ambassadors. The air was fresh and clear. Once in a while, we went to Marina Beach, which stretches six miles along the Bay of Bengal. To the grown-ups, the ocean was menacing and unpredictable, best to be viewed from a distance. We were only allowed to sit on the sand or the grass and couldn't go anywhere near the water lest we be washed away.

Madras, which was renamed Chennai in 1996, is the capital of the southern Indian state of Tamil Nadu, with an economy anchored by textiles, automakers, and food processing, and—more recently—software services. It is a city filled with prestigious colleges and universities. It's also the seat of South Indian classical arts that connect the community—ancient Carnatic music and Bharatanatyam, an expressive, rhythmic storytelling dance form. Every December the city filled with visitors for a renowned arts festival. We listened to the concerts on the radio and enjoyed the insightful critiques of each performance by the many relatives who were in and out of our house for the month.

We were a Hindu Brahmin family living alongside other Hindus and people of different faiths—Christians, Jains, and Muslims. We lived within the rules of a close, devoted family in the culturally vibrant, multifaith society around us.

To be Brahmin in mid-twentieth-century India meant we belonged to a class of people who lived simply, were devout, and were supremely focused on education. We were not wealthy, although the large house that we owned, however sparsely furnished, meant we lived comfortably and had invaluable stability. We came from a tradition of families who lived in multigenerational homes. We had few clothes—fashion was not something we desired. We saved as much as possible. We never

ate out or took vacations and always had renters on our second floor for extra income. Despite our modest economic standing, we knew that we were fortunate to be born Brahmin. We had instant respect because we were perceived as learned.

My mother celebrated every Hindu festival with the appropriate rituals, but no one acknowledged birthdays. My parents never hugged us, kissed us, or said, "I love you." Love was assumed. We never shared fears or hopes and dreams with our elders. They just were not the kind to have those conversations. Any effort might be cut off with the words "Pray harder. God will help you find a way."

My mother's favorite expression—often repeated several times a day—was "Matha, Pitha, Guru, Deivam." It was translated by her to mean "Your mother, your father, and your teacher should be revered as God."

She would constantly remind us to respect all four. For example, we couldn't put our feet up in front of elders; we couldn't snack while studying, as a sign of respect for books; we always stood when a teacher entered the room and sat only when permission was granted.

At the same time, as children at home, we were always allowed to express our points of view, fully develop our ideas, and argue them out but had to be willing to accept the adults interrupting us constantly, not allowing us to finish, and often declaring, "What do you know about this topic? Just listen to us. You will be fine."

Our Madras household was always noisy, with plenty of laughing, arguing, and shouting. It was a strict environment, and I was spanked—something that was quite common then in most families—when I misbehaved. Our life was steady and pushed me to learn both self-discipline and how to speak up. I

got the courage to branch out and prove myself because I was raised within a framework that gradually gave me the freedom to explore. There was always home to anchor me.

My childhood home was defined by particularly progressive thinking when it came to educating women. I was a middle child, dark-skinned, tall, and skinny. I had loads of energy and loved to play sports, climb trees, and run around the house and garden, all in a society where girls were judged on their skin tone, beauty, calmness, and "homeliness." I overheard chitchat among relatives wondering how they would ever find someone to marry "this tomboy." That still stings. But I was never deprived, as a girl, of being able to learn more, study harder, or prove myself alongside the smartest kids in our midst.

In our home, boys and girls were allowed to be equally ambitious. That's not to say that the rules were just the same. There was certainly a sense that girls were to be protected differently than boys were. But intellectually and in terms of opportunities, I never felt held back by my sex.

This came from the top—from our family's interpretation of centuries-old Brahmin values, from India's midcentury mission to prosper as a newly independent nation, and from Thatha's worldview. I was lucky that my father, whom I called Appa, was completely on board. He was always there to take us to any lessons and walked around with a proud smile if we did something well.

He told me he never wanted me to have to put my hand out and ask for money from anyone other than my parents. "We are investing in your education to help you stand on your own two feet," he said. "The rest is up to you. Be your own person."

My mother's view was the same. She is a tough, driven woman who, like many daughters-in-law in those days, was blamed by the elders for family conflicts, even if she had nothing to do with them. She handled those issues deftly and with a firm hand. She would have made a great CEO. She didn't get the chance to attend college, and she directed that frustration into making sure her girls could soar. It wasn't easy for her. I have always felt that she lived her life vicariously through her daughters, wishing for us the freedoms she never had.

Family, I learned from the very beginning, is fundamental to our lives on this planet. It is both my foundation and the force that has propelled me. The family that I created in the US with my husband, Raj, and my two daughters, Preetha and Tara, is my proudest achievement. I belong to an Indian family of a particular era and am defined by this heritage, but I know that family comes in every form. We thrive, individually and collectively, when we have deep connections with our parents and children, and within larger groups, whether we are related or not. I believe that healthy families are the root of healthy societies.

I know family is messy, with painful issues that can't be reconciled. I had twenty-nine first cousins, fourteen from my mother's side, whom I was very close to, and fifteen from my father's side, many of whom I barely knew because of historical rifts I cannot begin to fathom. I think these situations are a microcosm of what the rest of life is like, and they teach us about the difficulties that we must navigate and accept.

I was born in October 1955, four years after my parents married and just thirteen months after my sister's birth. My mom, Shantha, was twenty-two. My dad, Krishnamurthy, was thirty-three.

Their match was arranged. Shortly after my mother finished high school, a couple, who were distant relatives, approached her parents and asked whether she might marry their son. He had noticed her playing tennikoit, a popular sport for girls where players toss a rubber ring back and forth across a net. He liked her spirit, they said. Horoscopes were consulted, the families met a few times, and the alliance was fixed. Among the benefits for my mother, the sixth of her parents' eight children, was that she'd join a respected, educated family and that she'd get the comfort and safety of the big house that she'd move into right after the wedding.

At their first meeting, my mother and father barely spoke. When I came along, they were contentedly creating a life together, with income from his steady job. My dad, one of eight children, was set to inherit the house. My grandfather planned to leave it to him, his second son, because he was confident that my parents would care for him in his old age. He felt that this daughter-in-law was family oriented and would dedicate herself to him as much as she did to her husband and to her children when they came along.

When I was about six, my sister, Chandrika, and I were assigned daily chores. The most relentless began near dawn, when, on many days, one of us climbed out of our shared bed at the first sound of a grunting, bawling water buffalo at the front door. A local woman would arrive with the big, gray

animal and milk her for the day's supply. Our job was to make sure she didn't bulk up the milk by adding water.

My mother, whom I call Amma, used that buffalo milk for the yogurt, the butter, and the delicious, aromatic South Indian coffee that were staples of our vegetarian diet. A vendor came a little later in the morning, selling fresh vegetables—cauliflower, spinach, squash, pumpkin, potatoes, onions. Great variety was available, for a price.

By the time I turned seven, I was often sent to the grocery store a few blocks away to drop off a list of items for home delivery or to pick up a few things. The clerk would wrap the lentils, rice, or pulses in a newspaper curled into a cone and tie it with twine at the top. Large orders would be delivered to the house in more newspaper cones. The grains were poured into glass or aluminum canisters in the kitchen, the paper folded, the twine made into a ball, and both left on the shelf to be used again. Nothing was discarded.

I think of Amma as busy all the time. She'd be dressed and in the kitchen when the milk was carried in and would soon deliver the first cups of coffee to Thatha and my father. Kids were given a cup of Bournvita, a chocolate malt drink. Then she'd make breakfast, usually oat porridge with milk, sugar, and cardamom powder. On very hot days, we drank kanji, cooked rice soaked overnight in water and then blended with buttermilk.

By 8 a.m., she'd be in the garden, working alongside Shanmugam, our gardener, tending flowers and pruning the bushes. She picked flowers to adorn the prayer room, a large alcove in the kitchen, where she said her daily prayers, often while she was cooking. She also listened to Carnatic music and

sang along. Amma always wore flowers in her hair, a string of white or colorful blooms around her dark bun or ponytail. Once in a while, on weekends, she tucked flowers into our pigtails.

Once my father and we kids had left home, she'd be back in the kitchen, preparing lunch for Thatha, Chandrika, and me. The stove was fueled with kerosene, and the fumes could be overpowering. Despite this, she always cooked us fresh meals that were packed into neat metal tiffin carriers and sent warm to school. Shakuntala would spoon out the food while we sat under a tree in the playground. Every morsel was consumed; if we didn't finish what was sent, we'd have to eat the leftovers at dinner, a situation we knew to avoid at all costs. Amma served Thatha his midday meal on a large silver platter with little bowls for the various vegetables and accompaniments.

In the afternoons, she'd take a rickshaw to her parents' house a mile away to check in, discuss family matters, and help her mother in the kitchen. Then she'd head back home to cook again. Day after day, each meal was uniquely prepared, eaten, and cleaned up, with no leftovers. We had no refrigerator.

Chandrika and I returned home from school at around 4:30 p.m. and were greeted by Thatha and Amma. We got an hour to snack and play until Appa came home at about 5:30 p.m. Then we sat on the floor at Thatha's feet to do our homework, even though we had our own desks. He checked our work regularly. If we struggled with math, he'd pull out papers on which he'd already composed practice problems. On many days, we also wrote out two pages in handwriting notebooks to work on cursive—usually the phrase "the quick brown fox jumps over the lazy dog" because it includes all twenty-six letters of the

alphabet. Thatha believed that "a good handwriting meant a good future."

At around 8 p.m., we ate dinner together, although Amma would serve us first and eat later. Then there would be more schoolwork, chores, and lights out. Often, there would be power cuts, and the house was plunged into darkness. We lit candles and lanterns. Mosquitoes buzzed around, loving the dark and feasting on all of us. Capturing mosquitoes with a clap of the hands was a required survival skill. Before we slept, we had to say our prayers loudly so my mother could hear them—the Lord's Prayer, which we also recited at school, and then a couple of Sanskrit prayers.

When I was eight, my mother gave birth to a little boy, Nandu, through a complicated cesarean section. He was the pride and joy of everyone—someone to carry on the family name. I absolutely adored him. As was the tradition in families like ours, Amma and the baby spent a couple of months at her parents' home, a period when my father did a lot of the chores and got Chandrika and me off to school. When she came home with Nandu, Amma was busier than ever, managing a new baby and all her previous activities, even though she was still recovering from major abdominal surgery. As far as I could tell, she never missed a beat. How she did it, I'll never know.

Chennai, which now has more than ten million people, has always been water starved. The region relies on the annual monsoon rains to fill lakes and reservoirs, some hundreds of miles away and connected to the city by pipes installed in the 1890s. Water is also trucked in from rural areas, and residents wait in line with large plastic urns to collect their share.

Water was constantly rationed in our home. The Madras Corporation, the local water authority, would open the city valves very early in the morning. Water would trickle in and my parents would fill all available pots and pans to carefully deploy it for cooking, drinking, and cleaning.

We also had a well in the yard. It was attached to an electric pump that carried salt water to a tank on the second-floor terrace to then flow back down to the toilets. We bathed by pouring lukewarm water over our bodies with a small steel cup, and I'd scrunch up into a little knot to get the maximum soaking. We'd wash our hair using a handful of water mixed with shikakai powder, the ground-up bark and leaves of a common climbing shrub. Early on, we brushed our teeth using our index finger and a charcoal powder made from burnt rice husks. Then we graduated to Colgate tooth powder. I got an actual toothbrush and toothpaste when I was about nine. I didn't go to the dentist to have my teeth cleaned until I was twenty-four.

Our life was predictable. Our primary job was to study and get good grades. But Chandrika and I had evening tasks, too—putting away the dishes, grinding peaberry coffee beans in a two-handed manual mill for the adults' warm drinks in the morning, or, the toughest of them all, churning the buttermilk in the old, manual way to separate the butter. It was tedious and chafed our palms.

I began at Our Lady's Nursery School in 1958, the start of twelve years on the campus of Holy Angels Convent, an all-girls Catholic institution about a mile from home. For a couple of years, Chandrika and I rode to school every morning with my father on his bicycle or his scooter, first as little girls in gray

pinafores with white blouses and then in green-and-white uniforms with round collars and striped belts.

Every May, Amma would buy fifty yards or so of material, hire a local tailor, and order six fresh uniforms for the school terms to come. I can hear her telling the tailor to sew everything two sizes bigger than our current size so that we could grow into it. He also made us a couple of "frocks" for casual events and pavadais—colorful Indian skirts—for everyday use. They were all quite unshapely, but we thought they were high fashion and treasured them. Everything was folded neatly on shelves in a half-empty bedroom cupboard. For festivals and weddings, we'd get very special silk pavadais. Those were kept in my mother's cupboard and used sparingly. Amma would spend most of the clothes budget on us and then buy herself something simple.

During the day, Shakuntala would wash the men's shirts and dhotis, my mother's saris, and our uniforms and hang them to dry. And at night, after homework, Chandrika and I polished our black leather shoes, washed our knee-high socks, and ironed the correct creases into our clothes with starch we made from rice flour stirred with water over the stove. Lumpy starch left white blobs on the fabric, and we became experts at mixing it just right to race through the process. When it rained, we ironed the hell out of those clothes to avoid having to wear anything wet in the morning. If the power went out, which happened pretty often, we wore slightly damp uniforms to school. We weren't alone. I think many other kids at school were in the same predicament.

We had very few toys. My sister and I treasured our only dolls and included them in our many conversations. We also played what we called "house" with mini pots and pans and

"doctor" with crude medical equipment that we crafted out of wire and paper.

From the start, Chandrika and I absolutely loved school. School let us enter the world outside our tight family structure, and our enthusiasm was entirely sanctioned and applauded by the grown-ups. The whole arrangement set us free. We loved it so much that, some summers, even with cousins around to play with, we posted a calendar on our bedroom wall to count down the days until school started again.

At home, every activity was closely monitored. If we wanted to see a movie, my parents would insist they had to see it first, and they never seemed to have time to see movies—so we almost never went. We could go to the local lending library, a one-room structure a few blocks away with unlimited borrowing for a very low fee, but the books had to be returned the next day. (This is how I learned to speed-read!) Amma played the radio all the time, but, like the rest of India, we didn't have TV. The internet, of course, didn't exist. We always had visitors, but, other than seeing my maternal grandparents, we never visited anyone. One of us always had to be home to care for my grandfather.

At school, there was always something more to try. Between classes, I literally ran from one activity to another through the long, shady outdoor corridors. Holy Angels, started by the Franciscan Missionaries of Mary in 1897, had expanded to six buildings, an auditorium, a garden, a courtyard, a netball court, and a little-used tennis court. I often stayed after classes to play ball or volunteer for the teachers.

Early on, I joined Bulbuls, the junior level of the national Girl Scout program. I wore a different uniform, a pale-blue dress with an orange-striped scarf held tight with a ring, and after a couple of years, I was very excited to "fly up" to Girl Guides. I toiled at earning badges for sewing, knots, first aid, fire building, flag semaphores, and a dozen more skills that the scouts espoused. In grade eleven, I even went to a national scouting jamboree. I learned so much from scouting. It taught me about teamwork—how to give and how to get—and about how people have different leadership roles at different times. I learned about trust, with the great example of, literally, pitching a tent. I remember how everyone had to hold the ropes at just the right tension to get the poles to stand up and support the canopy or the whole thing would flop over. Everyone had to do their part or it wouldn't work.

We learned music at school and our teacher, Ms. Lazarus, had the gift of helping everyone fall in love with many school songs from the United Kingdom. Chandrika and I had Indian classical music and classical dance lessons at home a few days a week, too—absolute necessities for girls like us. These were considered prerequisites to finding a good husband. Chandrika, even then, was a very gifted singer and a dedicated student. I always longed to just go out and play.

Academically, Holy Angels was no picnic. We sat in classes of about thirty girls lined up in close rows of wooden desks. School started at 8:30 a.m. every day with an assembly and ended at 4 p.m. The instruction was brisk and thorough in English, history, math, science, geography, and essential women's skills like needlework and art. We had an exam period every few weeks that ramped up the pressure.

The teachers, including nuns who'd ventured from Ireland

to India to spend their lives devoted to God and education, were warm and formidable. They were also inescapable: dressed in habits with wimples around their chins, Sister Nessan, the headmistress, and Sister Benedict, who led the nursery school, were always walking the corridors. They also regularly stopped by our house to sip coffee and chat with my grandfather or my parents.

On report-card day, the last day of every month, Thatha would move a chair outside into the portico to receive the document the moment we approached. If we were not ranked in the top three in the class, preferably first, he was not happy with himself. He took our education personally. Sometimes, he questioned the teacher's assessments, not usually in our favor.

Amma, deeply committed to our learning, added her own tests. She drilled us from a general knowledge textbook on the Seven Wonders of the World, the great rivers, and country flags. Chandrika and I would sit in the kitchen as she ate her supper after the men and children had finished and get ten minutes to compose speeches on topics like "If you were prime minister of India, what would you do?" Then she'd pick a winner. The prize was a little square of Cadbury chocolate from a big block she kept under lock and key, and, if I won, I'd lick it for a good half hour. I loved those squares more than all the chocolate I can buy today.

I was a debater in school and signed up for every chance to make my case in local competitions. I picked Elocution as an elective, a course focused on speeches, poems, and public speaking. I was naturally good at debating and was not shy to get on stage.

In eighth grade, when I was almost twelve, we had to choose to focus on either the humanities or science, the next step in our curriculum created by the University of Cambridge. I began years of more intensive classes in physics, chemistry, biology—the whole works. This meant my grandfather, who was steeped in English, math, history, and the classics, couldn't be as involved as he might have liked in my work. I was on my own.

Biology particularly appealed to me. We dissected cockroaches, frogs, and earthworms in school and had to bring in the specimens ourselves. I would look around for large cockroaches and deposit them in a glass jar with chloroform so they were fresh for dissection the next day. Earthworms were aplenty, but frogs were extremely hard to find outside of the monsoon season. The whole family would get involved in the search. Fortunately, Holy Angels eventually contracted with a specimen supplier to provide frogs, and we got a much-needed break from frog hunting.

Also in eighth grade, Mrs. Jobard, my homeroom teacher, selected me to join a school team going to New Delhi for the first-ever United Schools Organization of India conference, a four-day event intended to build connections among schoolchildren across the country. This was an opportunity of unspeakable excitement both at school and at home. I was the youngest student selected and excited by how my whole family fussed over the trip—and by how quickly they agreed to pay for it.

So Mrs. Jobard, a small woman of about forty-five with intense eyes, and five Holy Angels girls, dressed in our uniforms, boarded the steam-powered train from Madras's enormous redbrick central railway station. We carried neat little luggage

and traveled north for two days, 1,350 miles (2,170 kilometers). We slept two nights in a narrow cabin with three berths folded down from each wall.

Delhi, India's capital, was like nothing I had ever seen. I was totally enthralled by the majestic buildings surrounded by lawns and gardens; and by the monuments; the wide, car-filled roads; the people on the streets wearing turbans; and the street signs in Hindi, the predominant language of a large swath of northern India, which I didn't understand. Our little group joined teenagers from more than thirty schools in a conference hall in Vigyan Bhavan for debating competitions, cultural performances, and lectures on peace and politics. We did an Irish dance about "good and evil," which, as I recall, confused the judges. They gave us a prize anyway. We ate in a giant mess hall and slept in dormitories.

My confidence was really built up by being part of this big group—and my eyes opened wide to the variety of cultures within India.

At home, as I entered my teenage years, our world was changing. My father had become a lecturer in the bank's training school, and, for almost three years, he traveled a lot. He was only home for two or three days a month, and I missed him enormously. He and I had a special bond, and I liked to think I was his favorite. He would share some of his thoughts about work with me and always made me feel very special.

Around this time, my mother installed a new Godrej almirah, a large metal cabinet made by the Indian lock maker Godrej and Boyce, to stockpile items for our marriage trousseaus. Whenever she saved a little from the family budget, she'd buy two of the

same items and put them away for Chandrika and me. She filled that cupboard with stainless steel pots and pans; silver trays, plates, and cups; and a few small items of gold jewelry. She bartered, sometimes taking old saris with a little gold thread to a vendor where she could trade the fabric for new cookware. Our house had three Godrej almirahs, one for my mother's clothes, one for family valuables, and one for the wedding stuff for her two girls.

I didn't pay too much attention to this. But I know that Chandrika, the elder daughter, beautiful with curly hair and a great smile, felt the pressure. I definitely benefited from being the second daughter in this case. I could operate below the radar.

One summer day in 1968, my adored father was hit by a bus while driving his Vespa. He was caught under the wheels and dragged down the road. I have a clear memory of Amma answering the door when the police came to tell us about the accident. We didn't have a telephone.

My mother and I jumped into an auto rickshaw and rushed to the hospital.

When we walked in, he was lying on a bed, bleeding profusely, barely conscious. He was holding his partially severed nose together with one hand. His leg bones were jutting out of his ankles. He had cuts and gashes all over his body. He looked at us and whispered that everything would be OK. Then he passed out.

After six hours of surgery and weeks in a medical clinic, he recovered at home. My mother was his physical therapist, helping him get back on his feet. The bills piled up—there was

no state medical insurance in India at the time—and my parents burned through almost all their savings. After several months, he went back to work, and our lives carried on, largely as before. He was forever covered in scars from this dreadful incident.

Had my father not recovered, I realize now that our lives would have been very different and difficult. Thatha's pension was small, and my mother, with three kids, had no means of earning money. None of my aunts and uncles could have afforded to take us in. With no government support systems in place, my mother may have added more tenants in the big house but would have run full speed into the deep-seated biases against the women of her generation, who almost never went into "business." Our education, as we knew it, would probably have stopped.

Family, as powerful as it is, can also be so fragile. Every family runs the risk of unexpected hardship. And without adequate safety nets from government or private enterprise, episodes like my father's accident can ripple through people's lives for decades or generations.

Most significantly, this event made real my father's urging for me, as a woman, to always have the means to provide for myself.

In tenth grade, a new girl, Mary Bernard, transferred into Holy Angels, and we became fantastic friends. Mary was the daughter of an army officer, and she was funny and adventurous. More important, she owned a shiny new acoustic guitar and took lessons.

I really wanted to learn to play the guitar, too, but Amma was just not going to buy me one. She was adamant and a little

horrified. Good South Indian Brahmin girls did not play guitar and sing English rock 'n' roll songs, she insisted. This was not appropriate; I should focus on South Indian classical music and instruments, she said.

But this wasn't going to stop me. And, in a lucky break, Mary and I found an old guitar in a storage cupboard in the school. We took it to Sister Nessan, who unexpectedly agreed to refurbish it for me to use. Contrary to my mother's attitude, I think she was a contemporary thinker who was not immune to the Beatles and was probably excited by the prospect of a new genre of music at Holy Angels.

Then, with two more friends, Jyothi and Hema, Mary and I formed a band for the school variety show. The nuns billed us the "LogRhythms," after the math tables we were studying, and we became inseparable. We practiced the five songs that Mary knew: "House of the Rising Sun," "Bésame Mucho," "Ob-La-Di, Ob-La-Da," "Greensleeves," and "Delilah." We were supernerds. But after we hit the stage for that first gig, dressed in white pants and psychedelic shirts, the school had to add two extra shows to accommodate the crowds. Sister Nessan and Sister Benedict sat in the first row, beaming. My dad was especially enthusiastic. He was back living in Madras with us again, and, even though he never saw us perform, he took up the habit of walking around singing our signature songs.

The LogRhythms lasted three years. We began as the only girl group in Madras, and we performed at school festivals and music concerts all over the city. We always started with our core five songs but added a few more—instrumental hits by the Ventures, like "Bulldog" and "Torquay," and pop hits like "These Boots Are Made for Walkin'" by Nancy Sinatra and "Yummy Yummy Yummy" by Ohio Express.

Our biggest fan and groupie was my brother, Nandu. He came to every concert and helped with the equipment. My conservative aunts and uncles, who I thought might be highly critical of my countercultural musical pursuits, bragged about me to their friends. It wasn't uncommon to hear them singing "Yummy Yummy Yummy" under their breath around the house. At every family get-together, I had to perform a few songs with my guitar.

After about a year, Jyothi and Hema, who played the bongos and guitar, opted out. We added a couple of guys, the Stephanos brothers, to help on drums and vocals. The Stephanos family became dear friends and have remained that way long after the band was dissolved.

I graduated from Holy Angels in December 1970, when I was just fifteen. There was no graduation ceremony. No fanfare. In fact, my parents had never visited the school in all the years we studied there. Teachers and nuns were given all the responsibility and authority over us. My extensive extracurricular activities had taken a lot of my time, and I graduated with decent grades, but I was not a top student.

Also, as was usual with all graduating high schoolers then, Thatha and my parents didn't get involved in my college search and admissions process at all. I had the comfort of knowing that they would pay for my undergraduate education and more. But the choice of college, a major, the long process to apply and get in or be rejected—it was all on me.

Chandrika, who always had top marks, had moved on the previous year to studying commerce at Madras Christian College (MCC) in a suburb called Tambaram, some nineteen

miles (thirty kilometers) away. MCC was one of the very few coed colleges in Madras and considered one of the best educational institutions in South India. It had a wonderful blend of academic excellence and hippy cool. It had a great music scene. Many observed that the college had something of a scaled-down Haight-Ashbury vibe.

I decided that MCC was the best choice for me, too, and I was happy when I was admitted. I joined the chemistry group, which included physics and math.

Chemistry fascinated me. I loved making one compound transform to another, one color to another, creating crystals of all shapes and sizes, watching precipitates, and learning the most basic information on how our universe works. The class had about thirty boys and eight girls, and I increased my focus on schoolwork to keep up. Wearing a sari every day, which was expected of girls in those days, made things a little harder, both during my ninety-minute commute to school each way and in the daylong labs, when chemicals splashed on our clothing. I spent a lot of time pinning my sari in the morning to cover the burn holes I'd put through it the week before.

I struggled in the advanced math classes. Most of my classmates had completed eleven years of school and then a year of pre-university courses. As a student who took the Cambridge exams, I skipped pre-university and went straight to college. I was OK in most subjects but way behind in math. This is the one time my parents stepped in to help. After hearing me cry over analytic geometry, differential equations, Laplace transforms, and Fourier series problems, they hired a professor to tutor me at home a few times a week. This was a major concession by my mother, who again had to deal with the stigma of my doing something a little out of the ordinary. She thought that

tutoring suggested there might be something wrong with me and, by extension, with my parents. This remedial help was absolutely critical though—without it, my life may have turned out differently. I'm not sure I would have passed these courses.

I also joined the MCC debating team, among the best in the city, and we won many intercollegiate and state championships. Debating freed me to study topics unrelated to science—world affairs, politics, social issues. This was time-consuming, but the variety of material and the caliber of my fellow debaters really lifted my game. Looking back, I can say that debating helped me build my confidence and hone my ability to persuade others to accept my point of view, and artfully push back on an opposing perspective. It was endlessly helpful.

India, of course, is a cricket-crazy country and ball-by-ball commentary on the radio brought life to a standstill. My uncles were all cricket fans who coordinated their vacations with five-day test matches and endlessly talked about the games and players. I came to love cricket, too, and played the game in our yard with my brother and his friends.

I attended some of the MCC men's college cricket matches, and, one day, on a whim, I declared to my friends that we ought to form a women's cricket team. To my great surprise, the idea took off. The college let us use the men's equipment, and a few male players started coaching a group of about fifteen women. We batted, bowled, and fielded three times a week; reviewed the rules; got injured; and picked ourselves up. Several women's colleges in Madras, it turns out, were starting to play cricket, and we organized the city's first-ever women's tournament. It was just four teams, but that was better than none.

I borrowed a white shirt and trousers from my father and managed to hold them up with belts and pins. Nandu was again my equipment manager. I haven't forgotten that wonderful feeling of walking onto the field to play Stella Maris College as the opening batswoman, fully suited in cricket whites, with at least fifty people—families, friends, and many strangers—applauding on the sidelines.

Chandrika and I were on different schedules at MCC, and we didn't interact much. She was part of the cool clique of boys and girls over in the humanities department. The last thing she wanted was to be seen with the nerdy science types, even if I was part of that crowd. She did very well in college and, when she was graduating, decided to take the exam to get into a top master's program in business, a gutsy decision for anyone but particularly for a woman. That choice had a huge impact on me.

India had four postgraduate management schools in the early 1970s, but only two were Indian Institutes of Management (IIMs). The IIM at Ahmedabad, affiliated with the Harvard Business School, was the best of them all. Tens of thousands of students chasing 150 seats took the brutally difficult entrance exam and went through grueling interviews. One of our uncles declared that getting into IIM Ahmedabad was like getting a Nobel Prize and told Chandrika she shouldn't be disappointed when—not if—she was rejected. Chandrika, always cool about her labors, wasn't fazed. She handled the admissions process as though it was no big deal.

When we heard that she was accepted—one of just a handful of women to get a spot because the school had so few rooms

for them in the dorms—the family was in awe. She was blazing a new trail. Thatha immediately set about paying the deposit.

Then came the drama. My mother drew the line. She declared that Chandrika would not go to business school in Ahmedabad, far away from Madras, unless she was married.

"Young, single girls don't go away from home to study, let alone to a coed college," she said. She wasn't wrong. That was certainly the norm in those days. But my grandfather ignored her concerns and noted that the tuition would be coming from his pension.

She was furious and quietly declared, "If you send her, I will fast until I die."

Chandrika was terrified. And my grandfather and father didn't help matters by telling the kids, "Don't worry, if she carries this through, we'll still take care of you."

A day or so later, thankfully, Amma came around. She dropped the fast and everybody pretended it hadn't happened. She busied herself getting Chandrika ready.

This episode is so emblematic of the pressure on mothers in India at the time—one foot on the brake to make sure their daughters were protected and well mannered, and the other foot on the accelerator to help their girls gain respect, independence, and power. Amma's social sense naturally gravitated to the brake; her dreams for us pressed on the accelerator.

A few weeks later, my father traveled with Chandrika on the train to Bombay and then on to Ahmedabad. I was sad to see her leave but not entirely unhappy about it. Nandu and I would have more space in the bedroom. I could take over her study table, which had a locking mechanism in the drawer. All my secrets could be kept from my brother's curious eye.

As I was finishing my own three years at MCC, my path had again been revealed by my sister ahead of me. I decided to apply for a master's degree to IIM Calcutta, on the eastern coast, an intense quant-oriented business program. Chandrika, rightly, didn't want me to trail her to Ahmedabad.

"You've been around for all my time in Holy Angels and MCC," she declared. "I need a break from you—don't you dare apply to IIM Ahmedabad!"

I replied, somewhat unconvincingly, that I'd be much happier in a program that was even more focused on math. "Ahmedabad is too easy—I'm applying to IIM Calcutta," I bravely retorted. The truth is, I didn't have a choice!

After a grueling admissions process involving a GMAT-type entrance exam, group discussions with other applicants, and a one-on-one interview, I was selected—and relieved. Had I not gotten in, I would have been viewed as the "failed" sibling, I thought.

This time, there was no objection to a daughter heading to business school and no more comparing this accomplishment with a Nobel Prize. In fact, it was sort of a nonevent. My dad took me from Madras to Calcutta on the Howrah Mail train, a thousand-mile (1,600-kilometer) journey.

I was super excited yet a little scared of what the future would hold.

2

In August 1974, I arrived in Calcutta, then a city twice the size of Madras and among the most densely populated places in the world. Calcutta, now called Kolkata, is a political center, the first designated capital of the British in India. My father and I, with my two small suitcases and an old handbag, took a ramshackle taxi from the train station to the campus. The city was congested. Buses and cars whirred by on crowded roads. I heard Bengali, the local language, for the first time. Everyone and everything felt loud.

IIM Calcutta—unlike the IIM Ahmedabad campus designed by the master architect Louis Kahn—occupied a few low-lying buildings on the Barrackpore Trunk Road, an ancient trade route that was now a busy four-lane highway. The classrooms were in nondescript, gray buildings, with peeling paint on the walls, scuffed furniture, and creaky fans overhead. The library was in a worn-out nineteenth-century mansion on the grounds called Emerald Bower. The whole place flooded to ankle-deep water during the monsoon season. Not a very aspirational setting.

I was one of six women in the eleventh class, or "batch," in the master's business program. Our little group lived with the six women of the tenth batch, doubled up in plain, simply furnished dorm rooms with a common bathroom at the end of the corridor. We ate in a big dining hall, together with the two hundred men in the program, on a strict schedule of three meals a day with no snacks. Once in a while, students escaped to little local restaurants for coffee or sweets.

The drab setting and food at school in Calcutta, however different from our home in Madras, didn't bother me. I was at IIM Calcutta—a famous educational institution in India—and I was pumped. My only regret was leaving Thatha, who was ninety-one and increasingly frail. I'd phone home just to talk to him.

But I was finally away, and there was no time to waste. I had my three-year chemistry degree from MCC and a well-honed sense that I could learn anything if I worked hard enough. I also felt I simply couldn't fail and bring that shame to my family. It would be a tough slog, but I had to figure it out.

I was a girl of just eighteen, and many of my classmates were in their early twenties. Most were engineers from the famous Indian Institutes of Technology and had already finished five-year programs. Their social backgrounds weren't too different from mine—middle-class kids, mostly from big cities, who spoke excellent English and had been prodded from birth to excel at school. We had all attended elite undergraduate colleges, and almost no one had work experience. I found the guys cheerful and erudite, dressed in jeans and T-shirts, hanging out together, playing guitar, or talking politics. They listened to Pink Floyd, Led Zeppelin, or Deep Purple; played cards; drank; and smoked a lot of grass, which seemed to be widely available.

IIM Calcutta was very ambitious. It was set up by the Indian government in 1961 with the help of the Massachusetts Institute of Technology (MIT) and was steeped in high-level math and statistics. I had grown up in socialist-leaning India, but the country was keen to groom the next generation in schools like this for a future of democracy and capitalism.

The subject matter at IIM Calcutta was classic MBA—a two-year program with required courses in the first and electives in the second. We studied finance, marketing, operations, strategy, economics, team dynamics—all taught with a huge dollop of quant. We learned supply-chain management, modeled factory schedules, reset production plans for multiple distribution centers, and prepared the routing system for a complex truck fleet. The faculty were renowned in their fields and were terrific teachers, too. They built a great rapport with the students.

One mandatory course was computer-board wiring. I'd never used a computer, and Calcutta had just two System/360 mainframes, the then-iconic IBM systems that helped globalize computing. We'd get a three-by-three-foot sheet of paper with dots and grids and had to solve a problem, first creating a flowchart, then writing a program in FORTRAN and translating it into a wiring diagram for a computer board. For the electrical engineers, this was second nature. For me, it was grueling. Our solutions were taken across town to the System/360 at the Indian Statistical Institute. If the diagram was right, we got an answer; if it was wrong, no credit. I have no idea why that course was useful at all.

While I struggled in some classes, I was well prepared in others. I'd grown up in a swirl of conversation and learned to argue philosophical questions in front of a crowd. Thatha had

often asked me to read him the newspaper because his eyes were tired. I thought I was helping him out. But he had usually read the articles already and just wanted to make sure I learned about current affairs.

As a teenager in Madras when I was in high school, I'd also been invited to three more important student conferences sponsored by the Indian government or international development groups. I don't know how I made these lists, but I suspect I was recommended by R. K. Barathan, the CEO of a chemical company who judged our student debates in Madras. He had sometimes pulled me aside and given me tips on how to improve my performance, so I presume he saw something in me. I can't think of another connection that would have elevated my name in this way. In March 1971, I was one of two students from India to participate in the Asian Youth Seminar on National Youth Policy in New Delhi. It involved classes and discussion on the future of health, education, Asian integration, and youth involvement, with delegates from Indonesia, Malaysia, Japan, Sri Lanka, and several more countries.

On the last day, we went to the glorious, enormous Rashtrapati Bhavan, the official residence of India's head of state, for tea with the president, V. V. Giri. I still have the invitation, embossed in gold with the state emblem of India, and my name, Miss Indra Krishnamurthy, handwritten at the top.

Later that year, I was selected to attend the Leslie Sawhny Programme of Training for Democracy, held in a lush rural military cantonment area in Deolali. That involved more classes and discussions on India's history, the Indian Constitution, free elections, and the media. Experts, including the constitutionalist Nani Palkhivala, stuck around after their talks. I particularly

remember Brigadier John Dalvi, who knew so much about what it took to draw the line between India and Pakistan in the mid-1940s. He was handsome and stern and chain-smoked while recounting stories of the struggles of partition. It all made for wonderful chats around an outdoor fire.

I was also picked to attend a National Integration Seminar in New Delhi, focused on issues related to governing one united India. What issues were state issues? Which ones were federal issues? Why is unity of the country important? The highlight of the week was tea with Indira Gandhi, the prime minister.

Each of these seminars attempted to train future Indian leaders on principles related to rule of law, capitalism, and national cooperation. They were very forward-looking and badly needed in the days when India was slowly transitioning to being a full-fledged free-market democracy. These experiences gave me a broad perspective and the foundational knowledge to better understand the country and my place in it.

At the end of my first year at IIM Calcutta, I landed a summer internship at the Department of Atomic Energy. The job was in Bombay.

Where Madras was quiet and Calcutta was political, Bombay, on the west coast, was the heart of commercial India—a city of tall buildings and shiny apartments, open late, crammed with workers rushing through the streets. I watched the incredible dabbawalas, men in white hats and striped outfits, riding their bicycles, or on trains and buses, moving thousands of lunches every day from homes to offices. Their delivery system, so finely tuned, has now become a popular case study on logistics management in business schools around the world.

I rode a double-decker bus to work near the bustling waterfront and the Gateway of India monument. I met up with business-school friends at midday and played bridge with them on weekends. I slept on a sofa in my aunt Lalitha and uncle Haran's apartment in Sion, a suburb of Bombay. They were full of love and told my parents they would be responsible for me, and set a firm 7 p.m. curfew, which I never violated.

I was teamed up with a student from IIM Ahmedabad to look at the construction schedules of six nuclear power plants and determine which would be completed on time. Over three months, we pored over lists of hundreds of equipment and engineering services for each plant to understand the delays and figure out new schedules. It was an exhausting process, but I think the vendors and partners gave us an honest assessment of the issues they were up against. The picture was troubling. We learned that some developed countries held back their state-of-the-art technologies from emerging markets to extract a little more return from outdated designs that were flawed and expensive. We also learned that large government projects could be pretty inefficient.

The internship left me with a sharper focus on the interdependence of business and society and convinced me that MBA students could play a constructive role in helping governments. But it didn't leave me encouraged about the motivations of wealthy countries toward emerging markets.

One evening in mid-June, my father called to say that our beloved thatha had suffered a stroke and wouldn't survive. I was told he was lying on his divan, unable to speak, with his left side numb. It was a picture I could imagine: my parents,

sister, and brother caring for him in the men's living room, family and friends filled with concern. I booked myself on the 6 a.m. flight to Madras.

By 9 a.m., I was in the back seat of a taxi rushing home from the airport. Half a mile from the house, I saw Thatha's funeral procession go by and my father, bare chested, wearing a dhoti and his Brahmin cross thread, leading the group of many of our male relatives. He carried a terra-cotta pot filled with coal embers.

I was crushed that I hadn't said goodbye to Thatha and furious when I got home that my family hadn't waited for me to arrive before moving his body. That's when a Hindu priest, who was performing funeral prayers, broke age-old rules by beckoning me to follow him to the male-only cremation grounds. It was too late. When we got there, my father had already lit the funeral pyre. Unseen, I watched the fire grow for a while and then left, tears streaming down my cheeks. To this day, that scene is etched in my memory. It fills me with overwhelming sadness.

I returned home to relatives huddled around the house, reflecting on Thatha's life. And I remembered the things Thatha told me: "If you take on something, you must give it your all" and "If you make a promise, keep it." He insisted on reliability.

He liked to say he was a lifelong student. "Even though I am in my eighties, I am a student like you all," he said. "The day I stop, my mind will atrophy. And then the body will follow."

And if he caught us loafing around, he'd say, "Satan has work for idle hands." That never left me. Still today I struggle to not be doing something useful all the time. Thatha remains my greatest teacher, and I refer to his life lessons in every aspect

of my adulthood. My dedication to work, regardless of the challenges, I think, comes from his pushing me to keep going.

I accepted Thatha's death, but I missed him. For a long time, we left the room where he spent most of his life with us untouched. Sometimes I'd walk in and start talking to him and then remember he wasn't there.

When I returned to IIM Calcutta that autumn, the school had moved to a new, modern campus in Joka, a southern suburb of Calcutta. My months in Bombay, working in a proper office on real issues, had spurred a sense that jumping into business school as a teenager with no work experience was a little premature. But it was too late to worry. I was halfway through.

I was drawn to thinking about how people shop, advertising, and the science of decision-making, and I decided to major in marketing. How do you innovate? How do you make products grab the consumer? I took electives in consumer insights, sales analysis, and organizational behavior. I was intrigued by all of it.

The new women's dorms, all single rooms with a set of common bathrooms, accommodated a slightly larger group of first-year students, including three women from Delhi with whom I became great friends, Sujata Lamba, Nishi Luthra, and Manjira Banerjee. Our social lives flourished. We played lots of bridge and table tennis. We went out to the local establishments with the men. We were becoming more mature, more self-confident. We studied together, relying on one another through the tough courses.

In class, I had to perform. Banks, consulting companies, government agencies, and industry players soon showed up to

review our grade cards and meet us for permanent jobs. IIM Calcutta graduates were a coveted group, but I wasn't "a topper" picked by the most prestigious firms. I was a good marketing student looking for a job with a great training program and excellent bosses.

I signed up to interview with Mettur Beardsell, a Madras-based textile company owned by Tootal, of Manchester, UK. The meetings were with S. L. Rao, the marketing director, and his head of human resources. Mr. Rao was notorious for his brilliance, ruthlessness, and low tolerance for mediocrity. He was a rapid-fire questioner who offered quick, harsh feedback. The interview began with a group of about twenty, and we were whittled down from there. I left after the third and final round, not sure how I'd performed.

Later that evening, the career office asked me to come back, and I was floored when Mr. Rao was waiting to offer me a position. I could have interviewed with other companies but decided against it. The mix of Madras and learning from Mr. Rao was too good to pass up.

Much later, I asked Mr. Rao why he picked me. He told me that I had held my own against all the men who were trying their best to impress; even though they tried to talk over me and interrupt me, I never gave in.

At IIM Calcutta, I was in school with men, taught by men, and studied the work of men to enter industries dominated by men. But the few women I studied with felt increasingly comfortable as the women's movement radiated across the globe. We spoke up, and I felt we were respected. We were never viewed as competition. The teachers and our fellow

students wanted us to succeed. We were outliers—the first generation of women to enter professional management schools and the world of business in any number—and we were special. We knew we were on the cusp of something bigger.

After World War II, women in India were encouraged to go to school and get degrees. Jawaharlal Nehru, the country's first prime minister, really pushed for this in all social strata, both to increase literacy rates among poor women and to tap the brightest minds regardless of gender. But young women were also severely restricted by their traditional families and by finances, and their brothers always took priority, irrespective of aptitude. My mother's family, with three boys and five girls, could only afford for one sister to attend college. Unfortunately, my mother lost out. She never hesitated to tell us how disappointed she was about this. "We'll make sure you go to college even if your father and I have to starve to pay for your education," she'd add with a flourish.

Once a woman graduated, she was still expected to marry, have children, run the household, and rely on her husband and his family for her security. Working outside the home was frowned on. Some women worked as teachers, in offices, as nurses, or in retail stores, but many quit when they were matched with a suitable young man. A few—especially Anglo-Indian women, women from progressive families, or women from homes that were financially strapped—continued in their jobs. Brahmin women were less likely to work outside the home, even if they were highly educated.

As a study in contrasts, India respected and worshipped women, and "mother" remained the most revered person in the family. But she was ignored in a curious way—unpaid

and toiling to keep everything going even when her husband retired. No one seemed to ask too many questions about any of this, even though it was the labor that formed the backbone of society.

I did have a few female role models with real power. The most prominent was Indira Gandhi, who was prime minister twice, from 1966 to 1977, and again from 1980 to 1984, when she was assassinated. Her politics were controversial, but we loved that she gave India personality and elegance. Indira Gandhi was Nehru's daughter, and Nehru's sister, Vijaya Lakshmi Pandit, was important, too. She was president of the United Nations General Assembly and, at various times, India's envoy to the USSR, the US, and the UK.

In my own orbit, female teachers, school administrators, and nuns—Sister Nessan, Sister Benedict, Miss Nigli, Miss Peace, Miss Meenakshi, Miss Saraswathi, Mrs. Jobard, and the rest—had showed me what it was to be an educated, working woman. At MCC, only my French professor and one chemistry professor were female. I had no female professors at IIM Calcutta.

By the time Chandrika and I were in college, my parents and grandparents saw that it was more acceptable for women to be in the ring with men. They would not have questioned us had we wanted to get married and settle down like many of our friends, but they didn't hold us back from wanting to do more. In fact, they encouraged it. We were lucky not to have our ambitions dampened.

Educating girls remains the bedrock of advancing women in our world, although poverty, violence, and ancient male-dominated cultures still stand in the way. The benefits are

endless. Educated girls and women are healthier, contribute more to the paid economy, and have far fewer children as teenagers themselves. They lead in their communities.

In the developing world, educated girls are also less likely to be married off as teens, in part because when they are elevated in their family by the confidence and wisdom that comes with education, they are more valued.

But educating girls and women—and what these women do once they get their degrees—are not just issues in the developing world. In the US, Europe, and India, where universities and community colleges are packed with women getting the most degrees, we still haven't smoothed the path to get the best and brightest into roles that serve them and our collective prosperity.

Even with a newly minted postgraduate diploma in management, as my IIM Calcutta degree was called then, no career in India in the 1970s started in an office. It always entailed working on the front line. For Mettur Beardsell, I went into a six-month sales-trainee program in the Alexander Thread division, back in Bombay. I was four months shy of my twenty-first birthday.

I started my new job by memorizing every kind of industrial and consumer sewing thread we made and the codes of every color in every shade. I studied how thread goes through sewing machines, how it behaves when washed, and which types shrink. I learned the uses and costs of one-ply, two-ply, and three-ply thread; of cotton, silk, and polyester.

Then, with a sample bag over my shoulder, I trudged all over the city to cut-and-sew garment makers, important cogs in India's massive garment export market. Some were big

customers, but most were little shops with five or six machines churning out T-shirts or madras-plaid, loose-cotton shorts and shirts with collars and buttons up the front. I was yelled at by shop stewards when the blue thread I sold didn't quite match the blue fabric or if the color ran. I didn't speak the local language, Marathi, and my Hindi was rudimentary, but somehow I managed to communicate.

Door-to-door sales is a humbling experience. It has stuck with me forever. To those tailors in the sewing shops, I was someone who would either help them deliver a great product or mess up their next order. I learned that business is done a few spools of thread at a time and that I owed my customers a duty of care. They were buying my product—and my word—and I had to listen carefully and deliver for them. I wanted the next sale. I was good at sales and enjoyed meeting people and hearing about their work. They tried to teach me their languages. They showed me pictures of their families. I got to know my customers as humble, hardworking, skilled people.

I liked the trudging around less, especially when some of the streets were flooded to my knees during the monsoons.

After six months, I was moved to Mettur Beardsell's Madras headquarters to assume a role as assistant product manager in textiles. Now I was in an office, with a desk and a shared secretary. My direct boss, the product manager, was a tough-but-fun guy, who believed in stretch assignments. I had to help him move the company into more colored and printed fabrics from its staple products of plain mull and longcloth, specialized white fabrics.

The first few weeks were hard. I did stints in sales, manufacturing, HR, and finance and then had to step right in

on helping choose the next season's palettes and sample prints. The sales department needed those choices within thirty days to start selling for the holidays.

As a first step, I asked to see sample swatches of everything we'd produced in the past couple of years. I wanted to make sure that I did not repeat old designs and that I understood which did well and which flopped. My new assistant pointed me to a big cupboard in the middle of the room and said, "It's all in there." Years of samples had literally been shoved into this cupboard willy-nilly. I rolled up my sleeves, took everything out, and sat down cross-legged on the floor to organize it.

At that very moment, the company's new managing director for India—Mr. Rao's new boss—showed up. He'd just moved from Manchester and wanted to meet the company's first woman from a management school. A colleague sitting at her desk pointed me out.

Norman Wade—six feet, four inches; white-haired and pipe-smoking—sauntered over, stared down at me sitting on the floor, and clearly thought I was crazy. This was my first encounter with someone who would become one of my most ardent supporters, an Englishman who'd steer me through the next couple of years. Norman wore traditional British suits and rode around town in a chauffeured white Mercedes-Benz. He introduced me to his wife, Alice, and told me about his grown children in the UK and his life in Macclesfield before he came to India. He always called me "Luv." Ultimately, he'd advise me to move to the US.

One day, Norman invited himself to our home and met my parents. After that, he often showed up for Amma's coffee and sat on the swing having long talks with my dad. I think

he found a home in our Indian family in some way. It wasn't always easy for me to have the attention of the boss, who was three levels above me at work. I know it ruffled feathers when Norman stopped by my desk to chat. I didn't think I could do anything about it.

I worked very diligently at Mettur Beardsell. For months, I accompanied salesmen with a sample book and price list to textile wholesalers in Madras, shops lined floor to ceiling with shelves filled with every type of printed and colored fabric. My job was to help sell bales of our material. I'd sit with customers for coffee, a sweet, or a snack, sometimes at six or seven stops on the same day. I'd take the time to explain the lineup of our products, demonstrating their charm by matching them with different colored blouses. I was the only woman they'd ever seen in the job, and they were very respectful. Interestingly, a few of them—or their wives—managed to find my parents and send over the horoscopes of boys they thought would make me a good husband.

We competed with fabrics from the more technically advanced North Indian mills. Our graphic artists would present designs—flowers, stripes, geometrics—and I'd help choose patterns and fashionable colors to sell for dresses, skirts, or shirts. Every six weeks, I traveled to the Anglo-French textile mills, our production partners in Pondicherry, a city about one hundred miles (160 kilometers) south of Madras, for quality control. I'd take a bus at 11 p.m. for a slow trip overnight, with stops in local towns, to get there by 6:30 a.m., then take a shower in the mill's guesthouse, drink coffee, and spend the day inspecting

fabrics as they came off the roller to make sure the prints were clear and not blurred on the edges.

I learned about five-color and six-color screen printing, roller printing, and different finishes, and I signed off before large orders were run. The business depended on attention to detail, and I tried to set the standard by showing a deep interest in the fine aspects of printing. The toughest part was rejecting finished lots when they didn't meet my standards and upsetting workers who felt they'd let me down. By 3 p.m., I'd be back on the bus and reach Madras at about 8 p.m. Those were long days.

My job at Mettur Beardsell—responsibility, authority, and a paycheck—gave me confidence that I could enter unfamiliar terrain and succeed. My earnings were reasonable, and, just as I'd watched my father do, I gave most of the money to my mother for the family. I did spend the bulk of my first paycheck on a red bicycle for Nandu, who was about thirteen. I just adored him and still remember his face when that bike was delivered. For the briefest of moments, I was the greatest person in the world.

My work also came with some perks, including a car allowance that I used to buy a secondhand, hunter-green, four-door Triumph Herald, with a taupe interior and a stick shift. I drove myself to work and zipped around on weekends, radio blaring, with friends and Nandu as my chaperone. We hung out under the trees at Woodland's Drive-In, a popular restaurant, where waiters scurried among the cars with trays that perched on rolled-down windows.

Still, I was twenty-two years old and not exactly free. Amma set a strict gas allowance for the car, and, on weekends, I had to be home by 7 p.m. I slept in my childhood bedroom and did my chores. Living on my own as a single woman would

have been unacceptable to society in Madras. The house ran as before, with Amma cooking and tending the garden, Nandu and his friends in and out of the house, and my father going about his business. Chandrika was in Bombay, thriving in a new job at Citibank and living in a "chummery," an apartment with others who worked at the bank and far fewer restrictions than living at home.

Everything was the same with one exception. With Thatha gone, the comfortable, airy space that had been his room became everybody's lounge. The divan was re-covered in a beautifully printed fabric. Black-and-white televisions had arrived in Madras in 1975 and we got one. Although the programming was scant, we'd have a full house for weekend movies, including the families of our maid and gardener.

Then another twist. Just when I felt on top of my work, in late 1977, a labor strike in South India's textile mills shut down Mettur Beardsell's production. Everything stalled. Workers journeyed to Madras from the main manufacturing plant in Mettur for a sit-in to get management to hear their demands. Meanwhile, I had little to do.

Around this time, Johnson & Johnson, the medical devices and consumer products company, called me, likely because I was an IIM-Calcutta grad. After one interview with C. V. Shah, an incisive executive who headed the personal products division, the company offered me a job in Bombay: product manager for India's launch of Stayfree feminine protection.

Norman encouraged me to take the job. He was sorry and sad to see me go, he said, but keen to see me develop.

I moved to Bombay yet again, in October 1977, and rented a little furnished bedroom with an attached bathroom from a

family in a building close to the Johnson & Johnson offices. They, too, had strict rules. I had to be home by 7:30 p.m., and if I was going to be late, I had to call and explain why. Late arrivals were strongly discouraged. They felt responsible for my safety.

At work, for the first time, I entered an American workplace. The Johnson & Johnson headquarters in India was grand, with fancy offices and an entirely different scale of extras for senior executives. My pay doubled from what I was earning before. The work demanded long hours and some weekends—very normal at American multinationals, I later discovered, and a big difference from the hours at Mettur Beardsell.

In India at the time, packaged products for women to handle their monthly periods were perceived as unnecessary and expensive. Most women used wadded or folded cloths that were washed, dried, and reused. Johnson & Johnson had already introduced Carefree, a belted napkin. Stayfree was a step up, the first disposable maxi pad with an adhesive strip that stuck to underwear. It had been sold in the US for almost ten years and promised women a new kind of freedom.

The Stayfree team in India had a lot to do to tweak the product to make it widely acceptable. We had to manufacture the pads with the right layers of absorbent and waterproof materials suitable for the Indian market and undergarments worn by local women. We had to get the adhesive reworked for the humidity. The box illustration of a woman with long hair and a flowing pink dress wading in the sea had to be precisely color-matched with the global package.

We conducted extensive research, asking dozens of women in the office and their acquaintances to use a pad and then

leave it in the bathroom for me to see how it crumpled or leaked. The request was awkward, but many of the women trusted us enough to comply. I wanted those pads smooth, not visible through clothes. I felt this issue had purpose and that the product could make women's lives just a little better. Cloth was uncomfortable. This was some form of liberation.

My bosses were all men, and I had to routinely explain my research and progress. These were delicate conversations for me, but the men listened intently and had constructive suggestions. They knew this was the job.

Advertising feminine personal products was taboo in India at that time. We could only talk tangentially about the "experience" of using them. We had to go into schools and colleges to explain the benefits to young women. We also had to convince parents, especially mothers, to pay for this "freedom" for their daughters, which wasn't always easy. And there was an additional issue: These products were never displayed or talked about in a store. They were kept behind the counter and passed to customers wrapped in newspaper. To ask for sanitary napkins, a woman would typically wait for a shop to clear, then quietly whisper to the clerk, almost always a man, that she wanted something personal. The clerk understood but sometimes smiled in a way that made her uncomfortable. India had no self-service stores in those days.

Despite all these hurdles, we introduced Stayfree in two test markets in less than seven months. I felt like my efforts had paid off.

While I was busy at Mettur Beardsell and Johnson & Johnson, many of my friends, all men, had left for

America for postgraduate programs at universities in California, Illinois, Texas, and Minnesota. The US had a special draw for young people, and was viewed as a seat of culture and innovation. We listened to American music, watched American movies, and read American news.

Many of the best students from the IITs chose to go to the US for their master's and PhD degrees and then went on to amazing careers. In a way, the US got India's very best, students who had been educated in elite institutions subsidized by the Indian government. This was a tremendous brain drain that, unfortunately, continues even today. It's surprising to me that the Indian government hasn't helped foster more of an entrepreneurial ecosystem to incentivize this talent to remain in the country.

After IIM, I felt a steady drumbeat from these friends to come to America, too. But I was always quick to think that I had no real reason.

What was my place in America?

India, of course, can be excruciatingly hot but never more than in the humid summer months in Madras. As teenagers, Chandrika and I had discovered that the libraries at the British and US consulates had consistently good air-conditioning. We often sought refuge there and loved their full collections of publications from abroad—magazines, newspapers, and books.

In December 1977, during a visit to Madras over the holidays, I wandered the mile or so from home down the road to the American Library, as I had so often done before. I began to browse back issues of magazines. And there, in a September 1976 issue of *Newsweek*, with Jimmy Carter and Gerald Ford

on the cover, I read an article, titled "A Shade of Difference," about Yale University's new business school, which focused on public and private management.

That article was speaking to me. I was interested in a life in global business but felt that my chance of going to the US for a job was very low. I had been thinking that a degree from the US was probably the best way to move ahead, but I was reluctant to repeat an MBA. The various courses I'd attended and my summer internship all awakened in me the interdependence of the public and private sectors. Yale seemed to be creating the exact blend of what I was eager to learn a lot more about.

Over the next few months, I sent away for the Yale application and took the GMAT. I told my parents about it, but no one was too optimistic. When I received an acceptance letter, no one really cared. We couldn't afford it.

Then, a few weeks later, another letter arrived. The university had decided to offer me financial aid—50 percent of the cost in loans, 20 percent in a work-to-pay program, and the rest in a scholarship. Suddenly, the excitement and nervousness in the family were palpable. The idea that I might leave India was becoming real. My father was abundantly proud; my mother was terrified about letting me go so far away.

Not surprisingly, both worried about how I would repay the loans. Converted to Indian rupees, my debt upon graduation would be much larger than my father's annual pay.

One evening in May 1978, Norman was in Bombay and invited me to dinner. He told me the mill strike was over and asked me to come back to Mettur Beardsell, this time to run the whole textile division. This was a major promotion. I

couldn't believe it. I'd be in charge of almost 60 percent of the company.

I told Norman about Yale and then asked him, "Norman, do you really think I should give up this Yale admission and come back to work for you?"

And he replied, "No, you shouldn't. I'm disappointed that you're going, but, if I was advising you as my daughter, I'd say, 'Go.'"

This, I think, was true mentorship. Norman was approaching his mandatory retirement age in India, and he must have thought that he'd train me as an executive for a couple of years before he returned to the UK. But he also didn't want to cap my progress. He was quick to support a different road for me. He was unselfish.

He also played a pivotal role in convincing my parents that I could succeed in America. When I told them he had offered me a big new position at Mettur Beardsell, they both immediately assumed I'd take it and come back to Madras. When I then said Norman thought I should go to Yale instead, they accepted that choice for me, too. They trusted Norman. I realize now that they trusted me, as well.

As I prepared to leave India, my two Mettur Beardsell bosses did one more thing that still astonishes me.

At that time, the US consulate in Madras approved about fifty student visa applications to the US a day and rejected more than half the people who applied. I was nervous about facing James E. Todd, the interviewing officer, who was well-known as a tough questioner and feared by potential US students like me. The system required lining up at 9 p.m. on Cathedral Road, outside the building's gates, for an overnight wait to receive

a token at 6 a.m. that granted time with Officer Todd. One night, I found a place in line, with nothing but a wall to lean on. There were about sixty people already in line at 10 p.m., all nervously clutching folders with their admission documents and uncertain about their fate. I was the only woman.

And then, every few hours, Norman or S. L. Rao showed up with food and encouragement. The others in the growing line were dumbstruck but impressed. There was Norman at 11 p.m. in his gleaming white Mercedes sedan, handing me a flask of hot coffee and asking what else I might need. Then his driver was back at 2 a.m. with coffee again. Then Mr. Rao appeared with breakfast at 5 a.m. to wish me luck. I will never forget the love these two men showed me. I got my token and later Officer Todd gave me the visa.

In August 1978, my parents traveled with me to Bombay to put me on a Pan American World Airways jet to the US. For months, I had overheard them at night discussing the pros and cons of my decision, and I think my father was the one who finally persuaded my mother to just let me spread my wings. I can imagine the overwhelming sadness they both must have felt to see their daughter go to a distant land, although they were nothing but cheerful and encouraging with me on that day. Amma later told me that they cried in private together.

My aunt and uncle and a couple of cousins joined us at the airport for a proper family farewell. I didn't know when I'd see any of them again, and I had a particularly hard time leaving Nandu.

And I really wished that Thatha had been around to bid me goodbye.

3

I clearly remember two things about my twenty-hour flight from Bombay to New York. The first is the soundtrack. The Boeing 747SP traveled west, over the Middle East, Europe, and the Atlantic Ocean. And Pan Am's Current Hits audio channel repeated a forty-five-minute loop of pop songs, including "Handyman" by James Taylor, "What a Wonderful World" by Art Garfunkel, "Year of the Cat" by Al Stewart, and "Stayin' Alive" by the Bee Gees. I heard them all at least fifteen times.

The second memory is a tip from a young American businessman I met in the Economy Lounge, a stand-up bar in the middle of the plane where I could stretch my legs and eat chips and peanuts. I told him I was heading to Yale University, in Connecticut. Quietly, he said, "Look, I'm going to help you with something. Connecticut is called 'Connett-ih-cut,' not 'Conneck-tih-cut.'" He made me practice saying it carefully. I'd never heard the state's name spoken correctly and had no idea that it is not pronounced as it is written. To me,

this was a gesture of kindness from a stranger that I've never forgotten.

When I landed at John F. Kennedy airport, I was wonderstruck—the number of aircraft, the hundreds of people from everywhere moving through the glass structure, the cleanliness and orderliness of it all. I found the Connecticut Limousine counter and got in a wagon-like car with several other passengers. As we rode along Interstate 95 in silence, I marveled at how structured everything was—the clean highways, the clear traffic flow, no honking, no animals wandering onto the road. It was all so very different. And so foreign to me. When we crossed from New York State into Connecticut, the driver loudly announced, "Welcome to the greatest state in the country!"

After about two hours, I was dropped in front of the Yale Office of International Students, which was then at the corner of Temple and Trumbull Streets in New Haven. It was a Saturday around midday. The streets were empty. I had a bulging suitcase with no wheels that was filled with saris, shirts, trousers, and one set of flat bedsheets; a carry-on duffel bag loaded with books; and $450 in cash. I'd spent $50 on the ride.

By late afternoon, after somehow carrying my luggage in two trips over six blocks, I sat alone on a bare bed in a high-ceilinged dormitory in the Hall of Graduate Studies, a 1930s building in Yale's Gothic style, with vaulted ceilings in the lobby, stained glass, and an imposing fourteen-story tower. I was two days early for my orientation. My roommates hadn't showed up. No one was around. I had no phone, no TV, and no idea where to procure anything. The dining room was still closed.

This was utterly unlike home and, strangely, not what I expected. Was it really going to be this quiet in America?

Where were the noisy taxicabs and screaming fire engines? Fashionable people on fashionable streets? Welcoming faces? What happened to the hustle and bustle? For the first time in my life, I was desperately lonely and frightened.

Before arriving, I had consumed every cultural export from the US that I could and had worked for an American company. I thought I was prepared. But, in every way, I was a complete novice. I started to cry, full of the sinking feeling that nothing about this was going to be what I had imagined. I contemplated getting on a return flight home the next day.

Of course, I didn't go back. My journey was just beginning. I now know that many immigrants' American dream begins with fear, awe, and loneliness.

I believe in the American story because it is my story. As a CEO, I once sat in the eighteenth-century, wood-paneled dining room at Chequers, the British prime minister's country manor, and was asked why I had immigrated, thirty years earlier, to the US and not the UK. "Because, Mr. Prime Minister," I responded, "I wouldn't be sitting here lunching with you if I'd come to the UK."

I was an unmarried Indian woman. The fact that I was in that dorm room in New England in the 1970s was a testament to my family in southern India: the focus, since my birth, on my education; my grandfather's and parents' faith in me; and their courage to defy centuries of cultural and social pressure to let their daughter fly. It was a testament to the nuns in my convent school, to my Indian schoolmates who encouraged me, and to an ambitious, newly independent India, which had elected a

woman as prime minister and signaled that women could reach any height.

It was also a sign of the times. Huge advances in technology, travel, and communications had companies and other institutions on the move around the world, seeking out markets and profit. Business education was thriving and the US was welcoming students like me.

I entered the US through the front door, with a visa and a seat at a prestigious university. It was my choice, and I knew it meant I had to work my way up. Maybe this prepared me for a tough life in the corporate world; it certainly required me to accept heartache and pain in my personal and professional lives and to just plow on. My duty was to honor this opportunity.

Mine is not an immigrant story of hardship—of fighting my way to America to escape poverty, persecution, or war. I don't know what it feels like to be a refugee, homeless because my own country is in crisis. I spoke English. I had landed in the US with $500. I was at Yale. And I had the safety net of my family in India, a place that I was familiar with and loved and that would take me back.

Still, I do feel connected to everyone who streams into America, whatever their circumstances, determined to work hard and to set in motion a more prosperous life for themselves and their families. I still have that fear—an immigrant's fear—that presses me to try to do well and to belong. In my early days in the US, I wanted my family to be proud of me and for whatever I touched in America to be proud of me, too. I felt like a guest in this country, and I wanted to be viewed as an upright person, a contributor, and not a liability.

On that first, lonely evening at Yale, my adventurous spirit slowly took over. I had traveled across the world for two days and I was hungry. I wandered over to the Wawa convenience store at the corner of York Street and Broadway, one block from the dorm, to find something to eat. The products, brands, and packaging were all new to me. I didn't know how to shop, because I'd never been in a store where you pick out what you want and pay for it at a checkout. So I watched the other shoppers to figure out what to do. What I missed most at that moment was South Indian food, and I thought I'd get some curds, a staple, to comfort me.

I searched high and low in that Wawa for curds, but I couldn't find them. I didn't know that curds in India are called yogurt in the US. Instead, I spent a few bucks on a loaf of white bread, a tomato, and a bag of potato chips. I squished the tomato onto the bread and ate it all like a sandwich, bland and unsatisfying. I missed my spicy hot chilies.

The next morning, luck came my way. An Iranian economics student named Mohsen Fardmanesh—small, slim, bespectacled—who lived down the corridor, knocked on my door with a big smile of welcome. What a relief. He knew about immigrants' loneliness, he said. I soon told him my troubles, starting with not being able to find familiar food.

"OK then," Mohsen said, "the simplest thing is to get you a slice of pizza and douse it with red chili flakes." We ventured out to Yorkside Pizza down the street, a typical New Haven restaurant with wooden booths and framed photos of sports teams on the walls. I had never tasted pizza. I had never tasted mozzarella cheese. Mohsen ordered me a slice to try, and, with the first bite, I gagged. Pizza wasn't for me. "But there's no

question of you not liking it," Mohsen told me. "You have to get used to it. Pizza is a staple in the US."

Mohsen was a godsend. Over the next few days, he helped me get a mailbox and a bank account. He told me about life in the US and at Yale for a foreign student, and how to bring some of my own background to my new life. He told me to take each day as it came and to enjoy it. "It will get better every day," he said.

For a month or so, as a vegetarian, all I ate in the Hall of Graduate Studies dining room was salad and bread. I was miserable. I was losing weight and perpetually tired, and schoolwork was ramping up. I knew I had to do something. So, with the housing department's help, I moved a few blocks away to Helen Hadley Hall at 420 Temple Street.

Helen Hadley Hall was—and remains—singularly unimpressive from the outside. It was built in 1958 to accommodate female graduate students, and it still bugs me that it was Yale's women who were relegated to this building. Vincent Scully, the famous professor at the Yale School of Architecture, once referred to it as "late modernist design at its most banal." That it existed among the Gothic and Georgian buildings that dotted the Yale campus, and even Temple Street, was surprising indeed.

The inside was equally institutional: single rooms with one square window each, hallway bathrooms, and two telephone talk rooms for each floor. The fluorescent lighting and gray floors made it look even more monotonous than necessary.

But this was a dorm filled with international master's and doctoral students on tight budgets—and the low-key building where it was easiest for us to mix Yale with the comforts of

home. We had big kitchens and dining rooms on each floor that breathed life into the dreary surroundings. Almost everybody cooked, and the aromas wafted through the halls—spicy Indian curries, Chinese food, Jamaican food. We didn't care about how we dressed or about anyone's accent or how they spoke.

My neighbor, Rob Martinez, was a Cuban American PhD student from New Jersey. Rob loved the variety of cultures in our dorm. He was worldly and a treasure trove of facts and figures on history and economics. He loved to argue politics with our Chinese and Polish friends while he ate Indian food. Rob helped many of us buy groceries, taking us in his green Subaru to the Stop & Shop grocery store a few miles away in Hamden, Connecticut. He was a great dancer, too. He taught me the Hustle, the disco dance that was a big hit at the time, and other line dances. His friendship, welcoming attitude, and empathy were so important in helping the students in Helen Hadley Hall build an incredible bond with America. One evening, a group of us even gathered for a ceremony making Rob an honorary Indian. He became a lifelong friend.

Life also felt better once I had access to the Hadley Hall phone. I couldn't afford a personal landline, and the central system, even if it was just for brief calls, provided a welcome respite. Friends from Madras reached out constantly from their schools in Illinois, Oklahoma, and California to get me through the initial shock.

After a while, I had to tell them to stop calling. I was grateful for their support, but I had work to do.

The School of Organization and Management (SOM), Yale's first new graduate program in fifty years, injected

new energy into the old-school business education dominated by Harvard and Stanford. Yale had created a hybrid program linking private business with the public sector in a degree called master's in public and private management. Many of the one hundred or so students in my class had experience in the political world, the military, or nonprofits. More than a third were women.

Our classes were in two beautiful old houses on New Haven's Hillhouse Avenue, connected in the back with dark-green, modern structures that looked like Pizza Hut restaurants. "Let's meet at the Pizza Hut building" was a common phrase.

At first, I was aghast by my American classmates' relaxed approach to almost everything, and then I was in awe. They exhibited a swagger that no one would have dared in India, where, for two decades, I had watched students stand up in respect whenever a teacher entered the room. Students at Yale put their feet on the desks, munched on sandwiches, called the professors by their first names—"Vic" and "Dave." They walked in late or left early and boisterously challenged the teachers' points of view. I found the free-flowing discussions spectacular. Topics were explored in depth; pros and cons debated. I'd never been part of anything like it.

In the first week, we were asked to form groups of eight by chatting with the people next to us, then told that this was our study group for the next two years. We named our group, with three women and five men, Don't Look Back. Together, we went through arctic- and desert-survival simulation exercises and had professors watch our group dynamics through a one-way mirror and then offer candid feedback. That experience was humbling. I realized that I had a lot to learn—how to

let others finish, to watch my body language, and to include everyone in group conversations. I had to speak clearly and deliberately and remain pithy with my interjections. After the first feedback session, I was a little disillusioned. But I started to perform better when I incorporated all the suggestions.

This was my second master's degree, but it was entirely different from IIM Calcutta: practical not theoretical. Actual cases were used to study business issues. Leaders of industry and government came to talk about real-life examples. I was surrounded by people with at least two or three years of work experience. Class was a two-way experience.

The faculty were simply superb. William Donaldson, who'd cofounded the Wall Street investment bank Donaldson, Lufkin & Jenrette and served in Richard Nixon's State Department, was the dean. Stephen Ross, who developed arbitrage pricing theory, taught microeconomics; Victor Vroom and David Berg taught individual and group behavior; Marty Whitman, the value investor, taught investments; Larry Isaacson, who'd worked for McKinsey and then CBS Records in California, taught strategy and marketing. Each was an expert in his field and respected by many. I found that they made the complex simple and understandable.

Larry, in particular, really believed in me and pushed me to do more. He let me opt out of some basic marketing classes and work for him on consulting projects. I taught a class for him to about fifteen women from the area who were returning to work and wanted to brush up on marketing, consumer segmentation, and advertising. I saw hope and fear in these women; they were optimistic that their new skills could allow them to return to paid work but afraid that they wouldn't get a job or that they

wouldn't be fully prepared for one. I taught them and, more important, helped build their confidence.

Once a week during lunch, the assistant dean would meet with students to hear our ideas and concerns. That the school's administration wanted to listen to students' input on quality of life at SOM and the curriculum amazed me. What a difference from the top-down approach in Indian educational institutions. The one commonality with IIM Calcutta was that business was still a man's world. We studied no business cases with women leaders, and I had no female professors. Women did not feature in what was taught to us.

In my second year, the coursework was magical—electives in finance and strategy, game theory, trade, and multilateral organizations. We parsed Burton Malkiel's *A Random Walk Down Wall Street.* We examined the rise of Gillette, the razor maker, and analyzed the troubled finances of the Metropolitan Museum of Art in New York, and Clark University in Worcester, Massachusetts. We learned about political polling and talked with Eric Marder, the pollster for Henry "Scoop" Jackson, a US senator who had run for president in 1972 and 1976.

Much as I adored the schoolwork, the social experience was equally powerful. With the student body, I was definitely an outsider and very aware of the cliques of young men and women who'd graduated from Ivy League colleges or Northeast boarding schools. Many were original preppies, who wore Sperry Top-Siders and took ski trips in the winter and headed to the beaches of Cape Cod or Long Island on weekends in the spring and fall. I was considered smart and hardworking, and people liked me fine, I think. But I was also largely invisible

and conscious of how international students, especially from developing countries, were grouped in people's minds. Diligent but no style, funny accents, socially inept. There was no explicit rejection of us but no deep welcoming. I wasn't shy, but I was careful about what I said.

I was uneasy about how I looked. Before leaving Madras, I'd gone to a local tailor with a pile of US magazines, and he'd sewn me a couple of shirts and tops that I thought reflected current American styles. But I soon realized those items were ill fitting and quite ugly. So I went to S. S. Kresge, the discount shop on Chapel Street that was the precursor of the Kmart chain, and bought three long-sleeved, easy-care polyester shirts to wear with my jeans. A few months in, Chandrika came to New York for her Citibank job and bought me a bright-blue down coat from Alexander's department store in midtown Manhattan—a real savior in the snowy winters.

Notwithstanding the Kresge shirts and Alexander's jacket, which I was proud of and were all I could afford, I was later told by some well-meaning friends that my clothes drew a lot of derision.

I had no money to spare. My scholarships and loans totaled about $15,000 a year, roughly evenly split, and I spent almost all on tuition, room, and board. I took a job working the front desk and the manual switchboard at Helen Hadley Hall three to four days a week, earning $3.85 an hour for midnight to 5 a.m. That was fifty cents an hour more than the daytime slot and $1.20 more than the minimum wage, which was $2.65 in those days. When the phone rang at reception, I'd buzz a resident's room and put the call through to the hallway phone. All night, students ran down the hall in their nightwear and slippers to get

their calls. I monitored the front door, sorted the mail, and did my homework.

Every four months or so, I sent a one-hundred-dollar money order home to Madras. The family did not need the money, but it felt great to contribute. I always earmarked twenty dollars for Nandu. He'd never been given pocket money before and loved me for sending him this huge sum to spend as he wanted.

That first fall, I also fell in love with the New York Yankees, a splendid and irrational affair that exists to this day. The 1978 World Series was a rematch between the Los Angeles Dodgers and the Yankees, who'd won the championship in 1977. The common room of Helen Hadley Hall—with its beat-up lounge chairs, fraying sofa, and the only TV around—was crammed every night of the playoffs. I was a cricketer missing my bat-and-ball sport and knew nothing about American baseball. But I was delighted one evening when a few guys asked me to sit with them and taught me the rules. I started reading everything I could about Reggie Jackson, Ron Guidry, and Bucky Dent and was over the moon when the Yankees won the series again. I cried when the captain and catcher, Thurman Munson, died in a plane crash in the summer of 1979.

This was the time I learned that the language of sports—and the details of particular games and players—was relevant in business. When students came together in the morning, they talked sports; in interviews, employers talked sports. If you weren't current on baseball or football, you didn't fit in.

This notion seemed connected with wisdom I'd received from my parents when I left India a few months earlier: "Be yourself, but try to blend in, too."

Shortly after our winter break, the race was on to land a summer job. I needed a paycheck, and I was a good student. My professors were ready to give me great references. They viewed me as hardworking and easy to work with. They felt I had a unique global perspective on issues that was sorely needed in corporate America. Companies were coming to Yale, and I had to impress them.

My only worry was that I had no business suit. I headed back to Kresge's with fifty dollars, my entire savings at the time, and picked out a dark-blue polyester outfit—a two-button jacket and matching slacks. I added a turquoise polyester blouse with light-blue and dark-blue vertical stripes. I went to try these on but had never been in a fitting room before and was uncomfortable about undressing behind a drape lest someone peek in.

So I held the pieces up in front of the mirror. The slacks were OK; the jacket seemed a little oversized. But I remembered my mother's advice to buy clothes a couple of sizes too big because I'd "grow into it." I was twenty-four years old but, just then, forgot I was fully grown. I bought it all, proud of handling this big purchase, and I used all of my money. This was the single biggest expenditure in my life thus far.

Leaving Kresge's, I noticed the shoe department, but I had nothing to spend on shoes. Never mind, I thought. My orange suede loafers with the chunky plastic base, which I'd been wearing all winter, would do fine. I could tuck my feet under the table. No one would notice.

On interview day, I put on the suit. The blouse fit nicely, but the slacks were a lot shorter than I had realized. The jacket hung awkwardly on me. But that's what I had, and I was stuck. It was too late to exchange the clothes for different sizes. I headed to the

SOM administration building where everyone was gathering in the career office to meet prospective employers. There were my schoolmates, pristine in their well-fitted Brooks Brothers suits, the women with silk shirts and elegant wool skirts and blazers.

I heard a collective gasp. Everyone was looking at me. I pretended not to care.

I met that day with Insilco, a Connecticut-based conglomerate that managed brands in prefabricated housing and office supplies, among other businesses. The interview went fine, but I left the room completely embarrassed and defeated.

I ran down the hall to the director of career development, Jane Morrison. I sat down on her sofa and burst into tears. "Look at me," I said. "I went to the interview like this. Everyone is laughing at me."

Jane was very matter-of-fact: "Yup, it's pretty bad," she said. "Pretty bad."

I told Jane about my financial predicament and how I bought a suit to fit my budget. "I wanted to fit in," I explained.

Then she asked me what I'd wear to an interview in India. A sari, I told her. I had many of them back in my room. Her advice: "Next time, wear the sari. And if they won't hire you for who you are, it's their loss. Just be yourself."

Insilco made two offers that evening. One was to me. It dawned on me that I was in a new environment—and that this might be a living example of the American promise of meritocracy. It was clear that Insilco picked me because of what I said and what I could contribute and looked past the horrendous outfit I wore. I had three weeks to accept the offer.

My next interview was scheduled with Booz Allen Hamilton, the consulting firm. Consulting was considered aspirational. The hours and travel were brutal, but the job paid well, and

the conventional wisdom was that the experience offered a three-to-five-year head start versus a regular corporate career. This meeting was too good to pass up, even with an offer in my pocket. I decided to carry on with it.

I wore my favorite turquoise silk sari with cream flowers and a turquoise blouse, and I met with a Booz Allen partner from Texas who put me at ease right away. He conducted a rigorous interview using a business case, and I felt he was judging my ability, not worrying one bit about what I wore or looked like.

Booz Allen hired me for a summer job in Chicago, with interns from Harvard, Stanford, Northwestern, and the University of Chicago. I joined a team developing strategy for an Indiana-based company that made food ingredients, a wonderful group of men who included me in all discussions and deliberations, coached me, and fully supported me.

I wore a sari to work every day but never visited the client. Taking me to a client meeting in Indianapolis in a sari would have been too jarring in those days. At the time, I fully understood and accepted my colleagues' leaving me behind. It seemed a small price to pay.

I was thrilled to be on my way as a working woman in America.

Work. It's not really optional. And that's good, because the benefits of paid work hardly need review: humans thrive when they are challenged; they are proud when they've done a job well and gain from being with people who share the same goals. And we all need money to live.

I believe that women's choice to work outside the home is integral to their well-being and their family's prosperity.

Somehow, some people in even the most sophisticated societies have continued to question whether women should engage in paid work at all. This perspective seems connected to the idea that children suffer if a job distracts their mothers from caring for them. In some places, it's just easier for the whole society to stick with the outdated habits they know.

I don't see it this way. In fact, working women's kids tend to do better in school, are more independent, and see their mothers as valuable role models. Besides, we have clear proof that women's paid labor-force participation is crucial to the whole economy. More women in the workforce makes us all more prosperous—cutting poverty, boosting wages, and swelling gross domestic product.

But, for me, the reason women need a clear path to paid work is more direct. We all deserve the power of the purse for our own freedom. The full acceptance of women as paid workers spells human progress. It unlocks them from being at the mercy of a male-dominated world.

I was happy to have landed in Chicago for my summer internship and open-minded about where I might end up after graduating.

I moved into a one-bedroom sublet in a high-rise building in Sandburg Village with a Yale classmate, Kimberly Rupert, another summer intern. The apartment belonged to a Chicago Bulls basketball player. It had a fish tank that hadn't been cleaned for weeks, a closet full of outsized men's sneakers, and a sink piled high with dirty dishes. The guy handling the rental agreement seemed happy to find reliable tenants who'd do the deep clean required to actually live there. Although his open-front shirt, multiple gold chains. and casual approach scared me a bit, over

time I grew to like and respect him. He was a helpful landlord and we were model tenants who kept the apartment spotless.

After a day of scrubbing and moving in, our living room with a big city view became a lively summer hub for the seven Booz Allen interns.

I had one other connection in Illinois. An Indian friend of mine studying in Dallas insisted I meet a guy named Raj Nooyi, a young engineer from Mangalore, India, who'd just finished his master's degree at the University of Texas. "He will help you settle in," I was told.

Raj was working at Eaton, an industrials company in Chicago's sprawling suburbs, and lived alone in a one-bedroom, sparsely furnished apartment near his office in Carol Stream, Illinois. I invited him over, and he quickly became a fixture in our tight group, hanging out in the Chicago apartment and taking us to his building complex to swim or play tennis. He was incredibly smart, well-read, and worldly. He was also good-looking, had a wonderful smile, and got along with everyone. Importantly, he could chauffeur us around in his car.

By the end of August, most of the gang had headed back to school, but I had a week left on the job. On a Friday night, Raj and I stepped out to the Sandburg Theatre, an old film house a block away, to see *Silver Streak*, a caper-on-a-train movie starring Gene Wilder and Richard Pryor. We loved it and laughed together at the slapstick comedy.

Then we walked to a restaurant and, as we finished dinner, decided to get married.

Who proposed to whom? Who broached the subject? What happened to the months of dating that were supposed to come before a proposal? I don't know. Forty-two years later, we are still debating this issue!

Before I flew back to New Haven, Raj took me to meet his aunt Jaya and uncle Ramesh, who lived about an hour away in Flossmoor, Illinois. Ramesh Adiga was a vascular surgeon at the South Suburban Hospital serving South Chicago, and his wife, Jaya, was a doctor in family practice. They were part of the wave of Indian physicians who had immigrated to the Midwest in the 1960s. Uncle Ramesh's sister and mother, visiting from India, were also in the house on the day I first met Ramesh and Jaya.

Honestly, Raj's family was apprehensive when we broke our happy news. They had long wanted to find him a bride. He was a catch—tall, highly educated, and based in the US. Now I was standing there, a complete unknown who spoke Tamil, not Kannada, his mother tongue, and whose horoscopes had not even been examined and matched.

At the same time, I was from a hardworking, well-established, highly educated, middle-class Hindu family. That was all good. Some of the objections melted away when Raj later insisted that he was going to marry me, whatever they thought of the situation. His relatives were then quick to see how we complemented each other and embraced me wholeheartedly.

Meanwhile, I told my parents over the phone that I was marrying someone named Raj Nooyi and gave them a few details. They were understandably scared and worried because they hadn't met him or vetted his family. But they also realized they had no choice. Again, they trusted my judgment, and acquiesced.

A month later, our two sets of parents and other relatives met in Madras and held a formal engagement ceremony—without me and Raj. My parents thought my new in-laws were

wonderful and concluded that meant we must be compatible, too.

My second year at Yale was full of looking ahead and the emerging reality of my life, married and working. I wanted a job at Boston Consulting Group (BCG), which was viewed as the top strategy consulting firm and was opening a new Chicago office. It would be perfect, I thought. By mid-autumn, after a series of six or seven tough interviews, I got the coveted offer.

My summer job also seemed to have elevated my standing among my peers at SOM. More students were welcoming of me, although I remained wary. I still didn't feel like I fit in.

Raj and I talked on the phone and saw each other every few weekends. I'd fly to Illinois and do my projects and schoolwork in his little apartment. We spent those months meticulously costing out our wedding and concluded that we could have only forty guests and that we would hold it in his uncle and aunt's basement. After paying for the flowers and the priest, we couldn't afford a single extra person.

In late May, my parents and Nandu came from India and joined Chandrika and Raj in New Haven to watch me graduate. It was bright and sunny—and an amazing day for me. My family was all together, and my mom and dad were excited and delighted to meet my future husband. They loved him.

I was heading on to a wonderful new stage yet somewhat sad to depart Yale and the academic life. The school had lived up to everything I had hoped for—I now knew so much more about how the private sector, the public sector, and nongovernmental organizations worked together to create a harmonious society.

I had learned about the US and felt well prepared to venture forth in American business. I had struggled a little to find my place but met wonderful, smart, committed thinkers. Many of my classmates have had incredible careers, and we still rely on one another. In fact, I now feel that the friendships that we all made at Yale SOM, after more than forty years, are stronger than ever.

After my goodbyes, the whole family piled into two rental cars and drove the 850 miles to Chicago for our wedding a few days later. My mother had brought my wedding sari and some of the jewelry she'd collected for me since I was a little girl.

Raj and I were married in a low-ceilinged, wood-paneled recreation room in Uncle Ramesh and Aunt Jaya's house in Flossmoor. The ceremony lasted about an hour. We then feasted on an Indian buffet dinner catered by a local restaurant. Rob Martinez, my Helen Hadley Hall neighbor, and Larry Isaacson, my professor, traveled to be there.

If we'd been married in India, our wedding would have gone on for at least a day and a half. My parents and lots of our relatives on both sides felt deprived that we didn't do it that way. But I didn't care. I was very happy. The fact that our families were together—all from so far away—was a source of great joy.

Sometime the following week, Raj's father, N. S. Rao, pulled the two of us aside. He gave us a pep talk about our life ahead—wishing us luck, advising us to work hard, and reassuring us that our families would always be there to share the load.

Then he said directly to me: "Indra, don't give up your job. You have all this education, and you should use it. We will support you in any way we can."

Part II

Finding My Footing

4

Moline, Illinois, on the Mississippi River, is 165 miles west of Chicago, surrounded by the corn and soybean farms of America's heartland. In 1980, it was also home to Servus Rubber, a sixty-year-old maker of industrial work boots struggling with new competition from overseas. Servus was my first client as a management consultant.

A week after our wedding, I traveled to Moline on a little plane with the brilliant Alan Spoon, who was in charge of recruiting when I was hired into BCG. Then I commuted for months, living two or three nights a week in a midpriced hotel; speaking to operations, sales, and marketing managers; roaming the factory; talking to workers on the assembly lines; and grasping everything I could about rubber and work boots.

Management consulting is the wellspring of so many global business careers for good reason. I learned more in six years at BCG than I could have anywhere else as a young MBA. I found it exhilarating, full of debate and fascinating people. Companies hire a firm like BCG to help answer fundamental

business questions: What are the value drivers of the business? How might they change? What are the strategic options to create value over time? What investments do they need to make? How should they organize themselves? They are buying the firm's way of thinking and experience from having been inside so many different industries.

Consultants dig in, devoted to understanding the art and science of an industry and of a particular business. BCG was heralded in strategy consulting. The firm's founder, Bruce Henderson, invented the "growth-share matrix" in 1970, the oft-taught model that rates businesses as cows, dogs, stars, and question marks, depending on their relative market share and growth rate. We were trained from day one to focus on addressing the client's real challenges with data and clear, objective thinking, not just telling them what they wanted to hear. We revealed uncomfortable truths and would then sit down with company leadership, go through our analysis, and figure out a path forward. I felt this process had an intellectual honesty that sidelined politics, although, of course, there was plenty of corporate politics to wade through, too.

The consulting business really suited me. I loved zooming in, digging deep into a business, learning growth and profit levers, then zooming out to determine how best to reposition a business or a company. Every project felt very personal, and I was busy all the time. I don't sleep much, and I easily put in the long hours needed when I was wrapped up in the analysis.

BCG's Chicago office was growing fast when I joined, and we soon moved from Monroe Street into one floor of a glassy skyscraper on Wacker Drive across from the 110-story Sears Tower. Dozens of graduates were hired every spring and

assigned to work that was flooding in. With just a few partners available for training, we taught ourselves and one another. We did all the complex modeling with calculators and No. 2 pencils and filled in hundreds of cells on paper spreadsheets. We plotted graphs by hand and then turned them into a production department with precise instructions as to how to make the slide decks presentable. It was painstaking, pre-PC, pre-Excel spreadsheet work. We often photocopied our sheets in sections and taped the pieces together to share them with colleagues and bosses.

The breadth of our projects was fantastic. I worked on trust banking, fuel additives, and dyestuffs. For LexisNexis, which was selling news and legal information stored on mainframe computers, I organized focus groups in fifteen cities to learn how people used the service and perceived its cost and benefits, and to determine what they didn't like about it. We translated this into an integrated marketing plan—tiers of service, pricing—all defined by meticulous consumer analysis. Finally, everything was expressed in terms of a revenue and profitability model.

Early in my tenure, BCG was hired by Trane, a company based in La Crosse, Wisconsin, that made industrial-sized heating, ventilating, and air-conditioner (HVAC) systems. Our team, led by a Scottish American BCG partner, included a Jewish man, an Italian man, and me.

After a few weeks, Trane's CEO, talking to the partner for an update, jokingly asked, "Do you know this is La Crosse, Wisconsin? You sent a team with a Jewish guy, an Italian guy, and an Indian woman. What's going on here?" To his credit, the partner responded, "You asked me for the best, and I gave you the best."

The Trane CEO was Bill Roth, a generous, thoughtful man who told me later he was delighted by that answer. I worked on projects for Trane for more than three years and got to know the particular generosity of Midwesterners.

Our job was to help Trane accelerate its growth and profitability. We first spent months talking with HVAC contractors who worked on enormous office buildings or small strip malls and apartments and then to general contractors, service technicians, and city building officials—all to understand Trane's position and how to improve it. We analyzed every job Trane had lost to the competition in the previous three years. The client was impressed with our unusually detailed approach.

As I became accustomed to consulting, I developed my own research routines. For a company that made citrus processing machines, I crawled through juice plants in Brazil and Florida and learned the intricacies of squeezing oranges with different commercial machines. I bought books to understand the terminology, science, and technology of any given problem, and I still have my annotated textbook on orange processing.

For a Japanese company, we had to scope out the US market for high-speed, state-of-the-art bottling lines. For G. D. Searle, a pharmaceutical company based in Skokie, Illinois, I worked on aspartame, the artificial sweetener discovered in Searle's labs in 1965, and helped the company think through how it should scale up its manufacturing process. As a second assignment, I had to research emerging zero-calorie sweeteners that could be commercialized in the next decade or two. My chemistry background came in handy here, but, for more relevant input, I

hired a professor who was an expert on sweeteners to visit labs in California and Europe with me.

I never anticipated that orange juice, bottling equipment, and sweeteners would become even more important to me later in life!

I worked on tissue and toilet paper. We built a cost model of every tissue manufacturing line in the country—the speed, the waste, the raw materials used, the cost. I learned the differences between Kleenex and Puffs and between Charmin, Scott, and store-brand toilet paper. I hung out in a bar in Green Bay, Wisconsin, nursing a lemonade, to listen to competitors' factory workers talk about their troubles on their tissue lines, and then drew lessons for my clients. I met equipment makers in Germany, Sweden, and Finland to understand the next generation of tissue-making machines and processes. Again, I hired an expert, a paper scientist from Miami University in Oxford, Ohio, who traveled with me to explain it all.

That led me to patents and figuring out what others were up to on the basis of their patent filings. I threw myself into an elaborate study of patents, using a framework developed by Battelle, an organization committed to using science to solve societal problems, and tracing the arc of technology investments in the industry. We analyzed thirty years of the tissue business to present insight into the entire competitive landscape.

The travel was unremitting. Week after week I hustled through the airport, lugging my briefcase and a Hartmann garment bag. The weight of that bag ended up misaligning my right shoulder—a memento I carry even today. I usually spent three or four nights away from home and then worked every

weekend crunching numbers, plotting graphs, writing presentations. I was learning all the time; it was an intellectual high and a physical low.

One night in Neenah, Wisconsin, I couldn't find a hotel room because of a very popular air show in nearby Oshkosh. I decided to drive the three hours home to Chicago and return the next day. Somewhere near the town of Fond du Lac, I was pulled over for speeding, and the officer said I could pay the $125 fine with a Visa card. I only had American Express and ended up in a Fond du Lac police precinct to call Raj. That's when I spotted a neat bed in a jail cell and—I can't believe it now—I actually asked if I could sleep on that bed for the night until my husband could come the next morning with the cash. I just did not want to drive to Chicago and back and was desperate for somewhere to rest. The cop told me to just go home. I paid the fine the next day by check.

As I threw myself into all of this, Raj and I missed our time together. But he was also working extraordinarily hard. This was the price to establish ourselves, we thought, and we worried that our luck might change. We'd have quick calls late at night to check up on our days. We spoke like we hadn't talked in ages.

Raj and I started our married life in his Carol Stream apartment. We economized and clipped grocery coupons from the newspaper. We balanced our checkbook every month, first setting aside money for my student loan repayment, then depositing some into savings, and finally sending a hundred dollars to each of our families in India to show we cared. They

did not really need it, but we felt good sending them that amount.

I had acquired two cream-colored pussy-bow blouses and two Evan Picone wool suits, one in camel and one in black; I wore the jackets and skirts interchangeably to create four combinations. I packed those same items into my carry-on bag every week, heading out to Neenah, Appleton, or La Crosse, Wisconsin; Baton Rouge, Louisiana; or New York. The clothes were often unrecognizable when I arrived, and I madly ironed them in hotel rooms before my meetings.

Raj was still working at Eaton as an industrial engineer in a manufacturing plant that made electronic controls. He, too, had just a few clothes in the closet—two or three shirts, a couple of trousers, and hand-me-down ties from Uncle Ramesh. Every night, he'd wash a shirt and hang it to dry and then press it the next morning. He always left home looking impeccably dressed.

Even though he already had a master's degree, Raj realized that to get ahead in management required the legitimacy of an MBA. Before long, he began the degree, taking the train to the University of Chicago's downtown campus in the early evening and getting home for supper around 10:30 p.m. Partway through his second year, he decided to resign from Eaton and became a full-time student for two trimesters. He graduated in 1983.

We didn't socialize much. We were busy and didn't really know anybody. We weren't invited to anything. Some weekends, we visited Raj's aunt and uncle. Or we'd go to Connie's Pizza on Twenty-Sixth Street, for a stuffed pie with tomato sauce on the side, or to a $5.99 all-you-can-eat Indian buffet on Devon Avenue. We still seasoned a lot of our food with hot green chilies or red pepper flakes.

When we stepped out, we looked for the longest entertainment for the smallest amount of money. For our first live concert in the US, we saw the band America at the Park West theater. We went to a couple of Cubs baseball games at Wrigley Field and to see the White Sox at Comiskey Park when the Yankees came to town.

We also once bundled up in thermal underwear and our thickest sweaters and coats to sit in the cheapest seats at Soldier Field for a Chicago Bears football game. The number of layers really didn't matter. The vicious winds off Lake Michigan that swirled around the stadium had us frozen in minutes. Raj was a big Dallas Cowboys fan after his time in Texas, and I had to learn the rules of American football fast to enjoy the games with him on the weekends.

After a year or so, we decided we should buy a house. We picked a lovely Tudor-style three bedroom in the village of Glen Ellyn. It was a new block, and the grass was barely planted; the trees were mere twigs. The house cost $125,000, with a minimum 5 percent down payment. We had $3,000 saved and Raj's uncle lent us $4,500. Even then, we had to buy mortgage insurance because we'd contributed so little. The interest rate was 17.5 percent.

The numbers did not scream that this was a good deal. But it seemed to us that the American dream meant we should buy a house and that we'd be saving money for the future because the value of the house would go up. We moved in but had no money for much else. So the breakfast area, family room, and master bedroom were the only rooms that were furnished. The rest of the house remained empty. We did buy a Toro lawn

mower at the local hardware store right away. We felt very American.

My parents had returned to Madras right after our wedding, and my dad told me he was eager to come back to explore the US with his grandchildren one day. I missed them a lot, but making an international call to India was expensive, especially during the day. So once a week after 10:30 p.m., I'd talk for half an hour with my parents and Nandu, and then we'd do the same with Raj's family.

Nandu, my brilliant brother, placed first in the state exams for high school students in Madras, and he applied to Yale College. He was accepted with a partial scholarship and some amount in loans. My sister had just been hired by McKinsey, the consulting firm, and moved to New York from India. Together, we agreed to pay the rest of the money that Nandu needed. He moved to New Haven in August 1981 as part of the Yale class of 1985. Raj and my plans to save for the future were shelved for the moment.

But then, on one terrible day in January 1983, my mom called to say that my father had had jaundice for almost a month. He'd lost sixty pounds, more than a third of his body weight, and he needed surgery to relieve the pain in his abdomen. He didn't want her to tell us about it for fear that we would interrupt our lives and come back to India. Even on our weekly calls, he'd never hinted that he wasn't well.

Chandrika, Nandu, and I decided to leave for India right away and to meet in Bombay to travel together to Madras. We rushed to the hospital from the airport, worried and scared. When we saw our father, we were shattered. He was a shadow of himself and suffering, yet he kept reassuring us not to worry.

The sight of my sick father took me back to those days after he had his Vespa accident. I knew I had to be strong for my mother, who had shouldered all the worries of his illness in the past months all alone. But he was in so much pain and again showing how completely dedicated he was to all of us. I was bereft.

The big house filled with relatives who traveled to support us. After a four-hour surgery, the doctor informed us that my dad had pancreatic cancer and that the outlook was grim.

And then, in the single most valuable corporate benefit I received in my early career, the head of BCG's Chicago office, Carl Stern, called to tell me to take up to six months off—with pay—to help care for my father. Carl, a friendly, wise manager who had recently moved from London, knew the toll of consulting work and went out of his way to create a nurturing environment for those of us who worked for him. He told me that the CEO of the Searle sweetener division, a client, said my projects could wait. A second client agreed to put my work on hold, too.

Not only was this a blessing at the time, but, with this generous act, Carl both acknowledged my value to BCG and gave me the chance to be the daughter I needed to be. I believe I would have curtailed my career—by quitting BCG to be with my dad and to help my family—had I not received this paid leave. With Raj in school full-time, we would have been in real financial trouble and unsettled until he'd found a new job.

It was also important that BCG initiated this process. I never would have requested leave, believing that, as a young consultant, I had zero leverage in asking for any kind of benefit that would help me through that difficult time.

This episode in my life underscores how paid leave to get through all kinds of personal situations—including childbirth and personal illness but also other circumstances—can be a game changer for so many careers. In many ways, it's only when you have experienced this benefit yourself that you can truly realize its critical importance.

After my dad's cancer surgery, Chandrika and Nandu returned to the US and I stayed on in Madras. I took my father to follow-up treatments and supported my mom, but there was little more to do in India to extend his life. Four weeks later, we decided to take him to Chicago. Raj's uncle had contacts at top hospitals who might help and we had the house, a place to nurse him back to health. Outwardly, my father remained optimistic, hoping the US would have a cure for him; what he was thinking on the inside, I would never know.

Raj bought a mattress and box spring for an empty upstairs bedroom, and my parents and I arrived in Glen Ellyn after a long trip through Dubai and New York. Nandu decided to take a semester off from Yale to be with us. Chandrika commuted every weekend from New York and called four or five times a day to check on my father and speak with him. For several weeks, we met with specialists, but there was no hope. Watching my beloved Appa deteriorate was incredibly painful, and I would sometimes lock myself in my room to cry. He died in the upstairs bedroom on a June afternoon with me sitting next to him. He was a very young sixty-one, a man who had worked hard and saved for his retirement, hoping to travel the world with my mother. But that was not to be. He

was my number one fan and meant the world to me—the man who played hide-and-seek, hummed our LogRhythms songs, took me to Calcutta, came to Bombay to see me off to Yale. Even though we'd had months to prepare for his death, I was devastated.

He passed away the same day Raj was set to graduate from the University of Chicago with his MBA, a ceremony that we all missed.

My mother returned to India with my brother, whose duty as the only son was to carry out the funeral rites. After thirteen days of mourning, they immersed his ashes in a sacred river in India.

In these same weeks, I discovered I was pregnant. I'd been able to share this joyful news with my father shortly before he died. He was so weak, but, in his final days, he urged everyone around me to make sure I was well taken care of. He would have been a spectacular grandfather.

His illness had moved quickly, and I didn't take the full six months of paid leave that BCG had so generously offered me. I went back to work after about three months, then immediately started dealing with a full project load and wretched morning sickness. I headed north to La Crosse with a suitcase full of snacks, knowing I had to eat a little something every two hours to keep from throwing up. Vegetarian fare in La Crosse, Wisconsin, in the 1980s was always a challenge. But pregnancy was a whole new ball game. I had to be prepared.

The next week, I arrived at Trane again with my special supplies, some spiced vegetables with rice that I could warm and quietly eat in my office or my hotel room. This went on

for a couple of weeks. But then one day I walked into the coffee room, and there it was—a calendar on the wall, filled out with a schedule and details of food planned for me. The secretaries in the office had banded together to help. They made sandwiches and soups that showed up as I worked and kept this up as the months went on. Their kindness blew me away.

For my last meeting with Trane, Bill Roth, the CEO, chartered two planes to bring his entire executive team to our offices in Chicago. The meeting would typically have happened in his own boardroom, but I was nine months pregnant and couldn't travel. Bill wanted me to be part of BCG's final presentation to his company.

My mother was just fifty years old when my father died. With her first grandchild on the way and all three of her children in America, she came to live with me and Raj. We soon put the Glen Ellyn house, which we had lived in for less than a year, on the market. It was full of painful memories, and my hour-long commute to downtown Chicago was tiresome. Raj had a new job at Hewlett Packard (HP) in Downers Grove, Illinois, as a sales executive in the manufacturing systems group.

We moved to a high-rise apartment on East Ohio Street, on the fifteenth floor with a view of Lake Michigan. The building was brand new and felt glamorous. My mother, who spent almost all her time at home, could walk to the store across the street and liked having more people and noise around. One of my BCG colleagues, Bill Elkus, lived a block away, and my mother quickly adopted his wife, Leslie, as another daughter. The two of them got along famously, and Leslie was frequently in our house. Another advantage was that the building was close

to BCG. I usually came home in a Flash Cab, a taxi service with cars that waited outside the office until midnight. I befriended one particular driver, a man named Patterson, who took great care of me as my pregnancy wore on. He'd wait in front of the office building for me, no matter how late I worked.

On one freezing January evening in 1984, I was at home when my water broke and I went into labor. I'd stuck with my suburban obstetrician, a friendly Indian American doctor who promised to be with me through every step of labor, but now I had to get to a hospital that was closer to our old house, almost an hour away. Raj, who was working late, said he'd meet me there. I called another BCG colleague, my friend Bob Solomon, who was the self-appointed alternate if Raj was not available. He showed up a few minutes later in a Flash Cab with Patterson at the wheel. Mom and I piled in. The temperature outside was about 4 degrees Fahrenheit (-15 degrees Celsius) but felt way colder.

For the next eighteen hours, while I was in labor, our little community watched and waited. Leslie Elkus showed up at the hospital to keep Amma company.

Finally, the beautiful Preetha Nooyi was born by cesarean section.

From her first breath, Raj and I adored our baby more than anything we could imagine. She slept between us or in a crib right by me for the next five years. I had three months of paid maternity leave and the absolutely priceless advantage, as a new mother, of my own mother there to help me. Raj had no parental leave and had to go right back to work. We didn't think twice about this.

Preetha was the first grandchild on both sides of our family and was immediately the center of everyone's universe. The details of her birth—the time, longitude, latitude—were sent to India to have a horoscope created that would give us a sense of her life ahead. It came back a few weeks later, assuring everyone that her future was bright.

We took hours of video of her every wriggle and burp with a huge VHS cassette camera on a tripod. Raj's parents came from India about six months later and stayed for several months. Raj would rush home from work to take her out in a stroller to a nearby park, endlessly doting on her. Chandrika came every other weekend to be with Preetha and phoned all the time just to hear her baby-talk. Nandu spent every holiday with us.

Life changed completely for me when I became a mother, with that rush of love from the deepest point inside that I'd never experienced before. Our transition into becoming a family was also profound. Raj and I had to care for our daughter, and we would no longer be alone. We'd have others living with us all the time: relatives and other caregivers for Preetha. There was no going back. We'd be making the choices for this whole collective.

Our growing family was a tether—a beautiful tether, but a tether nonetheless—and I wanted all of it.

I never once considered quitting my job when I had a baby. I was going back to work at the end of three months. Period. End of subject. This wasn't an emotional or philosophical decision in any way; it was an economic decision that was the right thing for us. We needed both of our incomes to pay the household expenses and to save for emergencies and our future.

And my path back to work was possible for one reason: my mother was home to look after Preetha. She did all that work, and I didn't worry.

The family support didn't end there. For the next few years, Raj and I forged ahead in our jobs because we had an extended network, on his side and mine, who stood by us and wanted us to succeed.

None of this meant that I didn't experience the constant heartache of being away from my child. I stopped breast-feeding after three months; I missed her first steps, her first words. But this was reality. I went back into my routines at BCG, traveling around the Midwest, meeting clients, and doing my best.

Then, one Friday afternoon in late May 1986, I was driving my red Toyota Camry home from Hoopeston, Illinois, about 115 miles south of Chicago. I pulled up to a stop sign on a hill where the highway was divided. I looked both ways and started to turn left.

The next thing I remember is waking up in intensive care in a Kankakee, Illinois, hospital.

5

For the next three months, I recovered from a car crash that crushed some bones in my hips and left me covered in cuts. I had internal bleeding, whiplash, and a concussion. In that first week, Raj went to the police station to retrieve my belongings, and, when the cop showed him my mangled red car, his legs buckled under him. The car had no airbags; the driver's side was completely crumpled. My leather briefcase, on the floor in the back, was smashed. It's a miracle that I survived.

The doctors at the Kankakee hospital, sensing internal bleeding, wanted to remove one of my kidneys, but Raj's uncle advised against it and had me moved to his bigger hospital in Hazel Crest, Illinois. The nurses later told me that he checked in every hour and one night showed up in his pajamas to treat the excruciating muscle spasms in my neck and back. The rest of the family flocked in again. Chandrika was working on an assignment in Puerto Rico and came immediately to Chicago. Nandu arrived from New Haven. Raj was there around the

clock. When my mother brought two-year-old Preetha to the hospital, my child lay down next to me crying and wouldn't leave my side, so afraid of seeing me connected to tubes in a strange room and bed.

I went home to the apartment after a few weeks, and my family took care of me, day after day. I had physical therapy; the concussion meant I had to relearn some people's names, and I couldn't watch TV or read much. I was told I couldn't have another child for a few years because of the internal injuries. Surprisingly, I took this news very calmly. I was so glad to have Preetha, and her chatter lifted me.

The intense rest I needed to heal forced me to slow down in a way I hadn't before. I slept a lot, and, on good days, I was eager to get back to work. On bad days, I was happy to be alive and intact. The accident was my fault because I had driven into the intersection without seeing the oncoming car. The signage at the crossing was very poor, as the police officer later noted in my court appearance. He'd seen many other accidents right there.

Once again, BCG stepped up when it mattered by paying my salary throughout this ordeal. We also had excellent health insurance through the company, and I don't know what we'd have done without it. But the time away from work made me reassess my priorities. I had a daughter now, and the endless travel and long hours no longer felt exciting. I wanted to be close to home.

Meanwhile, an executive recruiter kept calling, pressing me to consider a job in the automotive electronics division of Motorola. Finally, I shuffled into that company's Schaumburg, Illinois, headquarters for an interview, pushing a four-legged, aluminum walker.

Cars and trucks in the 1980s were being transformed from heavy steel, mechanical beasts to the lighter-weight, computer-guided machines we drive today. Motorola—a major player in developing two-way radios, pagers, semiconductors, cell phones, and satellites for government use—was inventing new systems for vehicles, from electronics for engine controls and antilock braking to intelligent navigation systems. The person running the automotive electronics division was Gerhard Schulmeyer, a German engineer and businessman who'd worked at Braun, Gillette, and Sony in Europe and had an MBA from MIT. Gerhard was rumored to be tough as nails. He needed a new head of strategy, someone to help him think through how Motorola's vast resources could radically upgrade personal transportation.

I knew Gerhard was a force the moment I met him. The interview was all substance, not about electronics or cars, but about my thought processes as a business strategist. How do I go about understanding what drives an industry I know nothing about? How do I keep current in the world of strategy? How extensive is my network of contacts? I liked Gerhard. He had an incredible ability to paint a picture of the future in words. He just wanted to know if we were a good fit. Shortly after the meeting, Motorola made me an offer.

I was surprised at how fast all this had happened and started to waver on whether I should pull the plug on BCG and consulting, which I so dearly loved. So I co-opted Raj to help me make a decision. We went to dinner with Gerhard and his smart and cheerful wife, Helga. The warmth and give-and-take between the two of them made a real impression on us. When we got home, Raj told me that if I really wanted to leave BCG

and work for someone who didn't care whether I was male, female, immigrant, mother, or whatever—someone who just cared about my brains—I should work for Gerhard. "All he'll care about is results," he said. I took the job.

I worked with Gerhard, on and off, for the next eight years. He was my teacher, coach, critic, and supporter and nourished my career with wisdom and care for my family that was fundamental to my ascent and ability to become a CEO. He taught me to simplify complex problems and to communicate them effectively. And he looked out for opportunities for me. He once sent me to teach a class at MIT when the university wanted him.

Yet again, I had the good luck of a boss who was a mentor, advocate, and friend. In return, I put in very long hours. My loyalty to him was unwavering.

In late 1986, still walking with a funny limp, I began commuting by car every morning from our downtown Chicago home to Motorola, about thirty miles away. A few weeks later, my mother told us that she just didn't want to face another Chicago winter, with months of frigid winds and below-freezing temperatures. The gently falling snow could be beautiful, she said, but she was feeling cooped up and really wanted to return to India for several months. Raj and I fully understood. We bought her the plane ticket. Preetha wasn't happy about it.

And then we had no childcare.

While Amma lived with us—through my pregnancy, as we adjusted to parenthood, and as I recovered from the terrible car accident—I had never once worried about Preetha being safe and loved. I didn't worry about her food or clothing or whether

she was being truly cared for. She was read to, talked to, picked up, encouraged, and signed up for baby classes. I was always in touch with my mother and knew the details of their days. Our daughter lived in the center of a full, devoted community.

But now, for one cold, dark season at least, Raj and I were on our own. And the next five months drove home how difficult it is for two working parents with young children to cope in an environment where quality, affordable childcare is not ubiquitous and where support systems for working families are completely lacking.

First, we put the word out to relatives, friends, and neighbors that we were looking for a caregiver and interviewed a few people. Like so many other parents, though, we didn't meet someone we trusted and connected with, and the whole prospect of a high-end, well-trained nanny was very expensive.

Then, thankfully, a woman named Vasantha, whom we'd met a few times at Indian music concerts, offered to help. She lived with her husband, three daughters, and one son, all teenagers, in a house in Oak Park, Illinois, about twenty minutes from our apartment and on the route to Raj's office. She would take Preetha every morning, she said, and either of us could get her on our way home. One absolute blessing of this arrangement, I know in retrospect, was that Vasantha let us pick up the baby any time in the evening.

So, every morning at 6:30, we dressed Preetha in her full-body snowsuit, hat, mittens, and boots and packed her bag of diapers, extra clothes, toys, creams, and little snacks. Then Raj carried her by 7 a.m. down the street to his car through the Chicago winter. He buckled her into her car seat and drove her to Oak Park.

In the evenings, it was often Raj who went back to Vasantha's house, making his way through the snowbanks to the front door. I was less available to pick Preetha up because, in my first year at Motorola, I had to travel to Phoenix fairly often to work with the Chicago-based executives who had their "winter head office" in Arizona. I remember a few episodes when I was stuck in a plane on the tarmac at O'Hare airport, panicked that I was late on my night to get my little daughter. Sometimes I didn't make it to Vasantha's house until 9 or 10 p.m.

Preetha loved Vasantha, but the early morning drives in the cold and the late night pickups wore on her. Some mornings, she just refused to leave the house and threw tantrums. That winter was not our most shining moment. By spring, Raj and I were exhausted with it all. Something had to change.

We chose to move back to Glen Ellyn, into a four-bedroom house with a semifinished basement, a front porch, and a double garage near a park and a Montessori school. The new house, in a brand-new development, was much closer to my office and had space for live-in help in addition to visiting family.

Our suburban American life began for a second time, now with furniture in almost every room, and a lively three-year-old girl. She loved to explore the nooks and corners and many stairs in the house and to splash in the bathtub. She had a couple of friends across the street, Mark and David, and they watched a lot of *Teenage Mutant Ninja Turtles* on TV. I never really understood this show, but Raphael, Donatello, Michelangelo, and Leonardo, the four main characters, became my new best friends.

Raj and I also asked our parents, uncles, and aunts in India whether any of them could take time off and come to the US

to help us with Preetha. Some agreed, and then we had to schedule them. We used a large, full-year calendar and worked months ahead to sort out all the travel times and tickets, as well as the visas and support documents everyone needed to get into the US and then go back.

For the next few years, my mother, in-laws, and relatives alternated living with us. Occasionally, we also hired a local babysitter to help get Preetha ready for her preschool classes, assist in cooking, and do some housework. In the evenings, Raj and I took over. We still didn't have a social life. Our neighbors were friendly but hustling to keep their work and family lives on track, too.

The Indian relatives each came for two or three months. They slept in a bright bedroom with an attached bathroom on the main floor and chipped in for Preetha's needs and activities. Frankly, they watched a lot of TV and didn't go anywhere except on weekends, when we showed them around Chicago or drove them to the mall or the movies. They struggled a bit in the quiet of suburbia, missing guests popping in and the bustle of home. We bought them each a Visit USA airline ticket, a deal for foreign visitors to fly around the country and see the sights. But no one used it. They came to Glen Ellyn just to be with us.

The men had decent midlevel jobs in government in India and had never taken much vacation, so they had paid time off to make the trip. Their wives hadn't worked outside their homes and didn't have many commitments of their own. Helping our growing family was viewed both as an intergenerational responsibility—and a joy. They felt vested in our success.

Crucially for me, they rejected the traditional Indian notion that the woman in the family, even if she earned money outside the house, was also responsible for keeping everyone fed, clothed, clean, and content. If I came home from work tired, they'd tell me to rest. I had stuck with my job—as Raj's father urged me to do after our wedding—and they were very proud of me. I was an educated, energetic woman making tracks in American business, and they talked about my career with their friends and acquaintances in India. Nooyi is a small village near Mangalore, and my in-laws loved that I carried the name in my pursuits in the US and put their tiny town on the map.

We didn't pay the visiting relatives or my mother for their help. Raj and I paid for everything in my mother's life when she lived with us but didn't give her a salary for the childcare, cooking, cleaning, and thousands of other small tasks she did to keep our household going over the years. Had we suggested we pay her, she would have been insulted.

Even though Raj and I juggled, worried, bickered, and coped during the one winter when we drove Preetha to the in-home childcare, I know our problems were pretty simple. The arrangement was short-lived, and we had secure jobs and a healthy child. Otherwise, when our children were small, Raj and I were very fortunate to be able to rely on a care ecosystem—made up of extended family supported by household help—to let our own little family flourish. And, of course, we could keep advancing in our careers.

But what of the millions of families who don't have this luxury? The travails of working parents who do this dance every day for years—through snowstorms but also through job loss,

divorce, illness, and the millions of other hurdles we all face—make me wonder why accessible, affordable quality childcare isn't a national priority.

The trusted care I had at home let me dive into my job at Motorola. In my first week, I sat down in my new office in the old Automotive Electronics building to read about the recent strategy work, and I soon figured out that Gerhard had burned through three or four chief strategists in the eighteen months before me. Not a good sign! I asked the head of HR about it.

"Yeah. That's because Gerhard is impossible to work with," he said. "He has an idea a minute and no one can keep up with him. We're hoping you'll last."

This was essential knowledge. Gerhard needed me to run fast with him and to help push his vision within the organization. He started stopping by my office every morning with new musings, and I started putting each into one of three buckets: (1) worth working on right away, (2) fine to take a few weeks to get to it, (3) not worth pursuing. Over time, I reordered the list, and he saw progress. He never questioned my judgment on how and why I had prioritized his ideas.

Gerhard hired me, a total outsider, because I had been exposed to so many different industries and could apply a strategic framework to understand what drives value in a business. I was outspoken and willing to challenge the status quo.

Still, I knew nothing about cars and electronics. So, I had two community college professors come twice a week to my office for lessons—one on how automobiles work and the other on solid-state physics and electronics. What is a microprocessor?

What is a semiconductor? What are electronic engine controls? What is a transmission? What is a carburetor? Without this extra training, I couldn't have succeeded. I had to establish myself as a curious and quick study who understood Motorola's whole portfolio, especially automotive electronics.

The company, founded in Chicago in 1928, was the first to develop car radios (hence the "motor" and the "ola," a typical 1920s suffix indicating sound). Six decades later, Motorola was loaded with brilliant minds helping lead the technology revolution. They worked with the National Aeronautics and Space Administration to build the radios that let Neil Armstrong speak to the world from the moon. They designed and built microprocessors and semiconductors to power computers built by Apple and others. They invented the first handheld portable telephone in 1971. When I arrived, the phone had become the DynaTAC 8000, the first commercially viable mobile phone. It was a $3,995 book-sized device with a thirty-minute battery life, and I was very proud of the one I got as a Motorola employee. I wore a pager on the waistband of my skirt, too, since executives like me certainly needed to be buzzed at any time. It was a sign of importance—even if the only people who buzzed you were family and friends.

For two years, I worked with Gerhard to reposition the automotive electronics division for sustained growth. Then, at his suggestion, I was asked by the CEO's office to lead a company-wide project we called "Control and Communications for People and Machines on the Move." We had three task forces to examine how technology might move with a person through the day—"Car of the Future," "Truck of

the Future," and "Home of the Future." We were to examine how people could transition seamlessly between a technologically advanced home and a car or truck to make life more convenient and connected.

I loved the mandate and the far-reaching nature of the assignment. I got a generous budget and assembled a team of several Motorola executives and seven MBA students who took a semester off to work on the project. We had so many ideas about how technology could and would shape our future: dashboards with integrated entertainment and navigation, built-in mobile phones, remote management of a home from the car. The list went on and on. We had to think about how Motorola should craft investment strategies for years to come.

The highlight was a daylong meeting with ten senior executives who said they were eager to cooperate across divisions and bring our conclusions to life. Personally, it was fulfilling to see my work so welcome.

In late 1988, all of thirty-three years old, I was promoted to director of corporate strategy and planning for Motorola. I started working with the CEO's office and felt included in that inner circle. Chris Galvin, who was in charge of corporate functions and later became CEO, advocated for me get the vice president title, a rarity for a woman in the company.

I moved into an office on the sixth floor of the big brown brick-and-glass headquarters building. This job came with a car and an indoor parking spot, a bonus because I could stop scraping the ice and snow off my windshield every winter night before driving home. I got a small raise, but I wasn't thinking about the money. I was excited to take on a bigger role.

My job was to rejuvenate corporate strategy, an underappreciated function in Motorola's executive branch. I

hired a half dozen people, including former colleagues from BCG and other parts of Motorola, and threw myself into the work. I loved managing people and explaining how we could grow Motorola and take on the agile companies in Silicon Valley.

As a leader, I could be very blunt in my drive to make sure we made all the right decisions. In some meetings, I would comment on plans directly and sometimes point out why I thought a unit's strategy wouldn't work. "Your strategy makes no sense," I'd say. "There's no way you can deliver the return you have assumed in your financial model." This wasn't popular—or effective.

At some point, George Fisher, the CEO, noted my style and pulled me aside. "Be careful about throwing hand grenades," he said. "You may turn people off even though you mean well." George coached me to take a different tack, by saying, for example, "Help me understand how this comes together. As I see it, this technology platform requires a lot of investment and patience. Is it prudent to factor in a quick return?" Much as I hated this new, softer way of asking questions, I found it got results. I appreciated how George spoke to me—one-on-one, straight, and in a constructive tone. Overall, good lessons.

Still, after a while, dealing with a complicated, top-heavy CEO's office, multiple division presidents, and other well-meaning managers who believed they, too, needed to influence Motorola's corporate strategy and planning made day-to-day work tedious. I figured out how to get stuff done in my strategy job by working through people who held informal power, but that seemed unnecessarily time-consuming.

One day in late 1989, Gerhard called me to say he was leaving Motorola. He'd accepted a job in Zurich at ASEA Brown Boveri (ABB), an ambitious new company formed by the recent merger of ASEA AB, of Sweden, and BBC Brown Boveri, of Switzerland. ABB would compete with General Electric (GE), Mitsubishi, and others to be the world's most important maker of heavy electrical equipment, including power generation and transmission equipment and industrial controls. Gerhard would commute to Switzerland. For now, Helga would stay in Chicago with their three children.

I was disappointed but not surprised. Gerhard had started running Motorola's European business a few months earlier, and I knew the global product divisions didn't like his direct style and were uncooperative. He was frustrated and heading on to greener pastures. Under his tutelage, I had grown enormously. I wished him very well and promised to stay in touch, but I knew I'd miss him a lot.

Meanwhile, at headquarters, the corporate strategy team was asked to take on a huge new endeavor—a complete portfolio analysis of every Motorola business. We worked day and night to examine the company's advantages and disadvantages, which segments should we invest in, and which long-term technology bets made the most sense. I found that all that earlier "of the Future" work was paying off. We had some great ideas to shoot for.

After almost a year, my team gave a six-hour presentation to the company's senior management, a top-to-bottom review with a clear plan of action. I was very proud of it all. It was the biggest and most comprehensive work I'd ever done. The discussion was exciting and revealing. Everyone was

complimentary, and the top brass said they'd get back to us in a few weeks with ideas on how to move ahead.

Gerhard called again. He'd arrived in Zurich and soon decided he wanted me to come to ABB. I told him that under no circumstances would I move to Zurich or start an international commute. OK, he said, he understood that. But since I wouldn't do the job, would I please help him find someone who could help him? He'd already asked his executive recruiter to find him "an Indra Nooyi." The recruiter had no idea what that meant and had to call me to create the job description.

I agreed to help and started vetting candidates. I even went to London just to meet four or five potential new strategists at Gerhard's behest. I'm sure they were puzzled as to why someone from Motorola was interviewing them for a job at ABB. But that didn't matter. Gerhard rejected them all. His secretary in Zurich also called me often when she was trying to figure out Gerhard's requests. We joked that I was her "Gerhard interpreter." I helped her through her early days.

Several more months went by. I was waiting for some direction on the next steps related to my portfolio analysis, but the Motorola bosses kept telling me to be patient. In the evenings, Raj started to hear me complain and, for the first time, saw me struggling with anxiety. It was an unusual situation for him—and for me. I was normally so determined, but now I was frustrated.

Given the culture of Motorola, maybe I should have known that big decisions about the company's entire future would be slow and careful. But I was impatient and stressed, and I

didn't know whether my impatience was—and is—a vice or a virtue.

Gerhard called yet again. ABB had been on a buying spree, he said, and had soaked up hundreds of smaller engineering and equipment manufacturing companies around the world. The company had grown to two hundred thousand employees and sales of about $20 billion a year. Now ABB was taking over Combustion Engineering, a company based in Stamford, Connecticut, that made power generation systems and other industrial equipment. Gerhard was adding the company's US operations to his job. He'd oversee about one third of ABB. He and Helga were moving to Connecticut.

Would I come, too?

Raj, at this time, was doing exceedingly well at Hewlett Packard. He was happy in his job as a sales executive and he was among the early winners of the company's President's Club Award, an accolade given to the top 0.1 percent of sales executives. He worked with people he viewed as close friends; he loved the business and environment.

Preetha was settled in her Montessori school in Glen Ellyn. We were both home most evenings at a reasonable hour, ate dinner together, played with our growing daughter, and read books to her. Some weekends, Raj took her to the Morton Arboretum, where they bonded over birds, trees, and flowers. Other weekends, we went to the science museum or the Shedd Aquarium in downtown Chicago. Our life was stable and fun. The trees we had planted in the yard were growing bigger. Yes,

I was frustrated at work, but there was so much equilibrium in our lives.

Still, Gerhard didn't stop. After talking to me, he reached out to Raj about the Connecticut plan and mapped out all the reasons why we should move: proximity to New York and my sister, better schools, lovely homes, more pay, and an action-oriented boss and company. He was quite the salesman. Raj took the call and listened patiently—a real tribute to the prince of a man he is.

One night, Raj asked me if I thought anything was going to happen with my Motorola portfolio analysis. I told him it didn't look good. The problem lay in the structure of Motorola's leadership: the presidents of each division, ultimately, had far more sway than I did over these decisions, and the CEO's office had to build consensus with them for major strategy decisions. My department was always going to be a sounding board, but our recommendations might take years to implement. How fresh would they be in the fast-moving tech world?

"OK," Raj said. "Then let's move. I want you to be happy, and it's clear you are not."

That my husband placed my happiness and career at the center of this discussion was touching indeed. He had clearly thought it through, and he was willing to have his wife and daughter move across the country while he stayed in Chicago and followed us later, God knows when. He knew he'd have to switch jobs in HP or move to another company. He was willing to make sure that I was fulfilled.

Raj's selflessness is all the more remarkable because he was taking on the conventions of the time in so many ways. He was an ambitious, educated man in his thirties on his own corporate

climb, with great financial and management prospects. He was also an Indian immigrant in the US, bound by both the behavioral expectations of his family and friends back home, and by the men he was getting to know in this new country. With this choice to change his life for the sake of my career, he was contesting all of that. His courage and devotion to me and to his family is why I adore him and view him as the best thing that ever happened to me.

When I decided to quit Motorola, Chris, whose grandfather had founded the company and whose father had been CEO, was visibly upset. He came to our house one weekend morning to convince me to stay. His most compelling argument was that I shouldn't leave an institution (Motorola) for an individual (Gerhard). I told him I didn't want to leave, but I didn't feel like I was having an impact.

All I wanted was to see the results of my work.

6

My mother, Preetha, and I uprooted to a small two-bedroom rental apartment on Strawberry Hill Avenue in Stamford, Connecticut, in late 1990. The building was a gigantic cement block; the walls were thin, the carpet was worn, and Preetha, now aged six, had nowhere to run around. At least it was temporary.

The plan was for Raj to commute from Chicago a couple of weekends a month while he worked with HP on a transfer to the Northeast. He was a top performer and set for a promotion, and he loved the work. He was optimistic, but, sadly, after a few months, we learned that the bigger job in Connecticut wasn't going to be available for more than a year. While Raj was OK with continuing to travel back and forth, I didn't want him away from us for such long periods. Preetha missed him, and I didn't think I could cope without him.

Raj reluctantly chose to move to Connecticut, unclear about what he was going to do next. It was a difficult choice and a sacrifice that he made out of love. He quit a great job in

a dominant company in the technology revolution right when he had terrific momentum there.

Separately, our house in Glen Ellyn sold in a few weeks, and we were fairly content about moving closer to New York. My sister and brother were nearby, and my mother had more friends from India in the area. New England was familiar. We were just an hour's drive from Yale, and I could engage more with SOM and maybe even go to Yankee Stadium to see games in person.

I was thrilled to get back to work with Gerhard—instantly satisfied to be in an environment where I could consult with him, make decisions, and take action. Our offices were on wooded grounds in a luxurious building with wide hallways and large rooms. My title was senior vice president of strategy and strategic marketing, and my portfolio included all of ABB's businesses in North America and the global industrial segment of the company. I was among the top fifty executives in ABB.

ABB was an acquisition machine at the time. In its heyday, Combustion Engineering, the company ABB had bought in Connecticut, had been an iconic American corporation, supplying steam generation and power transmission equipment to almost all the US utilities. Now it was a money-losing manufacturer of steam turbines with tens of thousands of employees. ABB wanted to boost its North American footprint and round out its power generation offering. I actually thought it was a terrible purchase, completed without much due diligence. Problems were everywhere. Gerhard had to streamline the whole operation and layer in the worldview of an ambitious European conglomerate.

ABB's CEO, based in Zurich, was Percy Barnevik, a young Swedish executive who had masterminded the merger of ASEA

with Brown Boveri three years earlier. Percy's operating style was unique: he decentralized the company into hundreds of legal entities and gave senior managers complete control. Then he'd come down like a ton of bricks if they didn't deliver. Percy had been named European "CEO of the Year" and his style was much talked about in the press. Everyone seemed impressed and a little bit afraid of Percy. I was far enough from him to just watch and learn.

Our biggest competitor was GE, led by the legendary CEO Jack Welch, who governed a sprawling corporate headquarters just twenty miles from our offices in Stamford. ABB studied every GE move with envy and fear. Jack Welch's GE was *the* company to emulate. The only puzzling thing to all of us at ABB was the reality that so much of its profit came from GE Capital, a risky strategy that could derail GE's performance if the financial markets turned volatile. This also meant GE's valuation was not being driven by its manufacturing business. We were benchmarking ourselves with the wrong company.

Yet again, I dove into the intricacies of the business. This time it was global industrial equipment for manufacturing facilities: textiles, paper, oil and gas, general industrial manufacturing. How do customers buy drives and motors, programmable logic controls, instrumentation? Do they buy systems or subsystems? Or do they buy independent products and integrate them using in-house engineers? My BCG training, especially my work with Trane on complex HVAC systems, helped me think this through.

I began studying the nuts and bolts of ABB's offerings. I started traveling regularly to Europe, mostly to Zurich, Switzerland; Mannheim, Germany; and Västerås, Sweden, to visit plants and work with global colleagues and customers.

In North America, the work was more holistic. Besides industrial customers, we had to deal with public utilities. What was power demand likely to be for the next twenty years? Which utilities will need generation capacity? Steam or gas? How old is the installed base? I created industry advisory councils and had experts help us craft strategy. Equipment suppliers and utilities were mutually dependent, and it was useful to get to know customers this way. My team, meanwhile, was a tight, productive, genial group.

Through it all, I also had the help of Anita Griffin, who planned my travels, kept my schedule, and was a great presence at work for all. She planned a surprise party for me in the office on the day I was sworn in as an American citizen—with little flags; a cake; and hats in red, white, and blue. She really understood that this was a big day for me: I was thrilled to become a citizen of the US, but I was giving up my citizenship of India, the country where I was born and a place so central to my identity. It was very emotional.

While I was very busy in my strategy job, I was also a critical extra set of eyes and ears for Gerhard. He was often at headquarters in Zurich because he was a member of the ABB Vorstand, the executive board. I became his intermediary in the US, passing messages to and from the managers trying to make his big ideas work. We talked several times a day.

Gerhard communicated in English, but his style was German. He liked simple frameworks, data neatly and logically presented, and pithy presentations. Sometimes, he'd sit through a meeting and then turn to me, in front of everyone, and say, "I take it you didn't review this material before it came to me." I could

sense when this was going to happen because his ears would turn red. I was the only one who noticed.

That sort of comment resulted in most of my colleagues' running work by me before it went to Gerhard. They appreciated my input, and it was another way for me to learn about issues for which I was not directly responsible. I had to use the power of my access carefully. I made sure people knew I was not speaking for Gerhard and that Gerhard knew that I didn't intend to carry tales.

There was a downside to this role, however. Chris Galvin at Motorola was right. My loyalty to Gerhard was complete, but I was really working for the individual, not the institution. My success and longevity in ABB were tied to Gerhard.

Strawberry Hill was not to our liking, and, after a few months, I started looking for a house to rent while we saved extra money to buy a permanent home. Raj and I carefully thought through this next step. We'd rent in a location close to where we wanted to buy a house, then put down roots there.

We chose Connecticut's Fairfield County, which is largely a bedroom community, lined with Metro-North train stations for the hundreds of thousands of workers who travel in and out of New York City every day. The county extends thirty miles up the Atlantic coast, from Greenwich on the New York State line, with big houses on winding, verdant roads, to Bridgeport, which, in 1990, was teetering on the edge of bankruptcy. In between are the smaller communities of Darien, New Canaan, Norwalk, Fairfield, Westport, and a half dozen more towns that epitomize New England suburban life: good schools, public

libraries, old churches, and pumpkins on the doorsteps in the fall.

When I didn't find a rental after a couple of outings, Gerhard had a suggestion. Helga and their children were moving from Chicago but wouldn't arrive for a few weeks. Gerhard and Helga had lined up a temporary house in New Canaan. Why didn't Raj and I take that house? The Schulmeyers would then find another one.

The place Gerhard and Helga had rented was gorgeous—bigger than we might have chosen—with mature trees and a lovely yard. OK, Raj and I thought when we saw it, it will cost a little more, but let's do it. But when Gerhard informed the homeowners of the switch to tenants of Indian origin, they reneged. "The house is not available to rent," they declared.

We can guess why these owners pulled out, but Raj and I just moved on. We needed to find a house and had no time or energy to dwell on this. The Schulmeyers didn't take that house either.

We found a place in Darien in a neighborhood called Noroton Bay, with wetlands all around abundant with birds and chipmunks, which Preetha loved to chase. The house was a large, contemporary structure that needed work but a perfect rental for us. We could see the glistening water from almost every room.

Raj soon landed a job in KPMG's consulting business, based in Stamford, focused on supply-chain management in the electronics industry. After less than a year, he moved to PRTM, another consulting firm affiliated with KPMG. He worked there for nine years and became a partner. The work energized him.

Preetha began first grade at the New Canaan Country School, and my mother lived with us and spent time with my sister, who was now married and living in New York with a new baby girl. My brother had graduated from Yale and was working on his PhD at MIT, in Cambridge, Massachusetts.

Soon enough, I was pregnant again. We were thrilled, although the cycle of wicked morning sickness began as it had before. I once passed out in my office and had to stay home for a few days. Gerhard sent his driver, Frank, to sit in our driveway in case I needed chauffeuring to the hospital. When I told Frank he should leave, he refused. "Mr. Schulmeyer won't let me."

And, again at this point, we needed reliable, affordable childcare for Preetha—someone to support a child in elementary school.

This time, we decided to hire a live-in nanny through a reputable agency, since we were eager to find someone who was screened and trustworthy and who could drive Preetha to school. We chose a young woman in her mid-twenties from upstate New York. We liked her, although Preetha seemed to watch a lot of TV when we weren't around. We spoke to the nanny about engaging more with the child, reading books, and playing, but nothing much changed. One evening, the nanny went into New York City with a friend to a party and informed us the next day that there was an incident involving her friend in the house where the party was held. She wasn't part of it, she said, but the police might show up to question her. We let her go.

We returned to the nanny agency, which charged a sizable fee for every placement, and picked someone else from the database who we hoped would last longer. She was from the

Midwest and appeared pleasant in her bio and photograph. We interviewed her by phone. She sounded capable and organized. After a couple of weeks, though, we realized that she couldn't keep up with the demands of the job. She was kind, but we couldn't be constantly worrying about how she'd get through the day. We had to let her go, too.

We felt desperate for these nannies to work out and had the resources to fit the right person comfortably into our family. But the process was so fraught and stressful, that, like millions of other working parents, we bailed out on any formal plan. Amma held the fort off and on, and we found a retired woman in the neighborhood who babysat Preetha when we needed her. Frank drove Preetha to school if Raj or I couldn't do it.

For me and Raj, this was a time of hope, stress, excitement, and trepidation. As my pregnancy progressed, I went from brutal morning sickness to intense fatigue—working, traveling, and trying to live up to the expectations of being a great executive, mother, wife, and daughter. My mother living with us brought great advantages and, over time, some difficulties. She had her own way of parenting Preetha. Sleep times and dining times were fairly lax, and TV watching was equally random. Raj wanted a little more routine and discipline in Preetha's life. My mother kept reminding us that she'd raised three kids and knew what she was doing. I didn't want to make her mad. Raj was right to want to organize Preetha's life a little more. I couldn't change my mother. I tried to intervene, with little luck.

There was a lot of tension in the house.

Multigenerational living, so natural in Asian households and many other cultures around the world, can be a tremendous advantage to working families. Mothers and fathers have an extra set of hands when they need them, and children and grandparents connect, building the kind of deep and lasting relationships that I had with Thatha and that Preetha has with my mother and Raj's parents. This model also works for caring for our elders and allows for young adults to rely on support from the home base when they are venturing out in the world.

I'm very aware that it's not easy. Living this way requires adjustments from all sides. It limits everyone's privacy and can lead to tussles that hurt elders and cause rifts within marriages. This is clearly not the intended outcome. Whole households have to agree on boundaries and behaviors to keep relationships healthy.

In some cultures where multigenerational living is common, it can be particularly hard on women who are caught in the middle as mothers, daughters, or daughters-in-law. These women may work outside the home but also have the tremendous burden of needing to be outstanding homemakers, parents, and caregivers to the elders. Every move can be analyzed and criticized. A woman's paycheck may be deposited against her wishes in a family fund, where she doesn't have control of her own spending. She ends up feeling guilty about not living up to anyone's expectations and doesn't have the freedom to make her own decisions.

Globally, with a rapidly aging population and a real need to support young families, figuring out the best way to set up multigenerational cohabitation, physically and practically, is becoming urgent. Doing this well—with inventive architecture and development and connected with community

infrastructure—could be a real boon to working families in ways that reduce the pressures but capture the wonderful benefits of living together.

Raj and I started looking for a permanent house in the vicinity of our Noroton home. We liked being near the water, the neighbors were friendly, and Preetha loved her school. Then, one day, I was flying to Europe and was seated beside another senior woman executive who also lived in the Connecticut suburbs. When I told her about our search for a home to buy, she responded, very plainly, "I hope you are not thinking about lily-white Darien or New Canaan."

I was struck by her comment but didn't ask her what she meant.

Curiously, a few weeks later, we were talking to a neighbor about our house search, and he used the exact same phrase. "What are you doing here in lily-white Darien?" he asked us. In the long run, he said, we wouldn't belong and we would feel unwelcome.

These two conversations, in rapid succession, opened our eyes to how our experience with Gerhard's rental house ran much deeper than we'd imagined. My father had always told me to "assume positive intent." But the message was pretty clear: these communities were not for people like us.

We moved our search to Greenwich, a larger town that is closer to the New York metropolitan area. Greenwich wasn't particularly diverse either, but we were told that more international families lived there. The real estate agent showed us everything that was available, and we found a lovely house within a short drive to the commercial part of town. It cost

more than we'd budgeted but met all our other criteria. We closed on the purchase. The home was now ours.

When we moved to Greenwich, we knew we were going to be living in a wealthy community—a sort of bubble quite different from the more unassuming house and surroundings we were used to in Chicago. We were a little ambivalent, but the quality of the schools, the safe neighborhoods, and our belief that we could protect our children all weighed on our choice.

Shortly after the purchase, we hired a contractor to do a few repairs before we moved in. A few weeks later, I returned from a trip and went to check on his progress and found that half the house had been stripped to its frame. The contractor claimed the building had much more wrong with it than expected. He started with a little demolition and then didn't stop.

What a disaster. We just didn't have the money for a big renovation. I was four months pregnant. We had to find a new construction team—this guy seemed dishonest—and we had to pull off this project on a very tight timeline. Raj and I felt completely out of our depth. This was a wood-framed house, and we'd grown up in the flat-topped concrete structures of India. We didn't know anything about two-by-four lumber or how to assess the required pitch for a roof to handle the snow. We were at the mercy of contractors. Thankfully, to tide us over, ABB lent us some money as part of a common company loan program at the time. And Helga, who was a designer and had renovated many homes before, knew what she was doing and stepped in. She was working on her own new house in Greenwich and added ours to her list.

We continued to be two families relying on each other to get through the demands of a broad range of work and family obligations—from building ABB into a dominant global company to making sure we all had a place to lay our heads at night.

In mid-December 1992, four days after we moved into our rebuilt home, I went into labor. The next morning I gave birth, via cesarean section, to a beautiful, healthy baby girl—Tara Nooyi. Once again, my love for the baby just overtook me. In the hospital, I didn't want her out of my sight and never let anyone take her to the nursery. I gazed at her in wonderment and prayed that God would give me the strength and ability to be a good mother to her and Preetha.

Our family was complete. Raj and I were delighted to have two daughters. We loved them dearly and felt the great weight of our responsibility. We wanted to protect them and to save for their educations and weddings, just as our families had done before us. We wanted to make sure they could dream big and fly high. We talked about how they would grow up to be caring, contributing citizens of their community and country and, perhaps, responsible parents themselves someday.

Two children are harder than one. It was clear in Tara's first months that the emotional, physical, and organizational work of parenting our girls was going to be far more complicated than we had anticipated.

I realize now, for instance, that I should have paid more attention to Preetha's adjustment to having a baby sister. She'd always been the family VIP, and she particularly treasured the joyful times alone with me when we sang and danced together.

She had already indicated that she missed me because I worked so much. When she was about eight, Gerhard once asked her what she wanted to be when she grew up. "I want to have your job," Preetha replied. "Because if I have your job, I'll always be with my mommy."

When Tara came along, Preetha was a third grader in a brand-new house. We'd been through months of a renovation, a pregnancy, our work obligations, and general rushing around. I thought she'd love having a little sibling. But now, in retrospect, I understand she felt jealous and upset about sharing her spotlight. She acted up and disobeyed. I was preoccupied, short-tempered, and, too often, ignored the fact that Preetha, too, needed me.

Meanwhile, little Tara began refusing to sleep unless she lay on my outstretched lower legs while I was propped up in bed. Pretty soon, I was spending my nights in this position, a habit that wasn't great for the mood.

Many times, as I tried to get some work done, with the baby sleeping on my legs and Preetha snoozing beside me, I wondered what I was doing. I started to ask myself: Should I keep working? What would be the consequences if I quit? Would I have regrets and resentments that would create a negative environment at home?

I had no idea how to take a break from work and then return a few years later. I could think of no examples of women who had done this. I was concerned that any hiatus would render my skills irrelevant and that it would be hard for me to reenter the job market, contribute to the economic well-being of my family, and stay intellectually active. There were also no young mothers around who were working from home, even temporarily. Going into the office was required.

I worried about all this and struggled to sleep. But I kept going.

My job at ABB remained relentless. I had three months of paid maternity leave, but, as a senior executive, I didn't feel I could disengage to devote that time to my family. The work didn't stop.

In fact, the day after Tara was born, Gerhard called me in the hospital to tell me about a project that would benefit from my input. I reminded him I'd just given birth and was recovering from surgery. "But it's your body that had the baby," he joked. "Your brain is still working."

Gerhard showed me he needed and appreciated me and that I was important to his work. He also knew that having a baby was a big deal and let me decide when I wanted to return.

But after he told me about the project, I brought my team together right away to talk about it. They were all men, but they, too, knew something about childbirth—and told me I was nuts to jump in so fast. They said they'd call me if they needed me. Nonetheless, I had them come over to my house regularly during my leave to discuss the project. This was all 100 percent my choice.

I wonder why I am wired this way where my inner compass always tells me to keep pushing on with my job responsibilities, whatever the circumstances. If I feel that I can help make something better, then I cannot stop myself from jumping in. I have a deep sense of duty and find it very hard to say no if someone asks for help.

I love my family dearly, but this inner drive to help whenever I can certainly has taken a lot of time away from them—much to their dismay.

I sometimes wish I were wired differently.

By this time, we had more money to spend on household help, which clearly smoothed my return to work. We hired a retired nurse to take care of Tara as a baby, help oversee Preetha's activities, and do some cooking. We also had a house cleaner. Our next-door neighbor, Mary Waterman, became a great friend. Her son Jamie was Preetha's age, and Mary got to know the nurse, Raj's parents, and all the other relatives, who continued to visit. Mary was a big help to them, answering any questions they had, and then filling me in on the proceedings.

Gradually in Tara's first year, this big collective started to work for all of us. We got into a routine where I felt there was a group looking after the girls, and no individual was carrying the whole load. That felt healthy and familiar to me.

For almost twenty years, Raj and I took very few vacations, although every year we made a trip to India as a family. We spent the time in Madras and Mangalore, and Preetha and Tara loved these holidays. They were full of fun and games and laughter with other kids that reminded me of my childhood summers. They roamed the garden without parents and never complained about mosquitoes, the power going out, or the persistent noise. The minute we got off the plane in India, it seems they assumed a certain Indianness. They were comfortable wearing Indian clothes and eating meals off banana leaves. They viewed it all as one big adventure.

For fourth grade, we moved Preetha to the North Street public school in Greenwich, close to our new house. After about six months, we got a surprising note from the teacher

saying that she wasn't turning in her homework. Preetha was smart, lively, and funny, and she enjoyed school. We'd been exceedingly conscientious about her education. She was surrounded by books and always had glowing reports. She was only ten—she didn't have all that much homework—but we were very concerned when we got the note.

When we checked her room, we found the work done but not submitted. We asked Preetha about it, and she had no real answer. She just shrugged. Given our tendency to trust teachers and school administrators completely, we were upset with her and gave her the time-out we thought was appropriate.

I discussed the situation with Mary, our neighbor, and she said she saw Preetha as an unusually diligent kid and suggested that something must be going on at school that was troubling her. Mary recommended we consult a child psychologist, and, with the permission of the school principal, we arranged for the expert to sit in Preetha's classroom as a silent observer.

It took just one day to learn the problem. According to the psychologist, Preetha put up her hand with an answer to almost every question in class but hadn't been called on all day. We were told one of her teachers, who was a man, simply ignored her. But that wasn't the whole issue. At lunchtime, Preetha sat alone with her meal, she said, while other kids sat together and chatted and carried on. Preetha did try to sit with the others, but they pushed her away and, when they were finished, made Preetha pick up after them. We later discovered that she had been bullied into this chore for weeks, and the teachers who were supervising the lunchroom had not intervened.

We were devastated. Raj and I wept, right there in the psychologist's office, when she acted this whole scene out for us. We couldn't believe that we'd put our daughter into a situation

where she was picked on like this, apparently because she was one of just a couple of students of color in the school. We had failed to protect our child in this wealthy bubble, which was much more exclusionary than we had expected.

We knew we had to make a quick move. We called Sacred Heart, the Catholic girls school in Greenwich, and spoke to the principal, Sister Joan Magnetti. Two days later, Preetha was enrolled and in class. Between Preetha and Tara, I was a Sacred Heart parent for the next eighteen years. Giving the commencement speech at Tara's graduation in 2011 was one of the most emotional moments of my life. I had dropped them off at Sacred Heart every morning that I could and seen their friends grow up with them. It was such a milestone for me to see Tara's class go forth into the world on that day.

Gerhard was restless. He was a great leader and very successful at ABB, but the politics at the top of the company—a regular clashing of the Swedish and Swiss-German executives' egos and ideas—were frustrating him. He wanted to run a company himself, and, in late 1993, he departed ABB to become CEO of Siemens Nixdorf, the information-systems wing of Munich-based Siemens AG.

I knew that our seven-year adventure together had ended. He tentatively asked if I wanted to join him, including taking the family to Germany, but I said no. It was too much upheaval. I was sad but totally comfortable with that decision.

I carried on at ABB for a few months, but the atmosphere soured for me. The new boss—hired from an American power-generation company—was uncomfortable working with women and regularly called me "honey." For the first time in

my career, I felt like I didn't belong. I began to plan my exit, including helping the half dozen people who worked for me find places in other companies.

Then I had a meeting with the boss. I recapped for him how Gerhard and I had worked as a team, and how I could help him manage the large business he was now responsible for. "But I'm not used to being called 'honey,' and I get this from you and the people who you brought in with you," I said. "I think that it's best if I go on to do something outside ABB."

Our conversation was friendly, but he told me he couldn't change. What I saw so far with him, he said, I had to accept.

I was glad to go.

Quitting ABB like this was not some act of bravado. I had a good reputation outside the company, and recruiters were always calling. I knew I'd find another job very quickly. Besides, Gerhard was always backstopping me. He soon arranged for me to have lunch with Jack Welch.

Jack, at this time, was halfway through his twenty years as CEO of GE and on the path to creating the most valuable US company. He'd fired tens of thousands of people and was labeled "Neutron Jack."

For two hours, we sat in GE's private dining room, talking about global business, the future of power generation and transmission, and the challenges of developing leaders. And, by the end of the lunch, he came up with a list of jobs for me to choose from, all to get my credentials as a GE operating executive. The management roles were in small cities such as Schenectady, New York, or Lexington, Kentucky. He said I could return to Connecticut in a few years and then join the office of the CEO.

I turned it all down right there. I explained that I had two young children and that my husband had started a new job. I was not moving. Jack then suggested I speak to Gary Wendt, the CEO of GE Capital, who was buying financial companies around the world to create a lending powerhouse. I could be useful there, too, he said, and the job would be in Stamford, Connecticut. That seemed plausible. I left the lunch and started thinking it all through.

Then I got a call from Bob Shapiro, the CEO of Monsanto, the agrochemical company based in Saint Louis, Missouri. I knew Bob from my BCG days, when he was the G. D. Searle client on the aspartame project. He wanted me to work with him at Monsanto in Saint Louis. I turned that down, too—again because I didn't want to move. I would have learned a lot working with Bob.

The pattern here is pretty clear. I had earned my way into the big leagues of executive recruitment and was being courted from all sides by important senior leaders who knew I could help their companies succeed. I had a devoted network of other important people, all men, who vouched for me. In this game, no one cared what I looked like or how much they had to pay me.

At the same time, all the jobs required me to upend my home life, and the same was expected of my husband and children. This was the cost of entry, and many men had made this choice themselves. Their families had gone along.

I couldn't do it. And I didn't want to.

The phone rang again. This time, it was a recruiter asking if I'd interview for the position of senior vice president of

corporate strategy and planning at PepsiCo, the beverage, snack, and restaurant company. The role included overseeing fifty high-potential executives, new hires who came into the planning department for eighteen months or so and were then rolled into management jobs throughout the company. Mentoring and training were to be a big part of the job.

I thought twice about going into a consumer business. Much as I knew I could learn anything, after eight years at Motorola and ABB, I was steeped in engineering, technology, and massive infrastructure projects. When I heard that PepsiCo also owned KFC, Taco Bell, and Pizza Hut, I wondered if the job was really for me. I don't eat meat. How could I relate to these restaurants?

Still, PepsiCo was based in Purchase, New York, close to home, and the nature of the job intrigued me. I drove over to meet Bob Dettmer, the chief financial officer, and Ronnie Miller Hasday, the head of corporate hiring. Bob and I had an instant connection.

A few days later, I met Wayne Calloway, PepsiCo's CEO. Wayne was notoriously quiet; he listened and nodded and never said much. That was his way. I think in my one-hour initial discussion with him, I talked for fifty-seven minutes and he talked for three. But he attentively took in everything I said. The time he gave me to speak and his brief interjections drew me out.

Shortly, both GE and PepsiCo were pressing me with attractive job offers. I was weighing my options, with Raj and my friend Orit Gadiesh, the chairman of Bain and Company, as my sounding boards. Preetha and Tara were rooting for PepsiCo after we received a large gift basket of goodies and T-shirts. Ronnie knew exactly how to capture the family's interest.

I needed some breathing room, and I told Jack and Wayne, who knew each other because Wayne was on GE's board of directors, that I would let them know my answer in a week.

Then I received a remarkable phone call from Wayne. He started by saying he'd been at a GE board meeting and that Jack had told him I was probably joining GE. "I understand why you would do that," he told me. "It's a great company, and Jack is a fine CEO.

"But," he went on, "I want to make PepsiCo's case one last time because you said you'd make your decision next week. My need for you is greater than Jack's," he said. "We've never had somebody like you in our executive ranks. I know that you can contribute significantly to PepsiCo. You will have all of our support to make sure you are successful."

I hung up the phone. I felt overwhelmed. Wayne's appeal had so much humility. And it was the most I'd ever heard him say.

That afternoon, this mother of two daughters—Preetha, age ten, and Tara, age one-and-a-half—and this wife of a consultant who traveled extensively, drove over to PepsiCo and accepted the job.

I couldn't wait to start.

Part III

THE PEPSICO YEARS

7

PepsiCo's world headquarters in Westchester County, New York, is a chic, midcentury modern, corporate landmark—a group of seven pale-gray concrete buildings designed by the architect Edward Durell Stone that are arranged in a U with three garden courtyards.

The office complex sits on 168 acres of green lawns, with clipped hedges and trees, a large pond, flower gardens, a reflecting pool with lilies, oak and birch groves, and a trail called the Golden Path, all created by the British designer Russell Page and later enhanced by the Belgian landscape artist François Goffinet. Monumental sculptures by Auguste Rodin, Barbara Hepworth, Alberto Giacometti, and a dozen more nineteenth- and twentieth-century masters dot the landscape. The gardens are open to the public. Thousands of visitors and schoolchildren visit to study the art and flora.

I pulled up to PepsiCo to begin my new job on March 30, 1994. But I didn't walk the Golden Path or go near the sculptures until 2014.

For twenty years, I just didn't have time.

In those first spring months, I settled in. I met my team and other department heads. My boss, the gracious and disciplined Bob Dettmer, answered hundreds of my questions about PepsiCo's structure, finances, and priorities. Frankly, I immediately fell in love with the place. PepsiCo was so full of optimism and vitality. It suited my upbeat spirit from day one.

In a way, I didn't know what I'd been missing. I enjoyed the challenge at ABB, where I worked on important infrastructure projects that took years to build. Motorola introduced me to the world of technology. I loved my consulting career, although I'd always moved on from the client companies before my ideas were realized. Now I had the opportunity to see, smell, touch, and taste the business. Our brands were household names; our consumers were everyday people; my kids could engage with it all. Tara once tried to explain my job to a young schoolmate—and simplified it by saying that I worked at KFC. "That's so cool!" her friend exclaimed. My job was totally relatable.

PepsiCo was very ambitious, friendly, and fun. I was excited and completely enamored.

Pepsi-Cola, the soft drink, was originally created in 1898 by a pharmacist in North Carolina named Caleb Bradham. By the 1930s, after a couple of bankruptcies, the Pepsi-Cola company took on the cola leader, Coca-Cola, with a radio jingle: "Pepsi-Cola hits the spot, twelve full ounces, that's a lot. Twice as much, for a nickel too. Pepsi-Cola is the drink for you."

The marketing wars were on. In 1963, in an advertising burst that celebrated a whole Pepsi lifestyle, images of sunny

youth declared the "Pepsi Generation." When Coke caught up to Pepsi with its own image campaign, Pepsi came back with the "Pepsi Challenge," cup-to-cup blind taste tests in stores and malls, which Pepsi, being slightly sweeter than Coke, tended to win.

Then, in late 1983, another coup: a $5 million contract with Michael Jackson and the Jackson 5, the first wave of supercharged celebrity endorsements that have now linked Pepsi and Diet Pepsi to Britney Spears, Beyoncé, the Spice Girls, David Bowie, Tina Turner, Shakira, Kylie Minogue, David Beckham, Sachin Tendulkar, and dozens more top stars around the world.

Pepsi also gained traction as an emblem of the Cold War. Nikita Khrushchev sipped the soda at a Moscow display of American innovation in 1959, and Don Kendall, who was CEO for twenty-three years, later landed a cola contract that started up bottling operations in the USSR. Pepsi was celebrated as the first capitalist product sold in the Soviet Union.

By 1994, PepsiCo was the fifteenth-biggest US company, with annual revenue of $25 billion. It sold drinks and food in more than 150 countries and employed 450,000 people. Advertising campaigns for Pepsi and Diet Pepsi had moved on to feature Shaquille O'Neal and Ray Charles. Cindy Crawford, the model, was featured studying our financials on the cover of that year's annual report with the caption "A typical investor looks us over."

Structurally, the company was a three-legged stool. One leg was beverages, including Pepsi-Cola, Diet Pepsi, Mountain Dew, Mug Root Beer, and fairly recent joint ventures with

Starbucks and Lipton for bottled coffee and tea drinks. The division's revenue was almost $9 billion.

A second leg was snacks, with revenue of $7 billion. That included Lay's potato chips, Fritos, Doritos, Cheetos, Tostitos, Rold Gold pretzels, SunChips, and Smartfood. We made Sabritas in Mexico, Matutano in Spain, and Smith's and Walkers in the UK. Frito-Lay, the US arm of the snacks business, was based in Plano, Texas.

Pepsi-Cola, the original soda company, and Frito-Lay, a Dallas-based chips company, had married three decades earlier to establish the core idea of PepsiCo—that salty snacks need a drink to wash them down. They are both "high velocity" products that fly off store shelves and need frequent replenishing. The merger unleashed important sales and distribution efficiencies and sparked much more business outside the US.

The company's third leg in 1994 was restaurants. PepsiCo bought the Pizza Hut and Taco Bell fast-food chains in the late 1970s and, a few years later, added Kentucky Fried Chicken, which was rebranded KFC. We owned casual dining brands like California Pizza Kitchen and East Side Mario's and a food-service company that distributed supplies to all the chains. The company operated or franchised twenty-eight thousand restaurants worldwide, serving more than six billion meals a year. Restaurant division revenue was about $9 billion.

Dozens more operations and activities made it all happen—seed farms, a contract-farmer network to grow potatoes, research and development and test kitchens, a direct store delivery system (DSD) that was already among the largest in the world with thousands of trucks and distribution centers. The company's sales force of about twenty-five thousand people

handled customer relationships—from the CEO of Wal-Mart to the individual managers of every 7-Eleven or independent corner store. It was all very complex and coordinated.

Wayne Calloway, the tall, redheaded CEO, was exactly the laconic leader I'd met in my interview. But he was also a fierce competitor, a former college basketball player who rode Harley-Davidson motorcycles. He'd served in the US Army before joining Frito-Lay as a salesman. PepsiCo was known as a talent academy, where rising executives took on tough assignments and either sank and left the company or swam and moved up. Wayne was focused on hiring and people development. He was determined to double revenue every five years. So far he was succeeding.

Wayne thought PepsiCo needed me more than GE needed me. He was astute. I had a rare international perspective and experience that would help his bottom line. He also sensed, I think, that a woman was long overdue in his executive ranks.

White American men held fifteen of the top fifteen jobs at PepsiCo when I walked in. Almost all wore blue or gray suits with white shirts and silk ties and had short hair or no hair. They drank Pepsi, mixed drinks, and liqueurs. Most of them golfed, fished, played tennis, hiked, and jogged. Some hunted for quail together. Many were married with children. I don't believe any of their wives worked in paid jobs outside their homes.

I am not detailing these characteristics to focus on these particular men. My colleagues were smart, creative, dedicated people and shouldered tremendous responsibility and stress. They built a beloved enterprise. The fact is that PepsiCo's

leadership mirrored almost every senior-executive suite in corporate America in 1994. Even the most accomplished women were still milling around in middle management. The number of female CEOs among the five hundred biggest companies that year was zero.

Men of this ilk flourished in the post–World War II US economy because they could be so-called ideal workers. In a society crafted around single-income families, with a female "homemaker" and a male "breadwinner," the men were, indeed, ideal workers for companies. They were completely available on a regular schedule, with no outside noise during set hours. This was usually Monday to Friday, nine to five, but shift times varied in the country's booming unionized manufacturing facilities.

The men who were climbing the management ladder, reaching for bigger titles, salaries, stock options, and board seats, could work more, travel more, study in the evenings, and spend hours mingling with clients, competitors, and friends. They were flexible because women were minding the home front. They could also pack up to go wherever the company needed them to go, with their wives and children on board. Society paved the path for these men to gain money and influence in companies, government, and global affairs. Everyone else supported them.

On the CEO floor of PepsiCo when I arrived, no one was expected to be a deeply engaged parent, let alone a great mother and wife. Dealing with teachers, doctors, dentists, groceries, clothing, cooking, cleaning, laundry, home decor, gardening, houseguests, birthdays, holidays, and vacations was just not their area. Maybe they were engaged—just a bit—in the emotional

health, academic success, and general good behavior of their children.

Even if they were interested in any of these things, these guys just didn't have time.

Importantly, the men I worked with didn't judge one another on how their work and family lives came together. They were plenty competitive but also caring and supportive of one another through crises, including divorce, illness, or troubles with their kids.

None of this crossed my mind when I met them. I was well aware that I was an outsider: I was still the eighteen-year-old girl at IIM Calcutta; the Indian immigrant in the polyester suit at Yale; the vegetarian, expectant mother in La Crosse, Wisconsin. At BCG, I had been inside many industries, but I'd never encountered a female client. I didn't think it was odd to be in meetings with dozens of men and no other women. At Motorola and ABB, my world was engineers, scientists, robots, and machinery. I'd never had a close woman colleague with a job like mine and had never seen a woman in a workplace who was senior to me.

When I got to PepsiCo, I was warmly welcomed. My new office was on the coveted "4/3"—the company nickname for building 4, floor 3—down the hall from the CEO and the rest of the top executives, and it had five large windows, a sign of status in the organization's informal rule book.

I was offered a reasonable budget to furnish my space, although I didn't spend it all. I selected a utilitarian cherrywood veneer credenza and a desk that came in a flat box, a conference table with six chairs, a white board, and a flip chart.

That June, about three months after I moved in, 4/3 was abuzz. Pizza Hut USA, with 5,100 restaurants, said that it would probably miss profit estimates for the second quarter and that the outlook was pessimistic for the rest of the year. The results for Taco Bell, KFC, and a few other of our eat-in chains also looked shaky.

Missing profit guidance was a significant crisis: PepsiCo shares were likely to fall, and they did. When the news got out, the stock plunged 15 percent, and three times the normal number of shares traded that day. Wayne acted fast. Within days, he created a new role—CEO of worldwide restaurants—and convinced Roger Enrico, a shrewd veteran PepsiCo executive who had stepped back to recover from a heart attack, to take the job.

I met Roger later that week when he walked into my office. He didn't smile. "Hi. I'm Roger Enrico," he said. "Normally, I would have interviewed the new head of strategy. You're the first one who was hired without my input."

"Hi, Roger," I said, cheerfully. "I've heard so much about you. I've been so looking forward to meeting you."

"I need to know everything about the restaurant business and exactly what the hell is going on in our restaurants," he said. "I'll see you in Dallas in ten days. You are now my chief strategist. Dettmer approved it."

That was the whole conversation. He left.

So now I had my original corporate strategy and planning job, reporting to Bob, and a second job, chief strategist of the restaurant group, reporting to Roger. My work was about to double; no one discussed my pay.

Roger Enrico was a tremendous leader and thinker who became PepsiCo's CEO two years later. He grew up among the iron mines of northern Minnesota, fought in the Vietnam War, and joined Frito-Lay in 1971 to help market Funyuns, the onion-dusted corn rings. Twenty years later, he would work in Japan and South America, run the Pepsi-Cola beverages division, and oversee a massive reorganization of Frito-Lay. Roger's favorite approach, and his claim to fame in PepsiCo, was that he made big changes to big things.

Roger's days started at 10 a.m., and he refused to read anything related to business after 9 p.m. He had lovely homes in Montana, Dallas, and the Cayman Islands and spent weekends in one or the other, fly fishing, horseback riding, scuba diving, golfing, or visiting museums. He was wily and political, and many people thought he was curt and gruff. But he was a showman at heart. It was his idea to sign Michael Jackson and his brothers to endorse Pepsi in the early '80s, and, when that campaign boosted our market share, Coca-Cola stumbled by changing its recipe to New Coke. Roger wrote a book called *The Other Guy Blinked*, declaring victory in the cola wars.

Now Roger was talking about restaurants because that part of the overall PepsiCo operation was, suddenly and surprisingly, faltering.

The problem was that the quick-service restaurant (QSR) business was overbuilt. Simply put, every new restaurant that opened ate into the business of all others. But PepsiCo couldn't stop expanding because our competitors kept expanding. For example, if we held off on putting a Pizza Hut in a new strip mall, Domino's Pizza or some other restaurant concept would

probably take the spot. Either way, Pizza Hut restaurants and other QSRs in the neighborhood would suffer.

This bind was showing up in the numbers, although we hadn't yet figured it all out. The business was enormous and very complex, involving real estate, franchisees, dine-in establishments, delivery, drive-throughs, complicated employee recruitment initiatives, food safety systems, marketing, and on and on.

I knew almost nothing about restaurants the day that Roger abruptly introduced himself. But I wanted to prove I could handle any challenge he threw at me. For the next week and a half, my seven-person restaurant strategy team worked around the clock to prepare for our meeting in Dallas.

The presentation—a few dozen slides and charts presented in the big boardroom beside Roger's office—was a detailed analysis that laid out the value drivers of the business, analyzed PepsiCo's history in restaurants over the past five years, and considered its future prospects. We concluded with a list of questions that needed answers right away. Roger was impressed, but he didn't say much. He did not believe in compliments. My team returned to New York, and, shortly after, his secretary called and asked me to meet him at 11 a.m. the following Monday at the private airplane hangar in Atlanta. I pressed her a little bit for details, but she had none. She suggested I pack for three or four days.

I filled up my over-the-shoulder garment bag and briefcase once again, flew to Atlanta on Delta Air Lines, and found my way to where the company planes park. Roger arrived on a PepsiCo Challenger jet. We got in a car with a driver and, ten minutes later, began stopping at every QSR on a busy commercial road

near the airport. We'd go into the restaurant, and Roger would order something, get the food, look at it, maybe taste a little bit, and throw it out, then get back in the car. As someone who grew up never wasting food, this sampling approach horrified me a little. I kept my opinion to myself.

After four stops, he turned to me and asked, "Well, what's the scorecard?" I was clearly puzzled. "What do you think we are doing here?" he exclaimed. "It's a market tour! We need to understand the business from the ground up!" He stepped out of the car to take a break.

I quickly called Richard Goodman, the CFO of Taco Bell, whom I barely knew, and explained the situation. Richard genially told me to track order times, wait times, food temperature, cleanliness, back-of-the-house and front-of-the-house staffing, and any other variable that might affect a customer's experience. I used this input to rough out a scorecard on a sheet of paper. For the rest of the day, I ranked any criteria I could think of on a scale of 1 to 5. This was my first experience with the PepsiCo sink-or-swim culture. I did not sink.

At about 5 p.m., we went back to the PepsiCo plane and flew to Chicago. The next day, we were back at it, visiting fast-casual dine-in restaurants like Olive Garden, California Pizza Kitchen, and Cracker Barrel—ordering, leaving, and scoring. On the third day, we did it all in suburban Washington, DC. I got comfortable with this discovery process and started to enjoy it.

As Roger and I flew back to Westchester County Airport, I chanced to open the local newspaper and came across the astrological forecast section. I am a Scorpio. My horoscope read "Today you will be traveling with someone who is very

difficult and will remain a big part of your life for the next few years." It was Roger in a nutshell. I circled it and gave it to him. He read it and, with a smile, passed it back, noting, "I am a Scorpio, too!"

Our three-day fast-food foray solidified my relationship with Roger for years to come. We barely spoke on that trip, but he saw that I was as curious about operational details as I was about the broad view. We both knew he was under the gun to learn the business himself.

In the next few months, Roger and I worked together on what drove the system's best restaurants. The answer, we found, was that diners need attention on a very personal level. Lifetime restaurateurs who loved their work tended to innovate for their own markets, with local promotions and other enticements. Their locations were cleaner, happier, more loved. The managers liked people and treated each customer as family. PepsiCo was a packaged-goods company that was approaching this very high-touch business in an impersonal way. We were good at adding units and hiring and developing menu items, and, as long as the restaurant business was growing this way, we did well. When we had to get more sales from existing restaurants, though, we struggled. We were not as good as we needed to be at the "touch" part.

In bold moves, Roger cut back on building new restaurants and franchised existing locations from all our QSR brands to our best operators. This immediately improved our cash flow and return on capital. With franchisees running restaurants better, sales and earnings started to climb. Roger was viewed as a hero. I learned so much in this process about a service business and how different it was from packaged goods. I also had my first

real experience on the front line answering to investors. Roger pushed me to start talking to the Wall Street analysts covering PepsiCo—there were dozens—and I enjoyed getting to know them. I thought they were smart and well-informed about the overall business model, although they were surprisingly lacking in operational knowledge, never really digging into the nuances of what drove sales or competition.

In early 1995, PepsiCo filed its annual 10-K, the detailed report on our financial performance to the US Securities and Exchange Commission. Under "executive officers," there was my name: Indra K. Nooyi, thirty-nine years. I was nervous and proud to be on that list. I remember the job's responsibility hitting me when I saw it.

In addition to all our restaurant strategy work, I was still heading corporate planning. That team now included forty-five people identified as emerging leaders who would work in headquarters for a few years and then "roll out" into management positions elsewhere in the company. Some had just joined PepsiCo; others had been with us for a year or two. About a third were women. Every three or four months, a few people cycled in and out.

The team I took on lacked international diversity. They worked hard and had great presence, but I was a little worried about a training program without much non-US representation in the group. After all, PepsiCo was investing heavily in international markets, and we needed to provide talent for those operations. I asked our internal recruiter for more diversity in the next group. Four months later, he proudly introduced me

to the latest hires. I was amused and dismayed. They were all Canadian.

Apparently, our recruiter was concerned about the corporate planning team's ability to play softball. The department had won the PepsiCo trophy several years running and wanted to keep it that way. Canadians, at least, knew the rules of softball and were ready to play.

After my initial disappointment, I sat down with the hiring team and specified exactly what I meant by diversity. The following year, they did deliver, with an excellent group of truly global hires, but the corporate planning team lost the softball trophy. PepsiCo still came out ahead.

In early 1996, after nearly two years of working like mad in strategy and planning, I was ready for my own operating role with responsibility for sales, profit, and loss. This was the career path for those rising in PepsiCo, and critical to my success, I was told. Wayne asked me to head Western European snacks, based in London, and Raj and I were excited about a move for a few years. We agreed that Preetha, now twelve, and Tara, now three, would have an amazing experience living abroad. Raj's company had a UK office, and it was possible for him to work from there. I went to London, found a house for us to live in, and toured and selected schools for both girls. We decided to rent out the Greenwich house; PepsiCo went into high gear to move us.

Sadly, in the weeks that this went on, Wayne Calloway learned that the cancer he'd battled before had come back. He decided to step aside, and PepsiCo's board of directors voted for Roger to take over as CEO.

To prepare for London, I was also vetting candidates to replace me in the strategy position, a hire that required Roger's approval. Then, just like Gerhard when he was looking for "an Indra Nooyi," Roger rejected everyone I sent over to meet him. Finally, I said, "Look, Roger, I am moving to Europe to run Western European snacks. You have to accept someone."

And, without blinking, he told me the move was off. "I have a lot of operating executives, but no one as strategic as you to help me," he said. It was high praise from Mr. Gruff. Our London arrangements had to be reversed, the house rental canceled, the schools notified, the movers stopped.

Raj and Preetha took the news in stride. But I was disappointed and not so sure how this would play out for me in the long term: on one hand, I'd be more involved in helping Roger reposition the company; on the other hand, I'd miss the opportunity to manage a business. It was great to be appreciated for my strategic thinking, but the people in the field with responsibility for profit and loss always got the most respect. Staying put would certainly restrict my career growth.

In senior management positions in most companies, staying in place or a lateral move may indicate to the organization that you aren't promotable and, very often, may be fungible. Once you cross into those vaunted ranks, there's no slowing down. I also knew, as a woman, I had to outdo the men.

Raj and I talked it over, and we agreed that this wasn't a time to worry about my own career but rather the good of the whole enterprise. The new CEO had made his decision; it was time to get down to work.

To be sure, it was a very tough time for Roger to take over. He had stabilized the restaurants but needed to determine their long-term prospects within PepsiCo.

A separate crisis was also brewing. Pepsi-Cola International, which accounted for a third of total beverage sales, was the next division to significantly miss profit estimates. Our Venezuelan bottler had defected to Coke, putting our 85 percent market share in that country in jeopardy. Our bottler in Brazil and Argentina was facing financial difficulties. A couple of key executives, including Bob Dettmer, decided to retire. Roger was forced to sort out this part of the company for the next six months.

At the same time, he asked that I confidentially begin a full, independent strategic review of the restaurant industry and our business prospects. I pulled together an experienced team and immersed myself in this work.

I didn't have an official profit and loss role at this time, but I was deeply involved with the financials of the whole company because my department ran multiple mathematical models to project quarterly sales and growth projections for every division. This work was separate from the individual divisions' own financial forecasts—and caused some friction. My department's numbers were sometimes a little different from theirs and, often, more accurate.

All of the forecasts were reviewed every quarter with Roger and the company's eleven senior leaders in a big meeting that I came to find very stressful. I was the only woman at the table. I would present our analysis from headquarters, which was used to manage investor expectations, and then the division presidents would weigh in with their own perspectives.

When the numbers differed, the criticisms of my department could be very mean. I was particularly insulted by accusations that "corporate planning was trying to run the company." In reality, the whole thing was a charade—some division presidents would be vocally upset if my department's models suggested they could do better, but also mutedly miffed if we said they were too optimistic. They just didn't want to upset the CEO by being wrong either way.

Quarter after quarter, I felt hostility from a few people in these meetings, and I was increasingly irked that no one else in the room ever backed me up. Once, we held the meeting in London, and, when the same scenario played out again, I left at midday and flew back to New York. This was completely out of character for me. Roger noticed, but he said nothing. As time went by, his failure to intervene started to bother me, too.

In September 1996, we finished the full restaurant business review and summed it up to present to the board of directors. This would be my first real exposure to PepsiCo's board, and I had no idea how I'd be viewed by these stalwarts of industry.

The day before that board meeting—on a day when we had one of the quarterly division-presidents meetings—I went to see Roger in his office.

"Roger, I'm ready for the board tomorrow," I said. "And after that, I'm leaving PepsiCo. I've put up with countless meetings where I've been humiliated. I won't deal with this anymore. I don't want anything from PepsiCo. I'm just going."

Even though I'd always been willing to push myself to the edge for my employers, I felt that I had to draw a line when it came to others respecting the sincerity of my work. On that

day, I didn't consider where my career would take me next; I just wanted to get out of what I felt was an unacceptable situation.

Roger flinched. He was holding a pen and twiddled it nervously back and forth on the desk. I could tell I'd unsettled him. But then he said, "I'll get back to you."

I don't know what he did after our talk. The meeting that day was delayed by several hours, and, when it happened late in the afternoon, the atmosphere was completely changed for me. Everyone was incredibly supportive.

The next day, I presented our strategic review of the restaurant business to the board and was very satisfied by how my work was received. I still remember Ray Hunt, who was then CEO of Hunt Oil, saying it was the best strategic presentation he'd seen at PepsiCo—or in any company. I was on cloud nine.

We now had two months to come up with detailed options for the business, including looking at getting out of restaurants altogether. That would mean hiving off a third of PepsiCo's revenue. Culturally, this would be tough on many people in PepsiCo: our three divisions were one family, and I knew the restaurant division would feel betrayed. But I viewed any form of separation as unfettering the restaurants from a packaged-goods company that was holding them back. The restaurants had to be an independent public company.

This was a moment for brutal objectivity. It's a situation I found myself in repeatedly over many years. Good business demands tough decisions based on rigorous analysis and unwavering follow-through. Emotion can't really play a part. The challenge we all face as leaders is to let the feelings churn inside you but then to present a calm exterior, and I learned to do that.

After that board meeting, Steve Reinemund, the president of Frito-Lay, an ex-restaurateur himself, came by my office brimming with enthusiasm. Roger showed up, too. "Let's get cracking," he said. No mention of our conversation. He obviously thought that the explicit support of the division presidents and the board over the previous twenty-four hours was enough to prove I was valuable to everyone. No further talk was needed.

Nine months later, we spun off the restaurant business into a publicly traded company called Tricon Global Restaurants. The company later changed its name to YUM! Brands and still owns and operates the thriving Pizza Hut, Taco Bell, and KFC chains.

Together with a young finance executive who impressed me in a division meeting, Hugh Johnston, we sold our food-service business and all our casual-dining chains. The work was punishing and intense, but this was my schooling in how investment banking and the process of spearheading divestitures, spin-offs, split-offs, initial public offerings, and other financial transactions really worked. I watched the lifestyle and modus operandi of investment bankers and deal lawyers through all of this. I was happy I wasn't one of them.

In January 1998, PepsiCo celebrated the one hundredth anniversary of Pepsi-Cola with an enormous gala on the Big Island of Hawaii. The party was magnificent: ocean breezes, incredible food, and hundreds of company executives and their spouses dancing into the night as the Rolling Stones performed on an intimate stage.

But the work wasn't on hold. Roger pulled me aside one morning and remarked that Coca-Cola's price-to-earnings ratio was around forty-five and PepsiCo was hovering around twenty. He wanted another in-depth analysis—now of Coke.

I returned to New York and, with a team of about ten people, dove into the global beverages business. We read every internal and public document we could lay our hands on. We hired Mars & Co., a consulting firm specializing in competitive analysis, and, over four months, worked through how Coke was making money and why investors valued their stock higher than ours. The final Mars report was three hundred pages, and I had to assimilate it all, summarize it, and present the conclusions to the board.

After much debate, we synthesized the message into six graphic, easy-to-understand posters and propped them up on easels around the conference room. In another important board meeting, I led PepsiCo's directors from chart to chart to explain it all and then rested my case: Coke's stock price was unsustainable. Our competitor's earnings growth was largely held up by onetime items, including regular sales of pieces of their minority interests in their bottling companies. Coke, many years earlier, had separated out their soft drink bottling and distribution system to independent public companies that mix the syrup with water and other ingredients to make the final bottled product. This ownership could be increased or decreased, within a range, pretty much at will.

In the meeting, I showed that Coke's return on invested capital, which drove the price-to-earnings ratio, was higher than PepsiCo's because Coke was focused primarily on making and selling the syrup.

PepsiCo owned our bottlers, but Roger was intrigued by our competitor's financial engineering. We started to discuss how we could spin off our North American bottlers, too. I was nervous about it because I thought that ceding control of our US beverage distribution could get difficult: independent bottlers would want to set their own growth goals, and I was worried that this could end up hurting us in the years ahead.

Still, I wasn't in charge. Roger weighed all the input and decided that PepsiCo should create a new, publicly traded bottling company, largely with our North American assets. We would retain 20 percent of this company.

Our strategic review of Coke revealed much to our executives and board about how our competitor was delivering its numbers. It also proved right in its conclusion. Once Roger decided to follow the same strategy, investors wised up. Coke's stock price fell as much as 34 percent during the third quarter of 1998.

The dealmaking for me in this period was nonstop. In the midst of the bottling transaction, bankers for Seagram called Roger and asked if we'd buy its fruit-juice subsidiary, Tropicana.

I thought this was a great idea. I now knew PepsiCo inside and out and could see the gaps. One was that consumers didn't engage with our drinks or snacks before ten o'clock in the morning. PepsiCo had once test-marketed a product for the coffee crowd called Pepsi A.M., but that was a bust. Tropicana, the number one orange juice maker, was a great grocery brand with a growing international business.

After an intense three-week analysis, where I hustled to Florida, Belgium, and England to complete the due diligence, we bought Tropicana in July 1998 for $3.3 billion in cash.

I started thinking more about how we should pay attention to the nutritional value of PepsiCo's offerings. Soda sales were slowing down. Consumers were shifting to noncarbonated and healthier drinks. Aquafina, our bottled water, was slowly gaining traction, and our teas and coffees were doing well. We no longer had the restaurants, and our balance sheet was primed to make substantial change.

Health and wellness, to me, was undeniably a category that offered huge opportunity. I'd seen this coming on the home front. I found it more than curious that a couple of children at Tara's birthday party one year asked if they could phone their mothers to get permission to sip the Pepsi we served. That sent up a real red flag for me.

One day, I asked our marketing team to help me think this through. We decided to set up a health-and-wellness advisory board of six experts from outside the company and added a couple of professors and nutrition experts to this group. At one point, we also took over a little-used conference room and created a mock grocery store with shelves full of healthier products that we imagined for our portfolio in the twenty-first century. Roger toured this setup and was intrigued. Steve saw it and was skeptical, in part because he thought it was a distraction. We took down the display and dissolved the wellness advisory board.

For several months, I wondered if I had caved in too early. Should I have come back with facts and figures to prove that health and wellness could be important for us? The reality was

that, given all my other priorities, this was a mountain I'd have to climb later.

From 1994 to 1999, I worked and worked and worked. I'd go home at night, take a shower, put on my flannel nightgown to show the girls I wasn't leaving, put them to bed, and sit up reading mail and reviewing documents until 1 or 2 a.m. I was almost never around for dinner.

I didn't exercise. I barely slept.

At least twice a month, I was traveling back and forth to our businesses around the world. I went to China at least eight times in this period—including several trips with Henry Kissinger, whose firm, Kissinger Associates, was helping us overseas—to figure out how to invest in a market where Coke had three times Pepsi's market share. Roger once asked me to accompany him to Asia for two weeks. We had business meetings from Monday to Thursday and spent long weekends bonding with local executives. Roger felt it was important to get to know these people in an informal setting. I wanted to be home with my family.

I did not stop. My own work responsibilities were huge, but I felt compelled to make sure everyone else's work was up to par, too. I coached and mentored, and I reviewed and rewrote presentations for dozens of colleagues.

Of all the times I overdid it, one day still stabs at me. Mary Waterman, our lovely next-door neighbor, died of breast cancer. But I skipped Mary's funeral because I stayed back at work rewriting slides related to the restaurant spin-off for the board, something that was really the responsibility of two others

on our team. These men had just dropped the assignment on me, saying, "You do it so well and Roger trusts you."

I should have just said no. I have never forgiven myself for prioritizing my work that day over my dear friend Mary.

Whatever toll my work life took on my role at home, I still had the lifeboat of Raj. He was now a partner at the consulting firm, working and traveling like crazy, yet a steady source of support. We also had a housekeeper, who drove and cooked for us, and a nanny, and they kept the house running and the children safe. My mother was spending more time with my sister's and brother's families in New York in these years, although she was always available to step in to help when needed. Raj's parents also helped out whenever we asked them to.

Tara started Montessori school before she was two years old and switched to preschool at Sacred Heart when she was three. She was busy and cared for during the day and also often came to PepsiCo in the evenings and hung out on the executive floor, running around and chatting with whoever was there. No one seemed to mind. Sometimes she curled up and slept under my desk.

Preetha missed me a lot in these years. She was an adolescent, and much of what she saw was a busy, stressed-out mother. All those times we had been singing and dancing together in Chicago, and our early days in Connecticut, were replaced by what she felt was competition from Tara. I was loving and present during difficult times but not really there day-to-day. Her angst was expressed by verbal outbursts, and I struggled to cope with them.

Tara was a calmer, quieter child, who once wrote me a note, which I still keep in my desk drawer, that lays bare the emotions of these years. On a big sheet of construction paper, decorated with flowers and butterflies, she begs me to come home. "I will love you again if you would please come home," the note says. In her sweet, crooked printing, the word *please* is spelled out seven times.

For many years when I traveled, I wrote notes and letters to Preetha and Tara and left them at home to open when I was away. I would grab time whenever possible to compose these missives—at my desk, sitting in cars or on planes, or at night in a hotel before I went to bed. I was always looking out in airport gift shops for stickers or little toys and knickknacks to include with the envelopes. We ended up with quite a collection of dolls in national dress—from Finland, from Japan, from Brazil. These notes and keepsakes were an ongoing, private little project for me as I carried on with my other duties. It kept me closer to my children, although I know it was a poor substitute for actually being there. For many years, the guilt of not being a full-time mother to my kids in their early years gnawed at me. In some ways, I think of these days with great sadness.

I often wondered why I kept going. The job was intellectually stimulating, and I truly loved what I was doing. I was sure I'd be miserable if I quit, and I wasn't willing to step out totally. On a more practical note, we were still paying off some debt from the house renovation, and our expenses were high with two private school tuitions.

We'd also set a financial goal: a dollar amount of savings for our retired life and more put aside to ensure the girls could be economically independent. And in the back of our minds, we

always worried what would happen if one of us lost our job. Raj and I both working was our safety net—probably more of the typical immigrant mentality.

One day in the spring of 2000, Roger casually walked into my office and said that Mike White, PepsiCo's CFO, was transferring to Europe to head up the snacks business. Roger was making me CFO, adding the role to all the other responsibilities I already had. I told him I had to think about it. I had too much on my plate already and was loath to take on more.

Two days later, on a Friday, he came by and said he was announcing my appointment the following week. Then he added, "You're already basically doing this job. Get your ass into that office."

Soon after, I packed up my things and moved into the CFO's office next door to the CEO's office. It had six panels of windows. Now nine departments would report to me: control, tax, treasury, investor relations, risk management, global procurement, information technology, mergers and acquisitions, and corporate planning.

That weekend, I dug out my old MBA finance books and started brushing up on everything I needed to relearn to be CFO. There was always so much to do.

Time was the critical currency in my life, and I spent almost all of it on PepsiCo. To succeed among the ideal workers, I had to be one myself.

PepsiCo's HR department offered work-share programs for some junior employees, and my first two administrative

assistants shared one job. No one else—certainly not at my level—seemed to ask for a reduced schedule, probably because they were nervous about a so-called flexibility stigma.

One other woman rose in PepsiCo's most senior ranks around this time. Brenda Barnes was named CEO of Pepsi-Cola North America in 1996 after twenty years at the company. She had three kids under twelve and, after less than a year in her new role, she quit. She moved to Chicago, spent eight years at home with her children, and served on boards. She was still a great executive. In 2005, she took over as CEO of Sara Lee.

Brenda's decision, like that of thousands of talented, ambitious women who've stepped out of big companies, made perfect sense. The rules of engagement in corporate leadership were absolutely unforgiving. Compromise to accommodate home life was unthinkable.

Brenda didn't have the same extended family support I could count on. And, in jobs with relentless travel, we had no technology to really connect with our children's day-to-day activities from afar. "The whole issue boils down to time," she told the press in 1997, when she was interviewed about her departure. "Hopefully, one day, corporate America can battle this."

Our days are still only twenty-four hours, and we must use them wisely. When we take on additional responsibilities, like caring for children or a sick family member, the best we can do is use the hours we have even more efficiently, without sacrificing our performance at work.

Now that we have tools for remote, seamless communication, I believe job flexibility and remote work for everyone who

needs it should be entirely routine. This will give families the chance to take care of home life obligations during the workday without feeling loaded with emotional consequences.

Shift workers have had to deal for far too long with last-minute calls or switches to their schedules that foul up their ability to plan their days and weeks. Stable work hours, aided by ubiquitously available scheduling technology, should be the norm for all shift workers, especially those who have any sort of caregiving responsibilities. Employers have no good reason to deny this courtesy.

Relieving the time conundrum includes one more factor, too: addressing the culture of urgency that consumes our economy and workplaces. Deadlines are incredibly important. But, too often, they are arbitrary.

I was involved in hundreds of projects with tight deadlines that probably could have stretched into a few more days. Would that have made a difference to the project? Most of the time, no. Would that have made a difference to my colleagues' lives at home, as caregivers or as members of their community? I think the answer is a resounding yes.

I had just settled into the CFO job, in September 2000, when Roger got a call from Bob Morrison, the CEO of Quaker Oats, asking if PepsiCo might consider buying his company.

This was a big one.

The Quaker Oats Company, based in Chicago for almost a century, was certainly a household name—known for its red-and-blue cylinders with a reassuring picture of a long-haired Quaker in a wide-brimmed hat. Quaker was a food company but, over the years, made plenty of money in other businesses,

too, including Fisher-Price toys, which it had sold in 1991.

Now, with sales of about $5 billion a year, its brands were Quaker Oats and Quaker granola bars, Life and Cap'n Crunch cereals, Aunt Jemima pancake mix and syrup, and Rice-A-Roni and Near East flavored rices, couscous, and other grains. Much more intriguing to investors—and the reason Quaker stock had doubled in value that year—was the surging popularity of its sports drink: Gatorade.

PepsiCo had long coveted Quaker Oats. We'd been in casual talks to merge two years earlier, but nothing came of it. We certainly wanted the incredible market share that Gatorade would give us in the isotonic drinks market. But we also loved the Quaker trademark, which would so beautifully blend with Tropicana for our morning lineup. Our own efforts to come up with breakfast options weren't going so well: some experimental Frito-Lay bars were squishy, didn't taste good, and were roundly unappealing.

Quaker's sale was not an open auction. PepsiCo was quietly asked to hear the pitch. Roger, Steve, and I and a few of our operating executives flew to Chicago for a full day of presentations. Bob Morrison and his team met us in a hotel boardroom and impressed us with their story. They'd stabilized the company after a few difficult years and believed Quaker needed a larger company's scale to grow outside the US.

We talked it all over and, a few days later, put in a bid. Within hours, the news leaked that PepsiCo and Quaker were in talks, and then the pressure was really on. Quaker agreed to our price but added a guardrail to the agreement that would protect its shareholders if PepsiCo's stock fell below a certain price.

We huddled with our bankers and discussed the pros and cons again. Roger had decided that the three of us—Roger,

Steve, and I—had to be in full agreement about everything related to this transaction. Steve was uncomfortable with the guardrail and we pushed back, but Quaker wouldn't budge.

After two weeks of negotiation, we walked away, much to Bob's surprise.

The next week, with the world aware that Quaker was looking to sell itself, Coca-Cola made the deal. Our rival would take Gatorade and likely sell off the other Quaker brands, we thought. We were a little worried but decided to not look back.

A few more weeks passed. Then, in late November—Thanksgiving week—Roger, Steve, and I were all together in Dallas at Frito-Lay's annual budget meetings. Quaker felt like it was in the rearview mirror, but we knew that Coke's board of directors was voting on its transformational purchase of Quaker that day. That evening, we flew back to New York, out of the news feed for three hours. When we landed, our BlackBerrys lit up. Coca-Cola's board, including a skeptical Warren Buffett, had voted down the plan to spend $14 billion on Quaker. We assumed it was because they didn't want a food business they knew nothing about.

The three of us were dumbfounded—for about five seconds. This meant the Quaker CEO Bob Morrison was out of options and would likely come back to PepsiCo. He really needed a buyer. We decided to go home to our families for Thanksgiving and think about it all.

Roger managed the situation perfectly. In long phone calls that weekend, he made the point that if we went back to Bob with a lower bid than we'd offered before, Bob would lose face. If we really wanted Quaker—the brands, the people, the customers, the image of the smiling guy in the big hat—we needed the CEO on our board for advice as we integrated the

companies. Roger proposed we stick to our original bid but ask Quaker to modify its demand for the financial guardrail.

A week later, we announced that PepsiCo would buy Quaker for $13.4 billion.

Unexpectedly, Roger added a management shake-up. He would step down as CEO and chairman of PepsiCo when the deal closed, and Steve would take over. Roger and Bob Morrison would serve on the board as vice chairmen. Steve and Roger also decided together that I would be named president of PepsiCo and join the board. I was in my office late on Friday, December 1, when Steve called me from Dallas to share the news.

I was over the moon. This was major. President of PepsiCo. The board of directors. Wow!

I packed up at work immediately.

I drove home. It was about 10 p.m., and the wintery roads were peaceful and dark. In those fifteen minutes behind the wheel, I let myself enjoy my accomplishment. I had worked so hard, learned so much, and earned my place.

I entered our house through the kitchen door and dropped my keys and bag on the counter. I was bursting with excitement—so eager to tell everyone. Then my mother appeared. "I have the most incredible news!" I exclaimed.

"The news can wait," she said. "I need you to go out and get milk."

"Why didn't you ask Raj to go get the milk?" I asked. "It looks like he came home a while ago."

"He looked tired, so I didn't want to disturb him," she said.

I picked up my keys, went back to the car, drove to the Stop & Shop a mile away, and bought a gallon of whole milk. When

I walked into the kitchen again, I was hopping mad. I slammed the plastic bottle on the counter.

"I've just become president of PepsiCo, and you couldn't just stop and listen to my news," I said, loudly. "You just wanted me to go get the milk!"

"Listen to me," my mother replied. "You may be the president or whatever of PepsiCo, but when you come home, you are a wife and a mother and a daughter. Nobody can take your place.

"So you leave that crown in the garage."

8

Buying the Quaker Oats Company for $13.4 billion was like riding a speeding roller-coaster, with Roger, Steve, and me buckled in together through the twists and turns—a little scary but, by the end, exhilarating and very satisfying.

PepsiCo shareholders focused completely on Gatorade, the number one sports drink in a booming, expanding market. They saw glittering possibilities for tie-ins with superstar global athletes. Michael Jordan, the best of basketball players, was already on TV as the face of the brand, inspiring young athletes to "Be like Mike" with a jingle that everyone was singing. Adding Gatorade to our lineup of noncarbonated drinks, with Aquafina water and Lipton iced teas, would more than double PepsiCo's share in that category to 30 percent of US sales.

I loved the Quaker part of the equation, too. Oatmeal, granola bars, pancakes, cereal—I imagined every one of them paired with Tropicana Pure Premium on America's breakfast table. Healthier food was on my mind. Preetha and Tara, now

ages fourteen and six, scrambled off to school every morning in their uniforms, buckling under the weight of their stuffed backpacks and grabbing a breakfast bar or little bags filled with cereal on the way out. I had a good sense of the meals that a busy, growing family might want—convenient, nutritious, delicious, affordable—and thought that PepsiCo could certainly help feed more people at more times of the day.

We announced the Quaker deal with great fanfare at PepsiCo headquarters. Roger gave investors a comprehensive presentation, which I had nervously stayed up all night perfecting. Then, unlike all the CEOs who claim multibillion-dollar moves as their own personal achievement, he talked about how our trio got it done. He celebrated me as a member of the inner circle and crucial to PepsiCo's future. It was the first time I was front and center at such a company-defining event.

We lined up for photos with Bob Morrison of Quaker Oats behind three dozen bottles of Gatorade and Pepsi. Roger proudly clutched Chewy granola bars, Steve had the Fritos, and I held up a half-gallon carton of orange juice. Was it a picture of the evolving face of American business—an immigrant woman of color taking her place in the uppermost ranks? Did this portend more opportunities for women in leadership?

Negotiating and announcing our big deal was the thrill ride. Now we had to make it work. We'd promised the world that adding Quaker Oats to PepsiCo would unlock tremendous efficiencies, with at least $350 million in cost savings over five years. That would cushion our short-term financial commitments and help PepsiCo invest in more big ideas, including expanding our snacks business outside the US.

Back on 4/3, we all knew that an ill-conceived postmerger integration could doom the success of the acquisition—we'd seen that happen in the industry before. Lousy execution would linger on our balance sheet and in the minds of investors for years to come, affecting our credibility. We figured we had about three months to come up with a very detailed plan to blend the companies, and we had to get it exactly right. We also needed US government approval, which required proving to the Federal Trade Commission (FTC) that Gatorade, backed by PepsiCo's heft in marketing and distribution, wouldn't block competitors from entering the sports-drink market or hurt consumers with higher prices. The biggest hurdle seemed to be that we owned another sports drink, All Sport, which was tiny and declining. Coke owned the only real Gatorade competitor, Powerade.

If the FTC blocked the deal, Quaker would remain a PepsiCo rival. So our planning team had to operate completely in private. We tapped Brian Cornell, who was running Tropicana Europe, and John Compton, head of Frito-Lay sales and marketing, to work with a handful of consultants, sealed off from the rest of the company. I talked with Brian and John several times a day. Every Friday at 7 a.m., we had a two-hour conference call to review every possible cost saving and how we'd land it. It was an intense time.

Meanwhile, Roger Enrico, the showman who summed up his own style with the pronouncement "make big changes to big things," was headed out the door. As CEO, he'd fixed the restaurant business and spun it off, separated the North American bottlers into a public company, and started PepsiCo

on the path to a more balanced portfolio of products. I don't think this broad rethinking would have happened without Roger at the helm, because he had the complete trust of the board. PepsiCo was also in good shape financially.

I learned a lot from Roger; he was intuitive and courageous. He took to very few people—his standards were "interesting," to say the least—but he took to me. He mentored me and, to others, that showed I was destined for bigger things. Even though Roger's style was confusing and annoying at times, I admired him enormously and we understood each other. His savvy and friendship propelled me.

Steve Reinemund, stepping into Roger's shoes as CEO, was a completely different character—a serious, upright, religious guy who wore shiny wing-tipped shoes and starched white shirts monogrammed with his initials on the cuffs. He had joined PepsiCo through Pizza Hut in the mid-1980s and created a home-delivery service that took on Domino's, our rival, and transformed the American pizza business.

In seven years as CEO of Frito-Lay, Steve had been ardently focused on operations. He knew everything about making salty snacks and distributing them, perfectly crisp and on time, to retailers. He was a terrific salesman, who visited retail CEOs and store managers and rode the delivery trucks. Lavish brand building and marketing were never his priority. While Pepsi-Cola was busy signing the British pop stars the Spice Girls to a multimillion-dollar contract on one side of the company, Frito-Lay's Tostitos were gaining share with ads featuring the Beverly Hillbillies making microwave nachos.

Even though he was now going to run the whole company, Steve hated spending much on corporate functions, such as IT or R&D. He believed in the decentralization and fierce

independence of every division. Steve was so cost conscious that he was rumored to have had the cleaning service at Frito-Lay headquarters cut to twice a week and the toilet paper switched to one-ply from two-ply. Roger, in typical fashion, nicknamed him "One-Ply."

Steve was born in Queens, New York; grew up with a single mother; and graduated from the US Naval Academy in Annapolis, Maryland. He served in the Marines for five years, including duties in full-dress uniform at the White House and Camp David for presidents Nixon and Ford. I once jokingly asked him whether he ever chilled out and let his hair down. An hour later, he walked into my office with his tie askew, his hair mussed up, and a broad grin. Steve could be funny and self-effacing, but he had to work at it.

At the same time, he always tried to do the right thing. He considered Pepsi-Cola's one-hundredth-anniversary celebration in Hawaii too extravagant and chose not to attend. When Roger took senior executives on the PepsiCo jet to Montana or the Cayman Islands for long team-building weekends, Steve usually chose to stay home with his wife, Gail, and their four kids.

I, of course, was never even invited on Roger's trips because they were always men only. For me, that was fine because I wanted more time at home. I was confident that Roger wouldn't pursue anything significant without my being consulted or involved.

Steve's frugal approach and attention to detail were just what PepsiCo needed when he took over in 2000. We were now a pure packaged-goods company—without the

restaurants—and had to earn superior profit from our new, streamlined core.

In 1999, when Steve was transitioning to the corporate offices, he had pushed me to learn more about what he called "the right side of the decimal point"—the pennies—by asking me to oversee a major Frito-Lay logistics project. He was right to do that. He knew I'd negotiated dozens of million- and billion-dollar transactions and easily handled big numbers on the left side of the decimal point. But I hadn't reckoned with how fractions of a cent, over huge volumes, drove PepsiCo profitability. Indeed, I hadn't really dealt with tiny increments in business since I walked from shop to shop selling thread and printed fabric for Mettur Beardsell in India.

The Frito-Lay assignment took me to Plano every week for seven months. I left home for the airport at 4:30 a.m. on Mondays and lived in a Marriott hotel room until Thursday night. I missed my family terribly, and, of course, the technology that connects us today with smartphones, texting, FaceTime, or Zoom did not exist. I talked to Raj or the girls on the phone, but those end-of-day calls were usually short, and our communication wasn't immediate or spontaneous. We had the services of a babysitter and a housekeeper, and Raj was home almost every night that I was away. We had agreed never to leave the girls without a family member with them for the night, whatever the circumstances. This required a lot of planning on our part. Preetha was just starting high school, and Tara was in first grade; it was a very precious time for me to have to leave them for several days at a time.

I threw myself into the task—a massive rethink of the direct store delivery system that was a hallmark of getting Frito-Lay products to market.

Lay's, Doritos, Walkers, and most other salty snacks are packed with air so they don't break, and that results in very large, lightweight freight. The products also sell fast, so store shelves need constant restocking. All this means the best way to move millions of bags of chips from the factory where they are made to the consumer is to deliver them directly to the store whenever possible, without interim handling. Frito-Lay had the largest, most sophisticated DSD system in the world, with forty-seven manufacturing plants in North America alone, supported by 230 large warehouses, 1,760 smaller bin warehouses, and a large truck fleet with sales representatives carrying handheld devices to record orders.

Throughout the 1990s, Frito-Lay was cranking out dozens of new flavors, shapes, and other line extensions, with product launches every three or four months. Consumers loved the variety, and offering new seasonings wasn't expensive for us at the manufacturing level. Almost everything was based on some variant of corn or potato chips. Besides, *new* meant *sales*: when we launched a new flavor and featured it prominently on the shelf, loads of people would give it a try.

All of this burdened the DSD system. Every type of store needed different packaging, and every new variant added to the distribution complexity. Convenience stores, for instance, wanted to sell Jumpin' Jack Cheese Doritos in 3.25-ounce packs for the grab-and-eat crowd; club stores like Costco, meanwhile, preferred multipacks for people who bought them in bulk once a month. We had to create and move hundreds of options.

Steve wanted to double the capacity of the DSD system and reconfigure it to handle 30 percent more varieties. We had to remove waste from the current operation to find that room and then upgrade everything, from the handheld computers to the

picking system in the distribution center to how we tailored shelf assortments by store and selling area. It was a Herculean task.

Of course, as I sweated the details at Frito-Lay, I had no idea that we'd be buying Quaker a year later. In retrospect, that Plano experience was really critical because it taught me how to look for the smallest cost savings. By the time I was working on the postmerger integration planning with Brian and John, I had some expertise in finding the nuggets.

Those two, working in their confidential bubble, figured out how we'd leverage the combined scale of PepsiCo and Quaker to pay less for everything from our packaging supplies to furniture to truck tires to ingredients like wheat and oats. They planned how we could consolidate offices and functions like HR, accounting, and legal. They detailed how Quaker's warehouse sales team could take on Tropicana and small-volume Frito-Lay items that didn't work well with DSD. They found almost two hundred projects that would save us anywhere from a few hundred thousand dollars to tens of millions of dollars. Each had to be scoped, score-carded, shepherded, and landed within a year. The bulk of it had to happen in the first four months.

Through these efforts, we delivered more than $700 million in savings to PepsiCo's bottom line over five years, twice the $350 million we'd estimated.

Unfortunately, government approval didn't progress quite as smoothly as we expected. After an initial examination, the

FTC's commissioners decided to take a second look at whether buying Gatorade gave PepsiCo too much power in the soft drink industry. We then had to provide far more data, detailed econometric modeling, and analysis to make our case.

One day, Steve dropped by my office and asked me to take over the FTC process, working with our legal team. What a minefield, I thought. The executive who was responsible for this project would be understandably puzzled and insulted. I had no experience with Washington regulators and was already flat out with other work, not to mention my family at home. I tried to talk Steve out of it, but he, too, was new to this and said he'd only be comfortable if I was on the case. If our hard-won Quaker deal fell apart, he said, at least the two of us could say we tried our very best.

I had to turn my efficiency up another notch.

I convinced my mother to come and live with us again full-time because Raj was also extremely busy at work. For the next few months, I was at my desk by 6 a.m. Then, at least three times a week, by 9 a.m. I boarded a PepsiCo plane that was on standby for me and, with the lawyers, flew to Washington. We met with FTC staff, discussed the case, and collected questions. By 3 p.m., we were back in the air, and I was in my office by 4:30. I passed out assignments to get the questions answered, reviewed the previous day's answers, and carried on with my other work. I went home about 10 p.m. and again sat up in bed until past midnight reviewing mail and making to-do lists. Our whole team worked incredibly hard in those few months.

In August 2001, PepsiCo's plan to buy Quaker Oats finally went to a vote by four FTC commissioners. The decision was as close as can be: a 2–2 tie. That meant our deal was approved. Steve and I were unspeakably relieved.

I came away from this process thoroughly impressed by the FTC staff. They were dedicated, focused, and quick to learn the intricacies of our business. They didn't start out knowing the business but read everything we sent them and asked difficult and insightful questions. These federal government staffers aren't as well paid as we are in private enterprise and, in those humid summer months, the people I worked with didn't even have air-conditioning, because their building was being renovated. Yet they carefully combed through almost two hundred boxes of our documents, with the sole intent of protecting the American consumer from the adverse effects of reduced competition. The transaction got a very thorough look.

At one point, I remember wishing that all Americans could see their tax dollars in action at the FTC because they'd be proud of this well-intentioned work. Years later, I happily accepted an invitation to deliver the keynote address at the FTC's one-hundredth-anniversary event. I recounted my experience with the FTC and belatedly thanked everyone for their yeoman's effort on this transaction.

A month after we closed the deal, I moved offices again—into a huge corner space with ten windows, seven on one side and three on the other. It was magnificent in every way—spacious, with lovely light-wood floors, and, at my insistence, the same furniture I had bought in my first week at PepsiCo. The room was so big and sparse that some of Roger's old furniture—a couple of couches and chairs—were moved in to fill the space. I felt like I had "landed," whatever that meant.

I also got a substantial raise. When Steve became my boss and I became president, he noticed that my compensation

hadn't been adjusted to reflect all of my responsibilities beyond CFO. Roger hadn't bothered with this; HR never brought it up, and neither did I.

I loved my job and felt it was a privilege to be sitting in that office. I felt I owed PepsiCo my hard work. Money was not my driver, and my salary was impressive, I thought, given where I'd started at BCG. I didn't compare myself with the men around me, some of whom, I later learned, had been getting generous special stock option grants for years. In my first six years at the company, I received nothing like that. Now the new CEO gave me a meaningful base-salary increase and asked the board to award me a special stock grant.

I still wonder why, over many years, I found it typical for the HR department to skate over the issue of women not being rewarded quite the same as men. Why did HR people tolerate it? It didn't seem to matter if the HR head was male or female. They were all very energetic about their worthy diversity programs yet defensive if I asked why a promising young woman executive wasn't getting the same salary as a similarly ranked guy.

We know that, on the whole, women's median salary in the US is about 80 percent that of men. In my world, pay disparity was expressed in smaller increments: a woman would get 95 percent of the base pay of a man doing the same work. If I asked why she was getting 5 percent less, I'd be told, "It's such a small difference, don't worry about it." Sometimes, I would fight back a little, with "then why don't we pay her 105 percent of what he is getting?" It was always an uphill battle when, in reality, HR should have been flagging these issues and systematically addressing them.

In any case, I found the very people managing salary budgets stuck on the idea that the men should get a little more. I wonder if it is because HR departments intrinsically still see men as more ideal. I have talked to friends in many industries, and this pattern persists no matter how outraged we claim to be about women being paid less.

Closing the Quaker deal with the FTC approval also ushered in a somewhat calmer period in our family life. The girls were getting a little older and more independent, Raj was working on a start-up and was in both the US and India a fair amount, and I was busy with US-based projects. Now, I also had the advantage of a company plane.

This was revolutionary for me. For my entire tenure at PepsiCo up to this time, I had witnessed other senior executives use the corporate jets for business trips and, sometimes, for personal travel. Until the FTC work, I always flew commercial. Even when I hauled alone to juice factories in Europe and Florida over two weeks for the due diligence on the Tropicana deal, Roger didn't offer me a company plane. I didn't ask, and maybe I should have. No one seemed to notice or consider my situation as a mom with two young kids at home for whom time was so dear.

I know there's more than a hint of elitism in discussing flying on company planes. But the reality is that thousands of jets ferry businesspeople around the world all the time, particularly if they run global companies. Once I was president of PepsiCo and I had that convenience, I was much more productive on the road. I could work quietly, with the privacy to read confidential documents or discuss proprietary information while I traveled.

My grandfather's entire savings went into this house, where three generations lived and cared for one another. The house gave us stability and comfort. Our family lived simply and we were supremely focused on education.

The swing in the women's living room, where we swayed and sang, and where my mother and her sisters sipped South Indian coffee and discussed the world around them.

My parents on their wedding day. My father had seen my mother in the neighborhood and was intrigued by her cheerful spirit. Their parents met and arranged the match. They had a wonderful partnership.

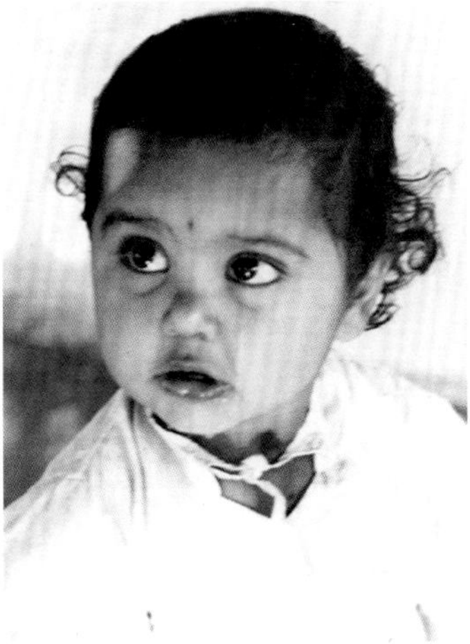

Me as a baby in 1956, not quite a year old. We didn't have a camera and my uncle took this picture. I have very few photos of my first years.

Thatha, my paternal grandfather, commanded the room just by sitting in a chair. He adored us and imparted a lifelong love of learning. He would say, "I am eighty, and I am still a student." I am at left, about age fourteen.

My maternal grandparents and some of my aunts and uncles. My mom and dad are standing directly behind her parents. Chandrika (left) and I are wearing silk pavadais, our skirts for special occasions.

I attended Holy Angels Convent School for twelve years, and literally ran from one activity to another. I especially loved science and music. Mrs. Jobard, in the center with short hair, was my favorite teacher and really encouraged me. I am in the middle row, second from right, with pigtails and bows.

At the airport saying farewell to my family before departing for Yale. My dad persuaded my mother to let me go. I was full of anticipation, and sad that Thatha wasn't there to see me fly.

The LogRhythms, our all-girls rock band, with Mary, Jyothi, and Hema. We began with five songs and became a hit at school fairs all over Madras. The boy in this photo, Kamlesh, was a neighbor who occasionally played the drums and took charge of equipment.

Raj and I were married in the wood-paneled basement of his uncle's house surrounded by all of our closest family. Here, our mothers are making sure Raj tied the wedding chain properly.

Carl Stern, head of BCG's Chicago office, gave me up to six months of paid leave when my father was terminally ill. I would have had to quit BCG to help my mother care for my father without that time off.

Raj and me in the early days of our marriage.

Preetha, my firstborn, taught me about love at the deepest level, and Raj and I doted on our beautiful baby girl. My mother, Raj's parents, and aunts and uncles from India lived with us off and on to help us care for her.

When Tara was born, I was again overcome with emotion for my child. I had paid leave and great health insurance, critical backstops. But we found that managing two kids was more complicated than one.

Raj is totally dedicated to our family and we have a real partnership as parents. He always encouraged me to keep moving and made many sacrifices in his own career for my sake.

My first day at PepsiCo, with CEO Wayne Calloway in his office. He was a man of few words, but he had phoned me to say he thought PepsiCo needed me more than General Electric needed me. That won me over.

Announcing our $13.2 billion purchase of Quaker Oats, with Bob Morrison, Roger Enrico, and Steve Reinemund. I had just been named president of PepsiCo and was proud to be in the inner circle.

Preetha and Tara in their school uniforms. For several years, I worked and traveled nonstop. I wrote notes describing the cities I was in and left them for the girls when I was away, but I missed them terribly.

Raj's parents with Preetha and Tara. My father-in-law supported my career and my mother-in-law, a gentle, loving person, was willing to help in any way. We traveled to India almost every year to spend time with family on both sides.

Tara's note, written when she was about six, begging me to come home. She later also sent me notes asking me to relax.

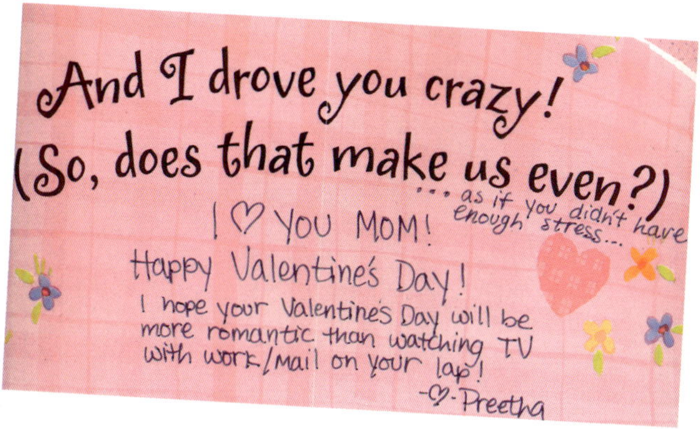

The inside of a card from Preetha. She knew I had a lot of stress, and hoped my Valentine's Day would be more interesting than an evening of TV and work.

With Steve Reinemund and his wife, Gail, in August 2006, when we announced I would become CEO of PepsiCo. I was excited and nervous, and the whole family wondered what this meant for us.

Indian president A.P. J. Abdul Kalam pins on the Padma Bhushan award in April 2007. I wished my father and grandfather had seen me that day. This was an incredible honor.

Jan Niski, Ann Cusano, and Barbara Spadaccia, my three assistants when I was president and CEO of PepsiCo. They kept my life together, protected me, and were deeply loyal to my family. I could not have managed but for these women expertly organizing the competing demands on my time.

Hillary Clinton came to PepsiCo when she was US senator for New York and I was ready to take over as CEO. She told me, in these few minutes together, that I could call her anytime. We are walking on the flat surface I had installed so people didn't keep tripping on the cobblestones, seen on the sides.

Shortly after taking over PepsiCo, I invited other female leaders to my home for a couple of dinners. We found we had a lot in common.

With Mehmood Khan, the person who probably made the biggest difference to Performance with Purpose. Mehmood elevated research and development, and led breakthroughs in cutting sugar and salt while maintaining taste in our products, and in saving water and reducing plastic.

The PepsiCo annual report cover of 2017 showing that more than 50 percent of our portfolio was now "better for you" and "good for you."

With Mauro Porcini, who was like no one who had ever walked into my office. He put words to my ideas about incorporating great design into the whole company.

The PepsiCo team worked hard, but we also had a great time together. Our karaoke parties, not surprisingly, could get pretty competitive. Here the men perform; the women sang next.

On a market tour in Guatemala. I went to stores to see how our products looked on the shelf, and wanted our frontline workers to know that I cared a lot about their efforts. In the foreground is Laxman Narasimhan, then the CEO of PepsiCo Latin America.

With Anne-Marie Slaughter and Norah O'Donnell at the 2016 Women in the World conference in New York. I loved speaking at events to boost women and build our sisterhood.

PepStart, our onsite childcare center at PepsiCo headquarters, soon filled to capacity, even with employees paying for the service. I see no reason large companies shouldn't help families with childcare for everyone's benefit.

President Barack Obama sought the opinions of business leaders as he navigated through the financial crisis. He was a great listener and welcomed all of our points of view.

With Derek Jeter of the New York Yankees. I fell in love with the Yankees during the 1978 World Series when I was a new immigrant and missing cricket, the bat-and-ball sport of my youth. Derek and I remain great friends.

My mother, Shantha, who always had one foot on the accelerator and one foot on the brake. She was both a catalyst for my career and my safety net.

My trip to South Africa in 2018 was the most memorable of my life. After I spent time with a group of teenage girls and heard about their difficult lives, they asked only for me to hug each one of them. We spent a long time embracing.

At the event announcing my retirement from PepsiCo. I was proud and grateful, and looking forward to my next chapter.

The loves of my life who give me so much joy—my husband, Raj, and my daughters, Preetha and Tara.

I was very honored to be included in the Smithsonian Institution's National Portrait Gallery with this painting by artist Jon R. Friedman.

FROM MY THANK-YOU SPEECH:

"I hope that any girl, any person of color, any immigrant, any American who looks at Jon's creation will not only see a portrait. I hope they will see that anything is possible. And I hope they will find their own way of bringing their spirit and talents to bear on the work of lifting up this country and our world."

The plane was a flying office. I could do many multistop, one-day trips.

I was home for dinner more often than I was earlier in my career and helped my daughters with their homework. Once they went to bed, I would read and go over work in our family room, often with the Yankees game on mute in the background.

Preetha was a gifted student, a National Merit Scholar semifinalist from her school, and a vivacious, witty young girl. But her teenage years were not easy. This is a difficult period for girls in general, but having me, her mother, whom she was so attached to, constantly traveling—and with zero flexibility to take time off to work from home when she just wanted me around—was tough on her. She also wasn't enjoying Sacred Heart anymore after so many years, frustrated by the cliques and petty fights that can arise when growing girls have been together too long.

To top it all, I realize that Raj and I were restricting her by referring back to our value system, rooted in 1970s India. The stylish clothes for girls Preetha's age at that time involved a lot of spaghetti straps, which we didn't like; we wanted her home on Saturday nights by 8 p.m.; we questioned why she couldn't just—always—have her friends to our house. It all seemed so reasonable to us at the time. Looking back, perhaps not.

It was all too much for Preetha. She chose to go to boarding school a few hours' drive away in Connecticut to finish high school. After she graduated, she went on to Hamilton College to major in geology and environmental science and developed an eagerness to protect our planet for the future. We are very proud of her.

Tara, in the elementary school grades, was happy at Sacred Heart, and I drove her many mornings on the way to the office.

As she got out of the car, I would roll down the window and merrily shout after her, "I love you best in the whole wide world!" I think she loved it, although, as she grew older, she did take up turning around and loudly whispering, "Mom, stop it. You're embarrassing me!" It never stopped me.

For several of these years, we also had a young teacher from the school come and hang out with Tara in the late afternoons and help her with homework. That arrangement worked out very well.

Raj helped Tara with math over the years, with mixed results. Often, I'd get panicked calls: "Mom. Help. Dad's way of teaching me math is not the way my teacher taught us. I'm getting more confused." I could hear Raj muttering in the background, "These teachers have no clue . . ." Obviously, the approach taken by his school in India was vastly different from the Sacred Heart approach.

The petty frustrations of working motherhood persisted for me, and I still felt plenty of nagging, low-lying guilt. The school, for instance, had a Class Coffee for mothers at 9:30 on some Wednesday mornings. I missed almost all of them. Preetha had accepted this reluctantly, but Tara started to express that she wished I could be a "real mom," too, and show up at the Class Coffees like the other moms. What could I do? I called a teacher at the school whom I was friendly with and asked how many mothers were actually attending. Then I figured out who wasn't there. The next time Tara mentioned it, I rattled off the names of the other moms in her grade who skipped it. It was my way of coping but may not have been a satisfying response for my young daughter.

For all my work stress, travel, and impossible schedules, I really tried to make sure I was a caring, involved mother to the

extent I could. Every one of my daughters' birthday parties was planned and executed with great love and attention to every small detail because I was aware that those days were special and fleeting. I went to every school event or competition that my kids were in and, for five years, was an active member of the school's board of trustees. I don't think I ever missed a meeting.

If anyone was sick or hurt, I was always there, which is in my nature. From my early years as a mom, when Preetha had chicken pox, infected me, and left me with a seriously scabbed face for months, I soothed my children beyond what Raj thought was required. I once dropped everything and raced to school when Preetha injured her ankle in gym and ended up standing to the side while this daughter, too, told me to stop embarrassing her. It didn't matter. I had to make sure she was OK.

Another time, I was in California and got a call from a hysterical Tara. She had two rabbits in a hutch in the backyard, and one had died. I did my best to console her. A half hour later, she called back. The second rabbit was lifeless, too. She was beside herself. I canceled the rest of my meetings and flew home.

I also can't overstate how much I relied on my PepsiCo assistant from 2000 to 2006, Barbara Spadaccia, a smart, loving, and incredibly generous women in her fifties with no kids of her own who took on my children and me as though we were her own kin. She was my unwavering supporter and a calm voice in everything I was trying to accomplish, often all at once.

I was always determined that the girls could phone me at work anytime, and they were regulars at the office. But I also got calls that I couldn't take, and then Barbara would step in. She sorted out all kinds of small crises, from missing school

supplies to forgotten assignments. Sometimes she'd take Preetha out for a late-day coffee or a walk just to talk about the pressures of school life. Barbara was basically a part of our family, and she worked very hard to make my life easier.

Barbara once stood in for me with Tara at the Mother-Daughter Liturgy event at the school, a special service in the chapel with a processional, singing, reflections by one mother in the group, and a sermon. Then all the moms and daughters exchanged letters with one another and had lunch. I always loved that day and made sure I was there. But this time I had an investor meeting that I simply couldn't skip. When I got home that evening, I was very apologetic to Tara, hugging her and tearing up at having missed our time together. Tara wasn't worried. "The day was amazing," she said. "Can Barbara do it again next year, Mom? She was awesome."

Steve and I also drew closer as friends when he was CEO and I was president of PepsiCo, partly because he had twins about the same age as Tara. He made a big effort to give them his complete attention every weekend. I remember driving out to see Preetha at boarding school once and Steve picking up Tara after school to get her home. I don't know of any other CEO who was quite so supportive.

Our surrogates—all those special people in our children's lives who support them, encourage them, and love them, too—have a profoundly important role to play for all of us. After all, it does take a village to raise a child.

My work at PepsiCo was essentially endless. I never went to bed at night thinking, "What should I do tomorrow?" I was always catching up, answering questions, moving forward.

I once flew to Moscow on a Friday night to help a young European team develop compelling logic for a Russian acquisition they wanted to propose. Boarding the plane home two days later, on a Sunday afternoon, I exclaimed, "Do you guys realize I gave up my weekend and flew all the way to Moscow to help you prepare for a presentation to *me* next Friday?"

"We know," one responded. "Thank you for being Indra Nooyi, our teacher. We now feel much better about how we'll do with Indra Nooyi, the president and CFO with extremely high standards!"

In these same years, I began an enormous redo of PepsiCo's entire IT system. The project emerged from crisis. One spring day in 2002, Frito-Lay's ordering system crashed, and we had to hire hundreds of temporary workers to process orders as we moved into the busy Memorial Day weekend. The backlog was huge: in a peak holiday period, Frito-Lay had more than 150,000 orders a day, and humans just couldn't do it all. We were coping with old legacy systems, and most of the people who knew how they worked—and how to fix them—were retired. We had to locate some of those people and call them in.

Across PepsiCo, we had many systems like this—piecemeal technology that was increasingly unreliable and expensive to maintain. We weren't alone with this dilemma. Many large companies were confronting the same problem and, to pay for technology updates, were taking onetime charges separate from their ongoing costs so that these expenses would be viewed as temporary and not affect underlying operating earnings.

I concluded that we needed a whole new enterprise system that could handle PepsiCo's growth, a major investment that would touch every part of our operation. We needed to set the

tone at PepsiCo that state-of-the-art IT was core to our success. I also had a personal reason to get this fixed. New federal financial regulations, the Sarbanes-Oxley Act, required that CFOs and CEOs sign documents every year guaranteeing the integrity of their company's financials. I told Steve we needed robust IT systems to be comfortable about signing.

Steve was reluctant. This was going to be really expensive and time-consuming. But he told me that if I found the money, I should take care of it. For several months, I worked with IT and external consultants on a plan that would end up costing \$1.5 billion—\$300 million a year for five years—just for phase 1. A couple of months later, a twenty-five-page approval document was on my desk, laying it all out.

Twenty people had already signed, and I was the second-to-last person who had to approve it. Steve was the last. I knew that if he saw my signature, he'd go ahead.

I couldn't do it. I couldn't sign off on a \$1.5 billion capital expenditure that was so technical that I couldn't fully comprehend it. So, just as I'd done in the old days, I hit the books. I bought everything I could find on enterprise systems, process mapping, data warehousing, and master data management. And over the next six weeks—through the December and New Year's holiday seasons—I studied it all. I canceled our annual trip to India, which the family protested but had to accept. In January, I went back to the team with a long list of questions and, once they had answered every one, added my name approving the spending. We paid for this system, which took more than seven years to build, by selling some shares that PepsiCo owned in our publicly traded bottling companies.

I think that leaders need to understand the details behind what they are approving before they affix their signature to

anything. This is not about trusting the people that work for you. It's about basic responsibility. Don't be a "pass-through." I think the people who worked for me came to appreciate that I read everything they sent me, both as a mark of respect to them and their work and because it was my responsibility. I know I drove people crazy with questions, but this was my job. I intended to do it well.

But what about leaving my crown in the garage?

Honestly, I wasn't even home enough in my first years as PepsiCo's president to think too much about how I was handling the relationship between my professional success and my role as a mother, wife, and daughter. I certainly didn't feel very royal, as I hustled from one project to another and made all those trips to Washington. I was just trying to keep up with the tremendous responsibilities of the job in a world with no one else like me.

Still, my mother's comment that night has stuck with me—just vague enough to interpret in myriad ways.

First, I think she said something deeply important about how we combine work and family. She was right, of course, that no matter who we are or what we do, nobody can take our place in our families. I was enjoying big success, but the stability of our home meant I would be equally valued and important whether or not I had been named president of PepsiCo, she indicated.

So should my mother have just let me share my great news? Yes. My excitement that night was not about my new title, per se. I wanted to enjoy the moment and my accomplishment with the people closest to me and to share in their pride. I have

a feeling that if I were a man, a husband, a father, I might have had a little more leeway.

I think women are held to a different standard from men when it comes to celebrating their professional accomplishments. No matter what we do, we are never quite enough. Getting a promotion or a prize outside the home sometimes seems to mean that either that prize was easy to get or that we are letting our domestic duties slide.

This zero-sum game for women when it comes to work or family achievements is pernicious. It's important for men, in particular, to see that this holds us all back. Why not just let women soar in every part of life? Why not celebrate what we do well when we do it? We all love to see our daughters win at sports or in spelling contests when they are children. So why do we undercut grown women who succeed on the career playing field by frequently adding commentary on whether they are equally fabulous at home?

To be sure, women don't help themselves or one another in this regard. I know it's easier said than done, but we really need to let go of perfection. I often felt that, even as I was gaining influence and power in the corporate world, I was failing my family because I wasn't home more. Looking back, I'm a little heartbroken that I spent so much energy worrying about this. I once felt so bombarded with commentary from my daughters about how my work was all-consuming, that I told them, "OK, I'm going to quit PepsiCo. My heart is with you two, and clearly it's all too much and I will just give it up and be at home." At that moment, it seemed to be a great decision. But then I got the pivot: "No, Mom! You can't quit!" exclaimed Tara. "You have worked so hard for this! Dream big, Mom! Dream big!"

Preetha wished there were two of me—a dedicated, always-present mother she could count on and a CEO mother she was so proud of. I wish this had been possible.

Somehow, I had to learn to let these waves of emotion among all of us just pass. This is also endemic to a mother's role perhaps. I am super committed and connected with my family, and, no matter what I was doing outside, I still had an important part to play in absorbing everyone's feelings. Sometimes I felt like a punching bag, with everyone's troubles attributed to my being a top executive at PepsiCo.

Even though I struggled with these feelings, I know I was supremely lucky to be married to Raj. In the crunch years for working women—with growing kids and a demanding job—I think our spouses do take a back seat, and they have to be able to handle it. Often, Raj would tell me, "Your list is always PepsiCo, PepsiCo, PepsiCo; then your kids [as if they were only mine]; then your mother; then, at the bottom, there's me." He was right. But my joking response was "At least you are on the list!"

In reality, Raj transcends lists. I am sure he knows it. The only way our marriage works and lasts is because we are on this journey together for the success of our entire family. But there were many demands on my time at PepsiCo, and I know that Raj often felt quite ignored.

For any working woman with kids, a supportive spouse can compensate for all that guilt we carry around. As I've often said, being a mom is a full-time job, being a wife is a full-time job, and being an executive is more than a full-time job. All of it requires constant prioritization and reprioritization, sometimes several times a day. And, depending on who we are talking to,

we feel like we never get it right. For me, Raj being there at every step grounded me. He never once made me feel guilty about not being home with the kids.

I also feel that a sisterhood of friends can make an enormous difference. There are times when we don't want to be told that we are wrong, and we don't want to be told what to do differently. We want to vent and be heard, not be judged. I have close, dear best friends—women I know in India, Israel, and the US—whom I can absolutely rely on to just listen to what's bugging me. They aren't in my family, they aren't in my work life, and in no way do I feel I have to impress them or prove myself in any way. They span multiple time zones, but that never seems to be a problem.

The "crown in the garage" comment also speaks to the broader relationship between power and humility. This is an incredible lesson for those who rise in their careers and end up in roles that give them real authority in the workplace and in society.

Over the years, I started to downplay my job with my extended family. When I was a midlevel executive, it was easier for them to talk to me and just let me be myself. Once I rose to the senior ranks, some started to treat me somehow as more of a stranger. They assumed I would be too busy to speak with them or too important to deal with "normal" people. Others simply resented my success. All of this created some unease in the family.

I adjusted by keeping my observations, experiences, and stresses to myself more than I might have otherwise and making sure I was in good spirits when I came home or was with family.

That was very hard when I was thinking about decisions that would affect hundreds of thousands of PepsiCo employees, consumers around the world, or an earnings report that could influence global markets. But I think that approach was necessary to maintain sanity and equilibrium in my life outside work.

At the same time, my career was extremely interesting, I was good at it, and I was trying to help steer a very large company. I loved PepsiCo and where we were going. I loved our products and our great ideas. I admit I was sometimes disappointed that I couldn't just celebrate all that without worrying that people would think I was some sort of egomaniac.

For instance, when I received the Padma Bhushan Award, the third-highest civilian honor in India, from the Indian government in 2007, I felt genuinely proud. I imagined how pleased Thatha and my father would have been to know that I was on a list that included prominent artists, scientists, lawyers, and social workers. I was handed the award by President A. P. J. Abdul Kalam in the imposing Rashtrapati Bhavan, in Delhi. It was the same building I had visited for tea as a girl of fifteen, and now I was being honored there. Raj flew from the US to be with me. My mother joined us, too. I was sad that Preetha and Tara were in school and had to skip the event. No one else in my family called to congratulate me.

The trappings of leadership in our world—money, travel, meeting famous and fascinating people, beautiful living and work spaces—become easy to adapt to and accept. But true leaders must keep their feet firmly rooted to the ground and focus on the responsibilities of their jobs. That's what I always tried to do. I felt I was a role model, with everyone watching me. I had very difficult jobs to do and tried to take everything else in stride.

Female leaders have this much tougher than male leaders because the world of power is designed for men. Women are always breaking ground as they navigate the upper reaches of business, government, or finance. We have to demonstrate our gravitas in a world where authority and brilliance, to many people, still look like an older gentleman. And we have to absorb dozens of the simple, little slights that show women are not yet fully embraced.

When I was head of PepsiCo, I once exited a plane in Mexico with a team of guys. We were each greeted by the immigration official: "Welcome, Mr. X." "Welcome, Mr. Y." "Welcome, Mr. Z." "Hi, Indra."

Women obviously have to spend a lot more time on their appearance and can't cut corners in that department without risking all credibility. But there is much more. I spoke at hundreds of conferences and always had to worry about whether I could sit comfortably on the chair that was set out because it might be too deep or too high for me in a dress or a skirt. I wore the same beautiful blue ball gown to two gala events in New York, two years apart, and heard comments from photographers who wished I'd bought a new dress so they could build their collection of stock photos of me. Every guy at that event was probably in the same tuxedo he'd worn for a decade.

I was once on the cover of *Greenwich Magazine* wearing my favorite Armani jacket that made me feel elegant and comfortable. I thought I looked pretty good. Then a saleswoman at the local Saks Fifth Avenue department store called and suggested that, in the future, I come to them for a more up-to-date look before any important photo shoots. "Wearing a jacket from last season," she observed, "is not OK."

Women's voices are too high or too low, or they are seen as too short or too tall, or too fat or too thin, to be great leaders. These judgments wear us down. We know that when we hear them about other women, there is plenty of talk out there about us, too. I think women can't escape the reminders that we must always weigh our power—whatever it may be—against society's expectations that we must, at all costs, remember that we are imperfect.

With all the ways that it can be analyzed, I also can't forget who delivered the "crown in the garage" line.

That night in the kitchen, my mother was the same woman she always was—torn between wanting to see her daughter soar in the outside world and making sure I lived up to my role as a dedicated wife who could be content looking after everyone else. When I was a little girl, she asked me to make speeches pretending I was India's prime minister. She also worried about finding me a husband.

One foot on the accelerator, one foot on the brake.

Go out and capture the crown but leave it in the garage.

In April 2006, Raj took a hiatus from his job to go to India and care for his father, who was sick with cancer. I missed him and was sad to know that his dad, who had always been so supportive of me, was dying. As the wife of the family's oldest son, I was expected to step in to help. But my ever-understanding in-laws insisted that I stay home to attend to the children and my important job. Raj was the primary caregiver for his father for almost six months until he passed away in November 2006.

In August of that year, with Raj in India, I decided to take a week off to spend some time at home on my own. My plan was to relax, organize the house a little, and hang out with Tara. Preetha was visiting friends in Maine. I had nothing else in mind and was just looking forward to sleeping in—if I could ever do it—reading and reorganizing closets.

But, on Monday morning, August 7, 2006, Steve showed up. He came into the kitchen, sat down holding the little notepad he always carried, and informed me that he was moving back to Dallas. PepsiCo's board was set to name me CEO, he told me.

In three months, the iconic American purveyor of Pepsi-Cola, first poured in 1898, would be mine to lead.

I was shocked. I knew that I was being considered to lead the place one day, but I had no idea that Steve would leave so soon. We had evolved a working cadence that was comfortable and productive, and we often joked that we would retire together.

Steve told me that a plane was waiting for me in the PepsiCo hangar at Westchester airport, and by 10 a.m., I was in the air flying to Nantucket, the island off the coast of Massachusetts. That's where John Akers, the chairman of the board's nominating committee, was vacationing, and he wanted to officially tell me the news. When I landed in Nantucket, John, dressed in his shorts and polo shirt, got on the plane, told me the board's decision that would be officially ratified the following Saturday, wished me luck, and said he was proud of me. We shook hands. He left.

Then I took off again and flew the fifteen minutes to Cape Cod, to see Mike White, the head of PepsiCo's international operations, at his summer home. We were good friends, and I knew that Mike was the other candidate for the job. In fact, a few months earlier, we'd been asked to sit out of a meeting when the board was discussing a "confidential topic."

With a few hours on our hands that day, we'd headed to Times Square to take in *Jersey Boys*, the Broadway show. Then we went to dinner and talked about all the great times we'd had over the years with our Pepsi and Frito-Lay colleagues. We'd enjoyed so many holiday parties, many hosted by me, that turned into karaoke nights or sing-alongs with Mike at the piano. I had compiled books with lyrics of 275 pop songs, and we all had our dog-eared copies just for those parties. We laughed about how Roger, on any given evening, always insisted on singing Frank Sinatra's "My Way" at least three times and Don McLean's "American Pie" at least twice. Our tight group had devoted much of our lives to working at PepsiCo. Despite all the pressure, we'd had a lot of fun, too.

Now, as CEO-to-be, I really wanted Mike to stay at the company, at least for a couple of years. I told him so, and we talked a little about potential leadership moves and the transition. Mike then sat down at his upright piano and we sang a few songs. We went out for ice cream and a walk on the beach, and he drove me to the airport, gave me a big hug, and assured me of his support.

When I got home, it was still midafternoon. I called Raj in India, and he immediately said he'd fly home for a day or two to make sure he was with me for the announcement. Then I sat down by myself, in tears, and let a rush of emotions wash over

me. I was excited, nervous, and worried about stepping into the spotlight. I thought about everything—where I'd come from, what I'd attained, what I should do with PepsiCo.

I thought about my beautiful family and that, for me, there would be no break for a long time.

Twenty-four hours later, everything kicked in. I was in charge of the announcement and had to help frame it. Changing CEOs is extremely confidential because of how the markets might react to a switch in leadership, and only a few people could know what was happening. I invited the general counsel, the head of public relations, and the head of HR to my house, and we crafted the outlines for the announcement and letters to our employees, retail partners, and affiliates. Every word was considered. We had to celebrate Steve's accomplishments. We had to demonstrate stability and orderly transition. We had to be optimistic, confident.

On Thursday, I called Preetha and let her know that something very important required her presence the following Monday. A little reluctantly, she agreed to show up, dressed appropriately. Tara was at home and curious about all the goings-on. I could not share my news with either of them.

On Saturday, I informed my mother, in confidence, who was in Manhattan with my brother. Her immediate reaction? "Oh no! Let me call Steve and talk him out of leaving," she said. "He will listen to me. You have too much to do and the kids to take care of. You don't need more responsibility." I gently convinced her to hold off.

At 6 a.m. on Monday, August 14, 2006, the news broke: PEPSI POURS IT ON WITH WOMAN CEO, one headline read. PEPSI

PICKS A WOMAN TO RUN THE SHOW, screamed another. My family in India told me I dominated the news cycle that day—both in print and on TV. The uncles and aunts who couldn't stop singing "Yummy Yummy Yummy" in Madras many years ago were very proud of their tomboy niece.

The day was a whirlwind. Employees crammed into PepsiCo's cafeteria for a global town hall meeting that was beamed across the company. Steve gave a speech about passing the baton to me. Then I spoke. PepsiCo was already a fantastic company, I said, and we were going to make it even better. Let's roll up our sleeves.

Raj, Preetha, and Tara lined up together nearby, watching the goings-on and wondering what this all meant for them.

I felt the weight of the job. I was upbeat and confident on the outside, but, inside, reality was taking hold.

9

I didn't want the rigmarole of changing offices again. I had a terrific corner office—my home away from home—sunny in the morning, a view of treetops that changed color in the autumn, and, far in the distance, an enormous red Alexander Calder stabile called *Hats Off*. I loved my simple desk; my big table for meetings, where Tara would come and do homework; and my few plants in large Asian ceramic pots. The glass shelves were filled with family photos and mementos of my travels.

Still, Steve was leaving "the CEO's office," a space exactly the same size on the opposite end of the corridor that had been Wayne's and Roger's corner, too. I'd been to so many meetings in that room, always deferential to the seat of power. On one side was a heavy mahogany desk; on the other was a sort of living room, with upholstered chairs around a glass coffee table, a Persian rug, and a fireplace. The space oozed traditional American corporate authority—hearkening back to the portrait-lined private men's clubs and smoky bankers' dens where, for decades, the real deals were said to have happened.

What should I do? I had to claim my place as CEO and chairman of the board for all to see. I briefly wondered whether I needed those old trappings. Then I decided to stay put. I had the fireplace and the wood paneling on the walls removed and that space renovated into two elegant offices for people who reported to me.

I felt I knew the rhythms and responsibilities of PepsiCo's CEO. I had worked faithfully with the past three leaders, deeply involved in all big decisions, from spinning off the restaurants to buying Tropicana to separating the bottlers into a public company and revamping the IT systems. I was sensitive to the pressures of managing an expansive, famous company and to the seasons and moods of the global economy.

In tune with my personality, I was probably overprepared. In twelve years as PepsiCo's corporate strategist, CFO, and then president, I had toured with truck drivers, walked through acres of manufacturing plants, and visited with retail partners in every corner of the world. I had tasted hundreds of experimental chip-and-dip flavors and sipped dozens of drink concoctions, and I could weigh in on every kind of mouthfeel. I was learning about how to grow potatoes in Inner Mongolia and cut water usage in rice fields. I knew every lever of our profit and loss statement and balance sheet and had credibility with our investors and analysts. I was as passionate about the spirit of PepsiCo as ever and completely intimate with its structure and foibles.

Most important, I was a dreamer and a doer, and I could paint a vivid picture of the future for PepsiCo and lead people to deliver on that vision. In retrospect, I understand why the board selected me as CEO.

But I also had butterflies in my stomach. When I walked into the building as CEO, on October 2, 2006, I had that strange feeling that many top leaders have tried to explain: I was "it," like in a game of tag. I felt like everyone was watching me and waiting for me to tell them what to do next.

I was catapulted into the wider public eye. I was the eleventh female CEO in the Fortune 500, a tiny club that included Meg Whitman at eBay, Anne Mulcahy at Xerox, and Patricia Russo at Lucent Technologies. I was also an immigrant woman of color from a developing market taking over a very well-known American consumer products company. And that made me a curiosity.

In the first few months, the press attention was constant and rather punishing. I had one chat with a senior New York journalist, whom I knew socially, that stuck with me. He said I'd be the focus of attention for some time. The press would gleefully build me up as a brilliant, different, new CEO so that when my inevitable troubles came along, I'd have farther to fall. That's the game, he warned me.

So far, my relationship with the media had been pretty good. In my early days at PepsiCo, I had no public persona, although I spoke with Wall Street analysts about our strategy and finances for their investor reports on the prospects for PepsiCo stock. As CFO, I presented PepsiCo's numbers every quarter on conference calls with the same analysts and with investment fund managers. I found it all very cordial and routine.

After the Quaker deal, my profile had ramped up. *BusinessWeek* ran a story contrasting Steve's leadership style and mine. Looking back, I realize this was a first taste of how I'd be persistently perceived and presented differently from powerful

men. We were an "odd couple," the story said. Steve was a former US Marine who ran marathons. I was a woman with an "unsettling habit of humming during meetings to calm herself." The article called my wardrobe "business Indian," including "anything from a flowing scarf to a sari." It goes on: "She'll make offbeat comments you'd never expect a high-level executive to utter," and "She has sort of a guileless, unencumbered quality."

In 2003, *Forbes* was preparing a feature article about PepsiCo under Steve and hastily arranged a photo shoot with me in our parking lot for pictures to accompany a sidebar. Then they used my photo on the issue's cover. Indra Nooyi has "feisty candor," the story said. It included a quote from Roger: "'Indra is like a dog with a bone,' says Enrico. He's being complimentary." I felt terrible about that *Forbes* cover story because Steve, as CEO, deserved the attention. It made no sense to me that I was the one highlighted.

This episode affected my approach to journalists ever after. I was always wary. I learned that, as hard as companies like ours may try to manage the message with vast communications and PR departments, it was an uphill climb. The media will write what it wants to, for better or worse.

Often, I found stories on PepsiCo in newspapers, magazines, and elsewhere fairly straightforward and factual, although the headlines could be sensational and far from our news. Some reporters published stories based on rumors that weren't true and created noise in the company that was difficult to quiet. Still, for all the challenges that the media poses for public figures like me, I remain convinced that the press is a critical element of democracy and must be celebrated and nurtured. I do urge journalists who cover companies to recommit to their core

mission of detailed reporting and analysis and to really spend the time to learn the complicated businesses and industries they cover. Writers also should not sacrifice the essence of a story for a dramatic headline. Accuracy is so fundamental to our system working.

When I rose to CEO in 2006, the press was again thrilled to celebrate my exoticism as a woman and Indian immigrant. I was presented in a sari and sometimes enhanced by bare feet. I hadn't worn a sari to work since my Booz Allen Hamilton internship in Chicago twenty-five years earlier. I did occasionally kick off my shoes in the office after 6 p.m., like almost every executive woman in pumps.

One *Wall Street Journal* story when I took over, with the headline PEPSI'S NEW CEO DOESN'T KEEP HER OPINIONS BOTTLED UP, describes me in the first paragraph wearing a sari and celebrating Harry Belafonte by singing "Day-O." In reality, I briefly introduced Mr. Belafonte and, as a group, we all sang "Day-O" at a 2005 diversity and inclusion event. I was wearing a business suit with my trademark flowing scarf. Maybe they thought that was a sari.

To be clear, since my teary conversation with Jane Morrison in her office at Yale after that uncomfortable interview, I had embraced the idea that anyone—including me—should wear whatever neat and respectful attire they feel comfortable in. I had adopted a philosophy that people should be able to bring their whole selves to work. I see this as fundamental to inclusivity in any organization. However, I admit it was discouraging that, as I stepped up to lead the second-largest food-and-beverage company in the world, I was often described as some sort of zany outsider with a penchant for traditional Indian dress.

Separately, I experienced a groundswell of support from the Indian and Indian American community. For so long, Indian immigrants like me had been viewed as nerdy people in science, only capable of running Silicon Valley startups. I heard from a friend at an investment bank who told me that he and other Indian Americans in US business were holding their heads a little higher and feeling they might be taken more seriously as potential leaders in their own firms because, for the first time, an Indian American was finally heading up a quintessential American consumer company.

In my first weeks as CEO, I had to put my team in place. This was tricky business. I wanted to surround myself with strong leaders to make sure I always had honest feedback. The management changeover from Steve inspired a few retirements, and that was OK.

In one surprise for me, my assistant, Barbara, left. Sadly, her mother had died a few months earlier, and she resigned to care for her ailing father. For a time, I felt like I'd lost my right hand, although I was fortunate to then hire Ann Cusano, a PepsiCo veteran who'd worked at PepsiCo for more than two decades and had been Steve's executive assistant.

Ann really knew how to handle the conflicting and changing priorities of a CEO's office. She always had a smile when anyone reached out to her but played the role of gatekeeper with great aplomb. She had grown children of her own and had deftly juggled motherhood and the pressures of her job, and, naturally, she endeared herself to Tara and Preetha. She was supported by Jan Niski, a lovely, caring person who seemed to be an extension of Ann's efficiency. Together, they covered the

CEO's office from 8 a.m. to 7 p.m. and handled the mounds of mail and all the calls that came in every day. Ann was with me until I left PepsiCo. I cannot emphasize enough how these women, for more than a decade, kept my life in order and contributed to my sanity.

I promoted Richard Goodman, the CFO of our international business unit, to be PepsiCo's CFO. He was respected, meticulous, and fearless in giving his opinions. In a similar vein, I persuaded Cynthia Trudell, a former General Motors executive who was on PepsiCo's board, to join as chief HR officer. I wanted an operating executive to help me rethink many of our HR processes and practices for the decades ahead. Cynthia had great ideas, which she frequently expressed at board meetings. I needed her around.

It was important that I retain Larry Thompson, a former deputy US attorney general, as our general counsel. But he had to be my choice, not a holdover from Steve, who had hired him. A public company's top lawyer is a CEO's closest advisor, privy to almost everything and heavily involved in board matters. Larry was pretty quiet, always listening and absorbing everything around him. But in one-on-one sessions with me, he'd say exactly when I was wrong or right, and he'd never hold back.

One day, I walked over to Larry's office and then, without really planning it, I told him he was fired. He was confused. Ten seconds later, with a big smile, I rehired him as general counsel. I know this was whiplash for Larry and maybe not stellar CEO technique. Still, he later told me that even though he was shocked for those few seconds, he understood how valuable it was for me to "rerecruit" him for the job. From that

moment, Larry was my general counsel and energized to be part of my new team.

Finally, to keep my CEO office running smoothly, I continued a practice Steve had started—rotating in an up-and-coming executive to serve as my chief of staff for eighteen months at a time. I began with John Sigalos, whom I'd worked with in the corporate strategy office and who was now in Bangkok. He moved back to New York, and his arrival brought needed order and structure to keeping track of the new demands on me.

For the next twelve years, I relied on a treasured group of outstanding, rising leaders in this role. From the beginning, I intended to travel a lot and I expected my chief of staff to travel with me. These trips would involve spending time with our businesses, of course, but I also wanted roundtables with young employees, separate meetings with women, visits with local government officials, and, very often, at the request of our local teams, public engagements with chambers of commerce or women's groups.

For every meeting, I required this person to prepare a detailed briefing document. In addition, all my speeches had to include my early input and then careful work with a speechwriter to ensure every word was culturally correct. This person also kept a list of follow-up items to make sure they were addressed.

If that wasn't enough, my chief of staff had one more very important duty: worrying about me in a public setting. Is the chair suitable for a woman? On a dais, should I wear a dress or trousers? What was the background color so I didn't blend in or clash? Could I get a vegetarian meal? Most important, I also needed breaks so I didn't get overwhelmed by nonstop activity. I think they were all pretty burned-out at the end of

their stints, but each one left with a deep understanding of the inner workings of a global CEO's office.

As I stepped up, I could sense supporters and detractors, enthusiasm, resentment, and some skepticism. The company's international team was happy that I had a global view and that Mike White would remain their boss. I was easily accepted by the Pepsi beverages and Frito-Lay executives, whom I'd worked with for years. Roger and Steve were both on hand, although they let me be. I always appreciated that.

Of course, a few individuals were loyal to their own idea of PepsiCo. One wrote to Steve, furious that the board had elevated someone so different from past CEOs. Steve wrote him a wonderful letter back, outlining all the ways I was the best person to run the place.

In my dreams, I created a new era for PepsiCo. I imagined a defining corporation of the twenty-first century, one that would carry far into the future, proud of its American roots, yet global and nimble enough to reflect changing times. That kind of corporate longevity isn't very common. Of the five hundred biggest US companies in 1965, when Frito-Lay and Pepsi-Cola merged, just seventy-seven, about 15 percent, remained on the list fifty years later. I wanted to set up PepsiCo to be successful for decades and decades, not just fleetingly successful during my time as CEO. My instinct was that PepsiCo had to rethink its purpose in society and to develop a new model to conduct its business.

I was also influenced by my formal training in India—by the conferences that schooled me in democracy and capitalism and by my internship at the Department of Atomic Energy in

Bombay, where I'd seen how powerhouse Western companies interact with the developing world. Yale SOM had inspired me to cross oceans for an education focused on the intersection of business and society, and the cases I studied there opened my eyes to how companies are embedded in a world of politics, government, nonprofits, communities, and families. All must work together to create a better future.

In the months after Steve walked into my kitchen on that summer Monday morning, I pondered all this, even as I went through the busy work, excitement, and trepidation of taking it on.

The task was monumental. PepsiCo was an iconic company, making and marketing seventeen brands with retail sales of more than $1 billion a year each, the most of any consumer packaged-goods company at that time. People ate and drank more than one billion servings of PepsiCo products every day. We operated in more than 180 countries and territories.

But PepsiCo—and our whole industry—were also being bombarded with criticism that the sugar, fat, and salt in our products contributed to the scourges of obesity, hypertension, and diabetes in the US and, increasingly, the rest of the world. We had acquired Quaker Oats and had started boosting our nutritious offerings. We'd eliminated trans fats. We were adding omega-3s to Tropicana. We'd pulled full-sugar drinks from schools. Yet all this seemed marginal given the scope of our business. PepsiCo was still seen as a junk food company.

The pressure was intense from public-health experts, parent groups, and governments. But consumer trends were driving the health message, too. That was clear even inside our own

operation. I was once in Egypt having dinner with our local leaders and their spouses, and one of the women told me how she was reluctant to let her children consume our products because they lacked nutritional value. This was incredibly honest—and useful for me. That someone could be so blunt, even when her family's income counted on PepsiCo, amped up my sense of urgency to do something about it.

Even our executives' habits were changing. Sometimes I noticed I was the only person drinking full-sugar Pepsi in conference meetings. I'd get frustrated that I had to argue in favor of more marketing support for our healthier brands. More than once I pointed out that if we preferred low-calorie drinks and bottled water ourselves, why did we think others weren't shifting that way? We were all consumers. We should support consumer choice, for sure, but our marketing and innovation decisions had to reflect the changing times.

Our rivalry with Coca-Cola didn't help matters. Coke had no food division, but Coke versus Pepsi was firmly embedded in the popular imagination. Our strategies and stocks were repeatedly compared, and any divergence surprised or worried the market. This made change tougher for us. We were always pinned to the cola wars.

But, in reality, the two companies were very different. Unfortunately, the longtime beverage analysts and reporters who covered us were comfortably stuck on old comparisons as opposed to the new reality of our portfolios. It was frustrating indeed.

For example, in 2006, Coca-Cola's namesake drinks brought in about 55 percent of revenue. Pepsi-Cola, meanwhile, brought in about 17 percent of our revenue. Our beverage business, in total, made up only 40 percent of PepsiCo's sales. To be sure,

carbonated drinks were still a very profitable business for both companies, even amid declining popularity.

A few years into my tenure as CEO, we explored changing the company's name to a moniker related to Anderson Hill, our headquarters' address, to separate our huge, diverse portfolio from the soda brand once and for all. Some in our upper ranks felt a new name would give PepsiCo an image more befitting of its product lines. But, after thinking through logos and a rollout plan, and then calculating the cost, we canned the idea. We couldn't see spending hundreds of millions of dollars to retire the iconic PepsiCo name when almost no consumer buying Sabra hummus, Lay's potato chips, Quaker Oats, or Naked Juice realized the products were all linked to PepsiCo.

The health debate wasn't our only big test. I was also worried about PepsiCo and the environment—all those bottles and bags, all that squandered water and fuel. Everywhere I went, particularly in developing and emerging markets where trash collection wasn't organized, I saw discarded plastic and wrappers. It was impossible to avoid. I was embarrassed.

And I felt even worse when, around that time, I got two letters in the mail. First, a group of US legislators from East Coast states wrote to the heads of all consumer packaged-goods companies, drawing attention to the waste washing up on their shores. "How can you help?" I remember the letter asked. Then I got a picture in the mail of the North Atlantic Garbage Patch, a hulking island of debris floating in the ocean that had been tracked since 1972. The picture was filled with drink bottles and processed-food packaging material. I recognized some of our bottles and chips bags.

The image of that garbage patch, which I much later saw written about in *National Geographic*, evoked an even deeper sense of responsibility in me. I had grown up in a household where one small bucket of waste a week was too much. Now I was captaining the "convenience culture"—where onetime use and a throwaway habit were the dominant leitmotifs.

When I talked about the letter and the garbage island with my senior executives, I didn't get much reaction. I felt oddly alone. It's not like this was out of the blue. Al Gore's documentary on climate change, *An Inconvenient Truth*, had just been released, and the whole world was talking about the planet. But I think that, for some key PepsiCo executives, the packaging waste problem just felt too colossal, something that would require a technological breakthrough to address. In addition—and they were right—the convenience culture was embedded in our society and would take a lot to change.

A second troubling environmental issue for me was water. The value of water is in my bones. Our lives in Madras were regulated by the flow of clear, clean water and the hours in the day when the taps were on or off. In my mind, I saw my dad at the kitchen sink, waiting for the trickle to fill our pans and bowls; I saw myself bathing with my little steel cup; I saw the women of Madras lined up, waiting their turn at a public well.

At PepsiCo, we were using 2.5 gallons of water for every gallon we made of Pepsi-Cola and our other beverages. Just fifteen miles outside Chennai, I saw our plants drawing water out of the aquifers using powerful pumps while the people in the city were parched. On my watch, I had to figure out how to make our factories extremely water efficient and, more important, to use our water management methods to help whole communities improve their water efficiency.

The more I thought about PepsiCo's future, the more I felt it was incumbent on me to connect what was good for our business with what was good for the world.

I needed a relatable, universal plan. It had to reflect our youthful culture and signal a wise evolution of our historic company. I needed to bring along tens of thousands of employees and bottling partners, many of whom had worked for PepsiCo for decades and loved it just the way it was. I started reading everything I could about transforming large organizations, about managing change, and about the responsibility of corporations. I consulted with board members and with trusted friends at BCG.

Finally, I decided the way forward was to rethink the company under the umbrella Performance with Purpose.

This was my opus. We would deliver excellent performance, as was expected for PepsiCo, but would add three imperatives to our work ahead: *nourish* humanity and the communities in which we live, *replenish* our environment, and *cherish* the people in our company. This wasn't corporate social responsibility or philanthropy focused on giving our money away. PwP would transform the way PepsiCo made money and tie our business success to these objectives: *Nourish. Replenish. Cherish.*

Nourish was focused on human sustainability. We had to feed people and societies responsibly and contribute to healthier eating and drinking by nudging consumers into making informed food choices. We had to keep supporting the items we called Fun for You, like original Pepsi-Cola and Doritos, but figure out how to cut their fat, sugar, and salt levels. We needed to dial up our Better for You products—our zero- and low-calorie options, including pretzels and diet sodas—and we had to step up innovation and marketing of our Good

for You products, including our range of juices, teas, and oatmeal.

Our new goal was noble, but we had one big obstacle: taste. Everything we made had been optimized over the years to taste fantastic. Now I was proposing that we tinker with recipes and ingredients to reduce the very elements that contributed to that taste—the fat, the sugar, and the salt. This posed both a complicated technical challenge—and a huge opportunity.

Replenish meant ensuring environmental sustainability. We had to rethink how we used energy and water, reducing plastic in our packaging and setting up recycling systems; we had to help our farming partners use less water in their agriculture. We had to cut greenhouse gas emissions. We needed to join the global effort to restore the health of the planet and couldn't wait any longer for more evidence on global warming. We had to be very open-minded, seeking out and embracing completely new ideas for our business in these areas. Hybrid and electric trucks, solar power, updated bottle-washing and irrigation methods: the list of ideas to explore and implement was long and growing.

Cherish was all about ensuring talent sustainability. PepsiCo had to be a supportive, empowering workplace, where all people could prosper. This was inextricably linked with another pressing issue—attracting and keeping top talent to make it all work. We knew that the millennial women and men flooding into the workplace would not choose PepsiCo unless we turned the corner on health and the environment. These were critical table stakes.

Even more important, I thought, was helping these young people integrate work and family. Millennials were facing enormous stress related to balancing money, marriage, and kids.

They'd witnessed their parents struggle with the same issues. They had no idea how to navigate all of this. Any help we could provide would give us a competitive advantage. We had to come to the realization that when we hired someone, it was not merely a pair of hands, a person. The whole family came along. The company had more than 250,000 employees, and we had to cherish every one of them.

Perhaps not surprisingly, the word *cherish* sparked plenty of controversy over the years. It was too soft, too feminine, to be a business imperative, I was told. One colleague commented, in a note to me, that the word prompted "audible groans that accompany eyes rolling back in heads like slot machines" and had "absolutely *no* credibility and to the contrary is now the source of ridicule."

Well, I guess it struck a nerve.

Shortly into my new job, I traveled to Frito-Lay's triangle-shaped headquarters in Plano, Texas, for my first town hall meeting as CEO. The auditorium was packed. I talked about our hard work and challenges and celebrated Frito-Lay's clout in the company. I floated PwP, and, then, in a private meeting with the senior team, I laid it all out.

This was an experiment. Frito-Lay's managers were always the skeptics—usually rejecting ideas from outside their own business. But I knew I needed them with me, so I made them my protagonists. After an interesting discussion, they promised to come back to me with their thoughts the following week. I was cautiously optimistic.

Three days later, Frito-Lay's CFO and the head of strategy flew to Purchase and told me how much the entire team loved

PwP. They understood and agreed that the time had come for the hard work of making our products healthier while preserving their taste and all the fun of Frito-Lay. They were super enthused about hybrid trucks and solar power, in particular, and saw that PwP could be a great recruiting tool.

I also shared PwP and all its components with Derek Yach, a global-health expert who'd worked at the World Health Organization. Derek had been a vocal critic of our products and environmental impact. I thought that a critic inside our tent would help me do it right. I hired him to help me think through how to transform the company and communicate the changes to public policy experts. Derek thought the direction I was proposing was bold, and he endorsed it. That was an important seal of approval for me.

A few weeks later, in a hotel ballroom in Scottsdale, Arizona, I presented PwP again, this time to PepsiCo's four hundred top managers from around the world, who were gathered for our private annual conference. I talked for more than an hour, reflecting on our history, our performance, our brands, our capabilities, and our wonderful people. I then unveiled PwP in all its detail. I explained how PwP was not about giving the money we make to deserving causes. There was a place for that, but what I was talking about was a new way to make money. If we didn't transform our portfolio to meet changing consumers, we couldn't grow; if we didn't focus on the environment, our costs would rise, and some countries would deny us license to operate; if we didn't let people bring their whole selves to work, we wouldn't get the best employees.

And if we didn't deliver performance, we couldn't fund purpose. Performance and purpose reinforced each other. It was a virtuous circle.

I threw my head and heart into this speech: I wanted all to sense my deep commitment. It worked. You could hear a pin drop as I spoke. They were electrified. No shuffling in the seats. And, when I finished, the group stood up and cheered. I was relieved and ready to take it on the road.

I believe in companies. I think the world is better off with large, private organizations, not only because they add stability but also because they innovate. Companies create jobs and offer products that satisfy people's demands. They add to the tax base and create community.

But I also believe that companies must be good in the ethical as well as the commercial sense. Some thought it odd that a modern-day CEO would try so hard to move an organization beyond the idea that a good company exists to make shareholders happy and beat the competition, within the bounds of the law. But the notion that a company is just a profit center is very recent. Throughout history, companies have prided themselves on their roots in society and the legacy they leave to it. No business can ever truly succeed in a society that fails.

I believe that a company's impact on society needs to be written through all business planning, and that this cannot be an afterthought. What's good for commerce and what's good for society have to go together.

With PwP, I had a strategy—simple and thoughtful—to take PepsiCo into the future. I was quietly thrilled that Frito-Lay's managers bought into it early and that our global leaders liked it, too. When I walked through the details with our board of directors, I had four vocal supporters—Dina Dublon, the former CFO of JPMorgan Chase; Sharon Percy Rockefeller, a

philanthropist and the CEO of public-television station WETA in Washington, DC; Victor Dzau, then the head of the Duke medical system; and Alberto Ibargüen, the CEO of the Knight Foundation. Alberto wrapped up the conversation by saying this felt like the only sensible way forward for PepsiCo. I had the wind at my back.

Importantly, I was also excited that PwP resonated with our younger employees. I knew that friends and relatives grilled them about the ethics of working for a company that churned out treats and lots of packaging waste. Now they had an answer: we were working on evolving PepsiCo to address those very concerns. This initiative came from the top but drew in our newest hires and interns. They were proud of it.

The investment and media audience was a lot tougher. Shareholders wouldn't stand for anything that might affect PepsiCo's short-term profitability targets, and, when I told them the plan, the response was decidedly mixed. Some were very clear that they bought PepsiCo stock because they believed in soda and chips. They wanted earnings growth today, not a new strategy for tomorrow. If they were interested in a different food-and-beverage company, they said, they'd look elsewhere.

The most memorable comment came from a portfolio manager in Boston. "Who do you think you are?" he asked me. "Mother Teresa?"

I forged on. As it turned out, PwP informed all my decisions for more than a decade. The strategy held up through the global financial crisis, the soda-tax debate, and a failed multiyear campaign by an activist investor to alter our company's direction. PwP constantly tested my resolve—and delivered many of the

most gratifying, joyful experiences of my life. Twelve years after I laid out PwP, in November 2019, 180 members of the Business Roundtable, an association of CEOs of America's biggest companies, signed a statement committing to a stakeholder focus as opposed to a narrow shareholder focus. It remains to be seen how many will articulate specific plans and metrics in support of that statement, but the fact that they signed on to a broader, sensible mandate for business is gratifying indeed. I felt vindicated.

When I had the honor of being included in the Smithsonian's National Portrait Gallery in 2019, I sat for a painting with four objects on a shelf behind me in the composition: a photo of my parents; a photo of Raj, Preetha, and Tara; a Yale SOM baseball cap; and a PepsiCo annual report with the words "Performance with Purpose" on the cover.

Huge change has no shortcuts. It requires honesty, agility, and courage. Once I committed to transforming PepsiCo, I felt my education and experience merging to serve that mission. I was ready for it. I knew what to do.

The critical first step was to frame the message for all to understand and embrace. I talked about PwP everywhere, describing in straightforward terms why the shift was so necessary. "Society and consumers are changing, and we can't be left behind," I said in every possible forum. "This is about how we make money, not about how we spend the money we make," I added. "This is essential for our employees and their families. This is our route to thriving together."

This was all terrific. But I also knew that no one would take my grand plan seriously unless I hired the required talent to take

us into this new direction and put financial resources behind them.

So I went about building a completely new global R&D operation. Up to now, every PepsiCo division had its own small R&D unit, a few scattered teams that largely responded to what product managers and marketers asked for. They were expert at flavors, colors, and package graphics but had engineered no radical change since switching Diet Pepsi to aspartame from saccharine in 1983.

PepsiCo's R&D effort was never connected with nutrition, physiology, or the intricacies of how human beings actually eat. At a minimum, I thought we needed new labs and chemists to figure out how to reduce the salt in Lay's potato chips, cut the sugar in Pepsi-Cola, and add whole grains to Cheetos—while leaving the experience of eating those treats as satisfying as ever. But I was much more ambitious than that. PepsiCo's science could be at the heart of reimagining the global food system.

It was a venture, I hoped, that would far outlast me at PepsiCo.

We needed a chief scientific officer to oversee it all, someone who was part of the executive team, reporting to me. I interviewed a few people for the new role . . . and then I met Mehmood Khan. He was president of global R&D at Takeda Pharmaceuticals, the Japanese biomedical company, and had previously led the diabetes, endocrine, and nutritional trials unit at the Mayo Clinic. We had a fascinating conversation over a long lunch and I felt like we totally clicked. Mehmood exuded what PepsiCo needed—leadership, experience, enthusiasm, vision. Excited, I offered him the job.

Mehmood declined. Why would he come to PepsiCo to reengineer potato chips, he asked, when Takeda gave him so

much latitude for lifesaving work in the drug industry? Good point, I thought, but I had a response: "Because at PepsiCo, you can taste everything that you create." Drug research goes on for years with minute advances, I said. With us, Mehmood could build an entire wing of PepsiCo. He'd lead the conversation on what people eat. He'd have immeasurable impact on public health.

He wasn't convinced. A few weeks later, we spoke again, and Mehmood recapped how hard it would be to convince the outside world that PepsiCo was serious about science, calories, and garbage. "Do you have the stomach for it?" he asked me. I assured him I did. There was no going back. I didn't think we had any other choice for the long-term vitality of our business but to do this, and I really wanted Mehmood on board.

In December 2007, after six months of talking it over, Mehmood finally agreed to join PepsiCo, and he moved with his family to Greenwich from Chicago. He began with a fairly modest budget that tripled over eight years. He hired dozens of new people with knowledge and skills that PepsiCo had never sought before—molecular biology, physiology, pharmacology, computer modeling, environmental engineering. He brought in scientists from Merck, DuPont, and Unilever. He expanded our facilities in Plano, Chicago, and Valhalla, New York, and set up research centers in China, Mexico, and Russia, in part to broaden the background and ethnicity of those thinking about our health and scientific challenges. Mehmood's department defined how we should approach diet and culture in a whole new way and cleared our path to thinking globally and acting locally.

Over a dozen years, under Mehmood's creative, steady guidance, PepsiCo reformulated carbonated soft drinks, slowly

cutting the sweetness in Pepsi-Cola so that the same product now had, in key countries, 10 to 20 percent less sugar than it did in 2006 without affecting its great taste. We reduced the sodium in our snacks, in part by trimming the size of the salt crystals so the human tongue would experience the flavor in the original way but with significantly less salt. In many markets, a single-serve bag of Lay's now had less salt than a slice of bread. We explored new ways to formulate carbonated citrus beverages with Stevia, a natural, zero-calorie sweetener; we made gluten-free Quaker Oats and invented new manufacturing methods to make 3D chips like Lay's Poppables.

R&D, working with the operations team, also oversaw shifts in delivery, manufacturing, and packaging technology that sliced our fuel consumption and reduced water and plastic use. The division also came up with waterless bottle-washing technologies and new ways to incorporate higher levels of recycled plastic in soda bottles. The work of Mehmood and the team won us many accolades. We published honest, detailed sustainability reports every year.

In 2012, PepsiCo won the Stockholm Water Prize, the world's top award for the conservation and protection of water resources. With water-saving equipment and technology, water recycling and reuse, and new water-management plans in our facilities, we'd saved sixteen billion liters of water in five years.

This prize was symbolic for me. It underscored how no purpose-driven task is impossible if you put your mind to it. I told people about the lack of water in my youth and found plenty of others in our global company with similar experiences. Once the emotions took hold, the task got easier. We also had the great advantage of being able to commit developed-world scientific resources to an emerging market problem.

Transforming PepsiCo with the ideas of PwP was never going to happen in a vacuum. We also had to bring our industry along to confront the world's health and environmental challenges. I took that on, too. I accepted the invitation to deliver the 2008 keynote address at the annual conference of the Food Marketing Institute, an industry association representing grocery retailers, again in Scottsdale. I was back at the podium in a ballroom, now facing a sea of seasoned executives who controlled much of the American food supply, including the CEOs of the biggest packaged-goods, grocery, and agricultural companies. I briefly reintroduced myself to the crowd, for the first time as PepsiCo's CEO. I spoke a little about my goals for our company.

Then I started talking about obesity. The people in that room represented companies with a total of $900 billion in annual revenues, I said, making us, together, the thirteenth-largest economy in the world. We had to use our influence and resources responsibly. We had to confront the contemporary affliction of too many calories, too little exercise, and the devastating health and economic burdens on our society. We had to act together.

I suggested we all adopt sensible nutrition labeling and encourage portion control and physical fitness. I talked about walkable cities, legal reforms for playground safety, and tax incentives to develop "positive nutrition." I threw loads of ideas at the crowd and finally called for us to come together as business and civic leaders—and as parents and caring citizens—to change the trajectory of big food for a healthier population. This was a systems issue, I said, and we needed to collectively promote complex behavioral change.

"Let's be a good industry that does what it possibly can—not grudgingly, but willingly, not as a last resort but as a first," I concluded.

It was a rousing entreaty to the most powerful decision makers in our corporate universe. After the speech, I especially remember Steve Burd, who headed the Safeway grocery store chain for more than twenty years, and Ric Jurgens, the CEO of Hy-Vee, a Midwestern retailer, coming up to me, full of enthusiasm about pulling together.

I believe that speech, which sparked the food industry's subsequent initiative, the Healthy Weight Commitment Foundation, helped turn the tide on how the US food industry approached health and wellness. The foundation was set up as a nonprofit to help reduce obesity and grew to include more than three hundred industry and nonprofit partners. We committed to remove at least 1.5 trillion calories from the food system over five years and, three years later, had eliminated more than six trillion calories. We partnered with First Lady Michelle Obama's "Let's Move!" campaign and funded community health programs in thirty-four thousand schools.

This kind of pulling together to address a societal issue was very encouraging to me. It is possible. It just doesn't happen enough. Private industry—with its incredible ability to move fast and efficiently—in partnership with government, with its broad mandate, is perhaps the most powerful force we have for positive change in society.

Through all this systemic change for PepsiCo, I was still, of course, grounded by my home life. Tara was in high school, and Preetha, now in her twenties and working, was

considering graduate business school. I felt like I had more time for the family, but they didn't need me as much. My commute was familiar and easy. We'd done a few more renovations on the house and worked on the garden, planting trees and perennials. We put in a pool, although I had no inclination to learn to swim.

We had help at home. Antonia, our housekeeper, was dedicated, and Indira, who cooked for us, kept the family healthy, making us all delicious vegetarian food. Between the two of them, the house ran smoothly. Raj's travels continued, but we had to do less calendar coordination. Technology was slowly helping us. I had my BlackBerry to talk regularly with the kids whenever I was away.

My time, day-to-day, was pretty much my own to dedicate to my insanely busy job. But I never shook the sense that family was ever-present, including for the people who worked for me. We all came from somewhere. I loved hearing employees' stories when I traveled to PepsiCo facilities around the world and always took the extra hours to meet everyone, shake hands, give hugs, and take pictures. I tried to notice when one more person wanted to greet me on a factory floor or in a sales office. I felt it was great for the company that every PepsiCo employee knew me and felt I was accessible. I wanted to humanize my role and show that this was everyone's company. I enjoyed real meaning in my job as CEO because of the people I met and how they invited me into their lives. Cherishing is very natural to me.

It was not uncommon for executives to bring their grown children to town halls I hosted so that their daughters could meet me. Fairly often, senior executives would seek me out,

sharing details of personal crises that might affect their role at work. I always listened to their issues and made it a point to follow up.

In December 2007, as we had done many times before, Raj, Preetha, Tara, and I traveled to India for the holiday break for a couple of weeks to visit our extended family. One morning, in the house on G. N. Chetty Road, where my mother still lived a few months of the year, she asked me to sit with her in the men's living room because she had a few people coming by. I was still the relatively new CEO of PepsiCo and hadn't spent any time in India since my appointment. They were keen to see me, she said.

For several hours, I sat in a chair while my mother's friends came in to meet the corporate chief. Every one of them walked by me, nodded hello, and then went straight to my mother to congratulate her and tell her what a great job she had done raising me, this successful daughter, the CEO of PepsiCo. I truly enjoyed watching her as the center of attention and wished my father could have been there, too. How proud he would have been. I missed him enormously.

When I returned to the US, I reflected on that morning, connecting my life as a high-profile US business executive with my years as a girl given every opportunity by my parents and grandparents to learn and excel. I thought about all the people working for PepsiCo and how committed their parents must also have been to get them to the point of contributing to our company so faithfully and energetically.

I decided to write to the parents of my senior executives. Over the next ten years, I wrote hundreds of notes, thanking mothers and fathers for the gift of their child to PepsiCo. I

also wrote to the spouses of all my direct reports, thanking them for sharing their husband or wife with PepsiCo. I worked with my chief of staff to help personalize the letters for each recipient.

These letters unleashed a lot of emotion. Almost everyone I wrote to sent a reply—some long thank-you letters and some short, loving notes. I got cookies and a beautifully hand-knit shawl. Some parents started doing regular grocery checks of our products near their homes and sent me photos showing that they, too, were working on our behalf. Other parents, my executives told me, opened every conversation with the words "How's Indra?"

The mothers and fathers were overjoyed to get a report card on their child's progress, regardless of their child's age. The executives, meanwhile, were blown away by their parents' reactions. I received many letters like the following:

Indra,

I would like to take a moment to share a personal experience with you. I received a call from my parents last night, which is unusual during the week. They received the letter you sent to them and wanted to share it with me.

I have rarely ever heard them so emotional. They were deeply touched that, "Indra Nooyi, CEO of PepsiCo would take the time from her busy schedule to send a letter to them."

My mother, who is blind and recovering from being in the hospital last week, sounded more exuberant than I have heard her sound for quite some time. My father, who is quite reserved, said that he wished his parents were alive so he could share this with them . . . "a letter like this is more valuable than money."

I wanted to let you know that your letter had a tremendous impact on them. I very much appreciate the gift you've given them and, in turn, to me.

Thank you for your thoughtfulness and leadership,
Ken

One executive wrote me a year after I retired to tell me that his mother, who had brought him up alone since he was six, had recently moved into a retirement community. In her sparsely furnished living room hangs only one item—a framed copy of the letter I had written her.

Of course, transforming PepsiCo was only part of my job as CEO. I also had to run the company the way it was. That meant, in the short term, delivering reliable profit, quarter after quarter. Investors demanded predictable performance with no misses. Underpromise, overdeliver.

Earnings are a ticking clock for every CEO. Publicly traded US companies have to file quarterly financial reports that, preferably, always show good news. When I retired from PepsiCo, between the roles of CFO and CEO, I'd been through seventy-five quarterly reports. Each included weeks of discussion and preparation, formal conference calls, and news coverage.

Tara, as a little girl, become so familiar with my periodic comment to the family—"Leave me alone for a few hours. I need to prepare for our earnings release"—that she'd lovingly rub my back and say, "Don't worry Mommy. It's going to be

OK! It's just earnings release!" even though she had no idea what that meant.

In an expansive company like PepsiCo, meeting growth targets is an ever-changing puzzle. We had to grow the "top line"—the revenue—by 4 percent every year to keep investors happy. That meant creating about $2.5 billion more in net sales every year.

PepsiCo had performed very well under Steve, with net income bolstered by all those cost savings related to the Quaker Oats merger. Gatorade was a winner, too. With our marketing and distribution expertise, the brand took off as we had hoped, and sales grew by double digits in the first five years we owned it. Steve used trade spending—discounts and promotions—to gain share, which worked very well for a while. Gatorade, however, needed a reboot a few years later when sales flagged because all those discounts had undercut its premium status.

Our business also surged because Wal-Mart, the world's biggest retailer, expanded fast in the first part of the decade and sold PepsiCo products in every new store. Wal-Mart was our highest-volume customer by far, and Steve himself led the sales effort.

Unfortunately for me, just a year after I took over, the whole economy headed into a tailspin, and I had to learn in a hurry how to manage through a period of extreme adversity.

By the end of 2007, a crisis in the US mortgage market was rippling through banks and then threatened the whole global financial system. Markets plunged and took the US and European economies with them. The so-called Great Recession, which came right after, lasted almost three years and completely altered our business landscape. In particular,

Wal-Mart's expansion slowed, and demand for carbonated drinks in North America dwindled even more. Coke had made a major reinvestment in its business in 2004 and was reaping the benefit of this reset. Commodity prices, including oil, jumped, adding extra expense to our operations. A rising US dollar had the same effect. We needed to grow in emerging markets as a counterweight to the lull in North America but hadn't invested much to develop opportunities in China and India over the previous ten years.

Among my first big trips as CEO was a visit to several cities in China to better understand those opportunities and challenges. I'd been to China a dozen times before but always with a narrow business agenda. This time, with Tara along, I spent several weeks learning more about the cities, towns, and people. We visited homes, and I got a much better sense about package sizes, popular flavors, and how families stocked their small refrigerators. I absorbed how multigenerational households function in China, with various family structures and individual roles. I got a much fuller sense of how PepsiCo should grow in the region.

We stepped up investments in China, followed by India and Brazil, including committing more than $1 billion for marketing and distribution over three years. In Russia, we bought Lebedyansky, a fruit-and-vegetable-juice company, for almost $2 billion in early 2008 and later added 66 percent of Wimm-Bill-Dann, the country's number three dairy and juice maker, for about $3.8 billion. Wimm-Bill-Dann, PepsiCo's largest acquisition since Quaker, was very important to me because it added $3 billion a year in revenue from nutritious products, including milk, yogurt, and baby food.

Our Good for You portfolio was growing elsewhere, too. I got a call one day from Ofra Strauss, the CEO of Strauss-Elite Food, our snacks partner in Israel. She asked to see me in Purchase and showed up with a huge hamper of Mediterranean dips—hummus, baba ghanoush, you name it. She laid them all out with fresh pita bread on my conference table, and we enjoyed a picnic of products from Sabra, a New York–based company that Strauss had recently purchased. It was a delicious lineup—totally vegetarian—and a great potential mate to Stacy's Pita Chips, which we'd acquired a couple of years earlier. Less than a year later, Sabra and Frito-Lay signed a joint venture, and Sabra now leads the US hummus market. More important for me, Ofra is one of my dearest friends.

Those kinds of agreements were very satisfying and, in the grand scheme of things, not that complicated. But we also went ahead with a very complex negotiation: simultaneously buying back control of our two largest beverage bottling partners.

In 1998, I'd worked with Roger to spin off the North American bottling operation into a publicly traded company, the Pepsi Bottling Group. Ten years later, exactly as I had predicted, we were constantly at odds with this company as soda sales, its primary source of profit, continued to slow.

The fundamental problem was that our interests weren't totally aligned. The bottlers made more money when they sold each bottle of soda at a higher price. PepsiCo, meanwhile, sold the syrup to the bottlers and so wanted more bottles sold—at a very competitive price.

Over time, we had developed an uneasy compromise that included PepsiCo providing the bottlers more and more marketing money. But, in a declining soda market, that spending didn't actually increase sales very much. It only propped up market share. And we found the bottlers' appetite for this support difficult to handle because it shifted PepsiCo's consumer-focused marketing dollars to the bottlers to help them boost their bottom lines. The situation was unsustainable. We were eroding the beverage business.

In a very involved transaction, we bought back our two major North American bottlers for $7.8 billion, giving us operational control of almost 80 percent of our bottling system. This was time-consuming, in part because we had to negotiate with two different parties. PepsiCo had clear parameters for walking away, and we absolutely stuck with those. When the deal closed, we immediately saw cost savings, but, more important, our increased control over our beverage distribution meant we could grow our top line by calling on more food-service accounts, such as restaurants and others who sell fountain drinks. We were able to redirect the time spent arguing with the bottlers toward innovation, new marketing ideas, and selling our products.

I learned plenty from this experience. I wondered about backtracking on our rationale of just ten years earlier, when Roger had decided to separate the bottling assets into an independent publicly traded company. Some observers saw a flip-flop, but I didn't see it that way, and perception wasn't going to run the company.

I had to muster the courage to change my mind when the environment changed and required a different approach to the business. That was leadership.

10

In my early days as CEO, if I had a few hours on any weekend, I'd slip on my comfortable shoes and get in the car. I'd head somewhere in Connecticut or suburban New York, to communities like Mount Kisco, Ridgefield, Newburgh, or New Haven. I'd pick a strip mall or a main street and enter a Target, a Stop & Shop supermarket, or a family-owned convenience store. I was anonymous, a random woman, a mom buying for her family. I knew every particular of how store shelves came to be stocked and generally did my own shopping near home. But I couldn't resist the tug of a secret market tour.

I'd take in the whole store, maybe pushing a cart, picking out a few items, and noting the signage, lobby displays, and the other shoppers. By the time I got to the center aisles with the bottled Starbucks Frappuccino, the Oat Squares cereal, or the SunChips, my mind-set was almost completely that of a regular shopper.

I started to notice the clutter in the PepsiCo sections. Our company was churning out dozens of options—Lay's chips

in regular, kettle-cooked, lightly salted and oven-baked; Quaker Oats in quick, rolled, instant, and steel-cut; Tropicana in original, low-acid, Homestyle, and Grovestand, and all in multiple flavors or blends. We were absolute masters of variety, distribution, and display. I kept asking myself: What was the unifying message of all those bright colors and loud logos? How do our products look in pantries at home? What was right for this neighborhood's families? And what should get the coveted eye-level placement—Fun for You or Good for You? It bothered me that our shelves, even when very neat, looked a little tired.

At the same time, I was drawn to the upstarts—the simple bags of sea-salt popcorn by regional brands or the quiet fonts on bottles of artisanal drinks, all billing themselves as natural, low calorie, or preservative free. I started to see why a young woman might sample green tea kombucha or coconut water instead of picking up another bottle of Diet Pepsi, even if we had added a new splash of lime.

The business was in flux. Some snappy niche brands were growing very fast, but, if they couldn't expand, they nose-dived, a "boom-splat" phenomenon. Meanwhile, chains like Kroger, the biggest supermarket company in the US, were adding special health-and-wellness sections, and I worried that shoppers at these chains wouldn't see our nutritious products elsewhere in the store.

I loved observing grocery markets across the country. I once sat with Brian Cornell, then head of PepsiCo America Foods, in a car in the parking lot of a Publix store near a Florida retirement village, watching shoppers. They went in and out of the sliding glass doors—some helped out of their cars at the curb, others steering motorized wheelchairs. Shopping was

clearly a happy occasion for the older generation, with lots of greeting and chatting.

Then Brian and I went into the store to see our products on the shelves—the twenty-four-packs of Pepsi cans and Aquafina bottles. How could these people even get these cases home? I'd already been pestering our engineers about how tight the Aquafina plastic caps were screwed on the bottles and how tough they were to open, even for me. After that Florida stakeout, I was convinced we needed to think more carefully about the needs of boomers and the silver generation.

I later sent a PepsiCo team to MIT's AgeLab, a center for research on quality of life for older people. From MIT, we gleaned great insight on labeling, typefaces, ergonomics, and aging Americans' views of a grocery shelf. Through all of this, I realized the opportunity and imperative of innovating for more specific customer cohorts.

My store outings often drew me back to an absorbing visit I'd had with Steve Jobs in his office at the Apple headquarters in Cupertino, California, in 2008. My dear friend Dean Ornish, a doctor who worked on lifestyle medicine and health, was close to Steve and brokered our meeting.

I hadn't met Steve before and he was incredibly gracious. We started out talking about our shared vegetarianism. Then he brought up a few PepsiCo brands, and I explained how we were evolving the portfolio toward healthier foods and reengineering our flagship sodas and snacks to cut the salt, fat, and sugar. I explained my ideas around human, environmental, and talent sustainability. Steve said he thought we should just cut half the sugar from everything. "But we'd have no company left," I said,

laughing. The respectable, formal, food-and-beverage industry and its long-term investors won't tolerate the high drama that Silicon Valley entrepreneurs pull off, I said. Besides, people like sugar.

Then we talked about design. For two hours, I soaked up Steve's thinking about injecting great, authentic design into a company's products and culture. Design was how Steve lived and how he thought. Design is embedded in innovation from the start, he said, and can't come in at the end. At Apple, design was in everything. Steve worried about what the new, beautiful iPhone looked and felt like, but also about the interface, the accessories, the store, and who might innovate to partner with the company. Apple is an experience. Users didn't only see the product, he said. They were romanced by it. Design is emotional. It captivates.

Despite PepsiCo's stunning ad campaigns, graphics, and packaging, and all our delicious, ubiquitous food and drink, I knew we were nowhere near this holistic approach to fitting it all together. Design thinking would need to permeate every part of the company. It would be a new way of working—coordinated across R&D, marketing and advertising, manufacturing and distribution—and involve far more prototyping and testing. This would be a radical change for us. The design function had to be nurtured and protected, Steve said. "If you don't show CEO support, don't bother starting on the journey."

Inspired, I decided we had to use design as a critical differentiator of our products. But first I had to understand the gap between where we were and where we needed to be. I gave each of my executive committee members a copy of *Package Design Now*, a coffee-table book full of splendid examples of

great consumer-product design. Later that week, I ramped it up—passing out elegant, soft-brown leather photo albums and asking them to photograph anything that they were drawn to as good design. Anything at all, I said. It could be a chair, a pencil, a tea kettle. They could make collages of magazine images. I really didn't care what it was. Just think design. The albums were due back to me in three months.

This didn't turn out well. Of the fifteen people who got the albums, one delivered outstanding work—that she had prepared by a professional agency. A few more turned in travel photos or what appeared to be last-minute shots of toothpaste and a mouthwash bottle in their bathroom. Some men had their wives prepare the album. A few blew it off altogether. I realized that design thinking was almost nonexistent among my senior managers.

I set the returned albums aside in a cupboard in my office. But these ideas lingered in my mind.

By 2010, I really had my legs under me as CEO. PwP was our guiding principle; Mehmood was building out the science of taste; we'd safely navigated through the rocky economy and made some great international acquisitions.

Most important, we had resolved the troubling relationship with our largest North American bottlers by buying them back, and we could see the gains we'd predicted from that strategic move.

Next up, I had to contemplate talent. Who should lead big parts of our company in the coming decade? Who should, ultimately, take my job? On average, the CEO of a US publicly

traded company lasts about five years. That's roughly the time that Roger and Steve each led PepsiCo.

I wasn't leaving anytime soon, but succession planning was a fundamental duty—and critical to my vision of Pepsi-Co as a well-oiled organization that would prosper long after I was gone. Every year, the board reviewed what would happen if the CEO was "hit by a bus." This is good corporate governance, and we took it seriously, including precise details of the quick transition options if I was suddenly not available. But we also needed a systematic and rigorous effort to develop the next generation of C-suite executives. We had amazing people around the world.

Someone out there was the next person to lead PepsiCo.

We had a guidebook, of sorts. Over four years, I had handwritten and refined a confidential memo, more than twenty pages long, that I called "Future Back."

The memo documented the ten key global megatrends that we thought would shape our world through 2020 and beyond. Megatrends are dominant, undeniable forces that influence the economy and society. In thinking through PwP, I had studied demographic, sociological, scientific, and consumer trends. "Future Back" summarized that work and went further, laying out strategic actions and capabilities that PepsiCo would need in the decades to come. The memo also outlined essential characteristics for our future leaders, from digital savvy to a deep understanding of resource and environmental issues to non-US experience that we'd never prioritized before.

The megatrends memo, almost ten years later, is still fascinating reading. Number one on the list is the rise of the Eastern and Southern Hemispheres. Number two is the demographic and power shift toward the elderly, women, and youth, and the

rising influence in the US of immigrant communities in urban centers; number three talks about the shift to healthier eating and drinking; number five is the evolution of the all-pervasive digital world and shopper-consumers using the web; number nine addresses trust in capitalism and corporations. Each item in the memo includes my view of the consequences for the global food-and-beverage industry and for our company.

Over several months in late 2011 and early 2012, I met one-on-one with each of our board members to review the document, discussions that easily stretched to two or three hours each. They were all extremely engaged, and, from then on out, I felt the board's support as I worked to redesign our organizational structure and develop new business leaders for a different world ahead. When the going got tough, I could always refer back to the reasons we took on even more change—the meticulously crafted megatrends research.

PepsiCo had long been a decentralized organization, a company with divisions that wanted to do their own thing, populated with energetic, competitive teams. Increasingly, though, the world demanded that we become a much more networked company.

Some years earlier, Steve had built up an important coordinated sales effort across snacks and beverages for customers like Wal-Mart, Kroger, and Safeway, which we called Power of One. We knew that getting people to buy more drinks and snacks together would help the whole company's growth. He went about creating Power of One customer teams, which helped PepsiCo become one of the largest suppliers to almost every North American retailer. Similarly, PepsiCo in Europe got more favorable retailer status because we came to the table

with both beverages and snacks—lines that, alone, were not major players in that part of the world.

I had expanded Power of One to more accounts, but we had to take that coordinated view beyond sales to every part of PepsiCo. We needed so-called centers of excellence in traditional areas like operations, DSD, and consumer research. We also had to add new areas like digital marketing, e-commerce, design, and artificial intelligence in a way that every division and region had access to world-class capabilities without duplicating efforts. We needed people to communicate and collaborate across every function of the company.

I decided to change the lattice of titles and reporting lines in our senior ranks and give more executives global mandates. I was helped by a few departures. Mike White, who was running our non-US business, left the company to become the CEO of DirecTV, and I split his job into three. Richard Goodman, the CFO, retired, and Hugh Johnston, the head of global operations who'd had jobs in all our North American businesses, took over. He turned out to be a fantastic CFO and a great partner to me.

That left another senior opening. We elevated more internal talent and brought in a few stars from the outside. The people puzzle went on and on.

Our IT work, which began back when Frito-Lay's ordering system crashed in 2002, helped in this transition, too. With each "go live" of new software, we had more visibility into streams of information across the company, including retailer sales data at our fingertips. We could see what product, marketing, or manufacturing activities were going on around the world and how effective they were. That became a boon to efficiency. We could take the best idea from any country, revise it a little

if we had to, and implement it elsewhere. This lift and shift of ideas and best practices boosted both revenue growth and profitability, eventually contributing to at least $1.5 billion in productivity gains over three years.

All this new collaboration was liberating in many ways. We started using real-time data to make quick decisions and were catching up to many other companies leveraging similar systems. Unfortunately, some PepsiCo old-timers weren't accustomed to sharing much information and struggled with what I thought was a necessary, refreshingly open approach. A few senior executives and midlevel marketing managers in the US departed. Others were let go when they failed to embrace our new processes. In hindsight, I think I kept some people in jobs for too long, hoping they would improve or change. During a transformation as consequential as PwP, though, these people can be extremely problematic. I now realize that it's better to move them out sooner rather than later.

It was a difficult transition but clear to everyone, in the end, that these changes were essential and here to stay.

In February 2012, I announced my last big strategic move to let the PepsiCo that I envisioned for the long run fly—a huge reinvestment in our famous names.

In the ballroom of the Grand Hyatt hotel on Forty-Second Street in Manhattan, just after reporting 2011 revenue of $66 billion and profit of $6.5 billion, I announced that we'd be spending an additional $600 million of advertising and marketing money to boost our brands, including Pepsi-Cola and Mountain Dew. This move was directly related to buying back our bottlers. We now had more to spend on pulling

in customers because we no longer had to fund the bottlers' demands for extra "push" funds.

For five years, I had worked diligently to fix the underbelly of PepsiCo and set it up for this moment. But I had also been through withering criticism, vilified by Wall Street analysts and the media for not paying more attention to our short-term financial results and stock performance. In actuality, our results were pretty good—from the end of December 2006 to the end of December 2011, PepsiCo's shareholder return was 22 percent. That compared with the S&P 500 Index's decline of 1.25 percent in the same period.

Around this time, I also had to reassure one activist investor, Ralph Whitworth of Relational Investors, who had bought $600 million of PepsiCo shares thinking he might be able to influence us. I met with Ralph in the conference room of a Midtown Manhattan law firm, surrounded by lawyers and men of finance, and listened carefully to his concerns. He said he needed some clarity on why I'd bought back the bottlers. I explained the strategy in detail. Ralph was smart and friendly, and, after a couple of discussions, he endorsed our plan. He told me to keep going; he did not want to waste any more of my time. He later sold his stock at a profit and remained a friend and a supporter until his untimely death in September 2016.

When we announced the brand reboot, with a chunk earmarked for our core beverages in North America, I was again hounded. To some reporters and analysts, this new spending looked like capitulation—a reassembling behind traditional soda brands that flew in the face of our push to healthier fare.

I didn't see it that way. We were driving a very big car in a very long race, and we had to make sure the engine was in

good shape. Pepsi-Cola, Diet Pepsi, and Mountain Dew were critical. The $70-billion-a-year soda market in the US was declining, but we had to remain competitive in that business, a profitable category that brought in traffic for retailers. Our key competitor had increased advertising behind its soda brands, and we had to keep in step. The fun was about to begin.

What we didn't bargain for was the fun that came with our second activist investor, Nelson Peltz of Trian Partners, who, we learned, had quietly bought up $1.5 billion of PepsiCo stock, a little more than 1 percent of the company.

I'd known Nelson socially for years, and, one day, he was on the phone. "Indra, Indra, Indra, I need to see you," he declared. He said he'd stop by my home for a quick meeting. Soon, he presented me with a so-called white paper, a document prepared by his team with all the reasons why PepsiCo should be split into two pieces, each publicly traded. I took a copy of his paper and assured him I would read it carefully and discuss every aspect of it with the board.

The decade after the global financial crisis, starting in 2009, was a heyday for these kinds of aggressive investor moves. Activist funds—pools of money in search of huge returns—pursued companies with decent cash flow where they thought they could perturb the CEO enough to do their bidding. Activists don't actually have to hold too much of a company's stock to make it all work. They air their grievances so publicly and often that others invest along with them. I think they also look out for companies that are trying something new so they can take the credit if it works out.

Peltz was a billionaire expert at all of this. But his plan for PepsiCo was aggressive, to say the least. He wanted to break up our company into beverages and snacks and then merge the snack company, Frito-Lay, with Mondelēz, the Chicago-based maker of Oreo and Chips Ahoy! cookies, Triscuit crackers, and Cadbury chocolate. Nelson's fund owned about $2 billion of Mondelēz stock. He said he'd float PepsiCo's beverage division as a separate company.

Every aspect of this scheme was problematic. First, breaking up PepsiCo would destroy our very successful Power of One sales efforts. Second, Nelson's idea for Frito-Lay to combine with a cookie and chocolate company didn't make sense. Frito-Lay's business grows because it takes market share from sweet occasions—all those times when people reach for cookies and chocolate. A company that owned a whole range of both salty and sweet snacks would compete with itself. It would be a zero-sum game. In addition, breaking up PepsiCo would surely distract our individual businesses, and their momentum would stall. And Frito-Lay and Mondelēz would likely have to go through a yearlong FTC antitrust process with an uncertain outcome.

Nelson wanted us to spend $50 billion to $60 billion to do all of this and go through two or three years of chaos and disruption. It would have destroyed the competitiveness of PepsiCo. Our weakened company would have been a gift to our rivals.

Despite all this, PepsiCo's board of directors, our senior leaders, and I analyzed Nelson's white paper in great detail, engaged with him respectfully, and met with him whenever he asked for time. I reminded him that most of my net worth was

tied up in PepsiCo shares and that I'd love to see the stock soar. "If you have a great idea, I'd be delighted to listen to it," I said. "But I have no desire to destroy a great company."

Finally, in 2016, Nelson sold his shares at a profit of more than 30 percent after recommending we add a new board member, Bill Johnson, the retired CEO of H. J. Heinz Company. Nelson enjoyed the gains related to our expanded portfolio of nutritious foods and PwP.

The huge injection of advertising and marketing money to reboot our brands in 2012 launched a new era for global marketing at PepsiCo.

Social media and interactive ideas were upon us; celebrities with huge contracts didn't rule anymore, and our millennial employees and customers wanted authentic, fun, creative fare. Meanwhile, I was still thinking about great design and how to move the DNA of the company in that direction. Outside agencies and design operations set up by many of our country teams had left us with a jumble. I wanted real experts. It was finally time for world-class in-house design capability, a beehive of artistry and critical thinking that would work side by side with our marketers but also with Mehmood's team on new products, better packaging, and breakthroughs related to environmental sustainability.

I had pulled out the brown leather albums with my executives' ideas of design over the years and showed them to people who I thought might be sympathetic to how far we had to go. One of those people was Brad Jakeman, who'd joined us to lead global beverage marketing from Activision Blizzard, the

world's biggest video game company. When I later struggled to make my point to a team working on a confidential project to design a new beverage-dispensing machine, Brad and I realized we had to build an in-house design capacity fast. We needed a strong, collaborative, iconic leader for this new function.

After a long search for a permanent chief design officer, Brad introduced me to Mauro Porcini, an Italian designer working in Minneapolis at 3M.

I don't believe a more interesting person than Mauro had ever walked into my office. I couldn't take my eyes off his shoes: black slippers with red stones that worked elegantly with his eclectic clothing and genial smile. The first time we met, Mauro spoke with so much passion. I felt he understood exactly what I wanted to do with design—giving me words that I hadn't been able to find. I decided on the spot that this was the guy for us. I had visions of the company becoming Porcini-ized.

Mauro wanted me to build a space—separate from headquarters—that would attract the best designers from around the world. I agreed to it, and the PepsiCo Design and Innovation Center, on Hudson Street in New York City, opened a year later. It became a magnet for our executives to learn about design and the intersection with R&D and product and packaging development. A truly virtuous circle.

I started reading even more about what design could do for us and then gladly agreed to Mauro's suggestion that PepsiCo take part in the Salone del Mobile. Milano, Milan's famous annual design week. For three years running, the design team created incredible experiential exhibits to elevate the company in the minds of the top creatives in the world. Mauro used the event primarily to recruit new designers. He hosted conversations

on business, food, and design and showed off our ideas on the future of soft drinks with unexpected combinations, flavor shots, and garnishes. We had a Quaker truck for breakfasts, poured iced teas in Murano glasses, and built funky tanks with copper tubes dispensing soda. One year, he collaborated with designers, including Karim Rashid and Fabio Novembre, to create iconic displays of our products and had Lapo Elkann of Garage Italia Customs—a company that transforms cars into kaleidoscopes of color, detail, and design—outfit a Fiat 500 in Pepsi motifs. I would love to have driven that car.

I attended the fair myself three times for a few days each. The first year was awkward, to say the least. I arrived in Italy with my task-oriented CEO expectations and business attire, and I immediately felt like a fish out of water in the colorful world of global design. Later, I absorbed the particular pace of the event and just took in as many exhibits as I could. I came to understand how every idea, from Lavazza's café with its beautiful new coffee machines to a small exhibit full of watches, was about grabbing people by the heart. Mauro introduced me to so many people, and I began to learn design culture, something very new—and very exhilarating—for me.

I still get goose bumps when I think about where we came from and where we went with design at PepsiCo. We embraced it as a building block of innovation, shifting our attention away from just selling products to creating whole experiences related to our brands.

Our design capability started winning PepsiCo's sales teams coveted contracts. This was especially true in our relationship with the sports world. PepsiCo had long, great partnerships in both the sports and music businesses, arrangements that we

believed gave people immense moments of joy and reflected the spirit of Pepsi. We chose to partner with leagues that had annual seasons, as opposed to events that happened periodically, like the Olympics. We had a huge contract with the National Football League, renewed in 2011 for another ten years, that included deals with more than twenty teams. Our name was on the Super Bowl halftime show. Gatorade was guzzled on the sidelines. Quaker sponsored football's youth wing. Even though I did not grow up with American football, I came to love the game and developed a great rapport with Roger Goodell, the NFL commissioner, and with several team owners.

In 2013, I was asked to speak at a *Sports Business Journal* conference in Manhattan, a talk I remember very well for two reasons. First, I made my long-felt case for how I thought women were ignored in sports marketing, a topic I'd explored with the help of Jennifer Storms, PepsiCo's senior VP of global sports marketing, who was always thinking about how we could leverage sports to build our brands. Second, Adam Silver, then the National Basketball Association's deputy commissioner and COO and now its commissioner, was in the audience.

I started my speech showing a magazine advertisement from the 1950s for heavy wool climbing sweaters. The ad features two strapping gentlemen standing on top of a mountain and a woman below them grasping a rope. The copy reads "Men are better than women! Indoors, women are useful—even pleasant. On mountains, they are something of a drag."

Of course, the world has changed, I said, but the reality was that sports marketers, together with companies like ours, still didn't do much to recognize that women are athletes, coaches, and genuine fans. We had to do more than "pink it and shrink

it" when it came to capturing their hearts, and I thought there was huge—largely untapped—potential in doing much more sophisticated sports marketing to women. The audience was rapt. This was an approach I don't think the industry had heard from a consumer packaged-goods CEO before. Of course, there were probably no other female CEOs quite like me. I was a sports fan who'd received dozens of football, baseball, and basketball jerseys over the years, all customized with my name and the number 1 on the back—and all in enormous men's sizes that I couldn't wear.

When Adam and I talked after my speech, he knew I was looking at sports marketing in a broad and creative way, and he asked me some very pointed questions, culminating with "Why does the NFL get so much visibility and excitement with its beverage partnerships and we don't?" I told him he was partnering with the wrong company. Aside from its longtime affiliation with Gatorade, a PepsiCo brand, the NBA was largely pouring our competitor's product.

A year later, when the NBA's beverage contract came up, we pitched the business with stunning options—all curated by Mauro and the design team—for how PepsiCo could help promote basketball. We talked about the whole fan experience, from courtside engagement to how people interact with brands while watching games on TV. PepsiCo would do it all—lobby displays, local marketing, and special packaging for individual teams. Our mission was to bring the NBA's future to life, and our sales and design capabilities were unified and ready to go. At a lively event in a Manhattan warehouse surrounded by NBA paraphernalia, Adam and I shook hands on a five-year deal—subsequently renewed—that made PepsiCo brands the

official foods and beverages of the NBA, the minor league, the Women's National Basketball Association, and USA Basketball. It was a huge win.

We also signed a new contract with the New York Yankees that included far more signage in Yankee stadium. I watched games on TV whenever I could and soon found myself counting the minutes that our brands were on the screen instead of keeping track of the plays. A couple of times a year, I went to games in person, and our sales team would make certain we had extra visibility. Joe Girardi, then the Yankees manager, once joked with me that he might have to take out a player or two to make more room for extra Gatorade coolers in the dugout.

In 2015, we inked a partnership with the Union of European Football Associations (UEFA), helping lift brand marketing in European football by adding more of the flash and dazzle that mark American sports marketing.

Through everything at work and home, my love of sports had not waned. I was always excited to go to a few games, meet athletes, and celebrate the hard work that is so well exhibited in competitive sports. But this wasn't all about big league team sports. The Bowling Proprietors' Association of America, a trade organization, once asked me to speak at its Bowl Expo, an invitation our sales team said was welcome given our food-and-beverage contracts with the thirty-four hundred US bowling centers that belonged to the nonprofit group.

True to form, I really prepared for this talk. I went out bowling a few times, by myself, to get a sense of the sport and the flavor of contemporary bowling culture. I talked to the bowlers and the staff to understand the whole experience. It was useful. Two weeks later I felt like I could speak somewhat authentically about bowling to the Las Vegas crowd.

After eight or nine years in the job, I was well-known as PepsiCo's CEO. The company was doing very well, and business and functional leaders wanted me to do even more outside the company. I met with customers and became close with more top CEOs, including Mike Duke and then Doug McMillon at Wal-Mart, Jim Sinegal at Costco, and Arne Sorenson at Marriott. We still had independent bottling partners around the world, and they got to know me very well, too. I think we developed great respect for one another.

I spoke at hundreds of events: industry panels, economic clubs, women's conferences, and business schools. I was a popular voice on work-life balance. I was also asked to speak at corporate governance events and annual conferences hosted by big investors. I received many leadership awards and always encouraged a balanced view of companies doing well and doing good. I talked endlessly about PwP.

I was also pressed into service to speak with US state governments and others around the world on issues related to soda taxes. In our own backyard, Michael Bloomberg, the mayor of New York City, was lobbying to limit the size of sodas to sixteen ounces. Soda taxes cropped up in other states and areas of the world, too, including California, Mexico, and many other parts of Latin America and the Middle East. We tried to make sure they were sensible and suggested options such as exempting zero-calorie drinks and individual packages of fewer than one hundred calories. I felt these taxes were more about the revenue they generated for local municipalities than limiting sugary sodas. Taxes on plastic containers also started to emerge, and we found partners to develop closed-loop recycling systems—a difficult undertaking. I tried to look at these issues

through the eyes of the communities, an approach that gave me credibility with our critics.

Much of what I articulated with PwP was coming to pass, with hits and misses, but with a flow of enthusiasm from PepsiCo employees that energized me. We published our sustainability report every year and could show the world all the progress we were making on our various initiatives. I felt very strongly that these reports had to be meticulous in their detail, with no waffling on how difficult it was making real change in these areas. The integrity of our goals, our timeline, and our reporting was absolutely crucial to me.

We had also undertaken a renovation of PepsiCo's headquarters and moved out of the building for two years. The overhaul let us engineer new spaces, and we added an on-site childcare facility, called PepStart, with a special drop-off area, outdoor climbing equipment, and beautifully designed infant and toddler spaces for sleeping, eating, and learning. PepStart rapidly filled with dozens of babies and kids under five and a waiting list. Families paid for the service, but the benefit of offering this convenience and peace of mind was immediate and lasting. We also offered near-site and on-site childcare in many offices around the world and, if I had stayed longer at PepsiCo, I would like to have introduced this benefit at our factories as well.

On one hand, I felt vindicated by all of PwP's success. On the other, I wish we had moved even faster on some of our sustainability initiatives. Interestingly, one of the earliest and most vocal detractors of all the product changes I aspired to with PwP visited our office one day and gave me a DVD about the ills of sugar. He told me he'd cut down on his sugar intake massively. I wished him well.

As time went on, I met many world leaders. CEOs often have perfunctory photo ops with presidents and prime ministers, but I enjoyed lengthy discussions with heads of government and senior ministers all over the world. I think they appreciated PepsiCo's investments in their countries and were keen to work with us as we implemented PwP. Many also were also intrigued that I was a foreign-born female leader ambitiously repositioning a big American company. I hope that our conversations forced them to think about how women could succeed in their companies and countries, too.

In China, I found the leadership focused on agricultural development to keep their farmers viable. In Baotou, Inner Mongolia, PepsiCo initiated potato farming with water-efficient drip-irrigation systems to grow the potatoes we needed to make chips for the country, and these farms also yielded a surplus for export. The Chinese leaders wanted to understand how to prolong the life of agricultural commodities as the goods traveled across a vast distribution system.

My trips to India were fascinating, too. I always visited with the prime minister and other related ministries and was once invited by the Indian ambassador to the US, Nirupama Rao, to address Indian foreign service officials in New Delhi. I spoke passionately about something I strongly believe—that ambassadors and consul generals had to expand their efforts to focus on economic diplomacy as a key pillar of their political diplomacy. This was the first time they had invited a global CEO to address them, and I gave them a lot to think about.

I often reminded myself that I made these fascinating contacts and received these invitations because of my position, and that my "friends" list would shrink when I retired. A few

relationships evolved from positional to personal, but not too many. Being a CEO opens doors in the most dazzling ways, but no one is doing it because they are nice people. It's about what you can do for them. I was also very conscious whenever I got off the plane in an unfamiliar place that I had to think like a local. That was a useful framework for doing successful projects together.

At home in the US, I was invited to White House state dinners hosted by presidents George W. Bush and Barack Obama, and joined meetings of senior business executives with presidents Bush, Obama, and Donald Trump. In every encounter, I was treated with the utmost respect by the leaders and their staff. I also traveled with President Obama to India for a state visit, which included a US-India CEO forum. After the meeting, he invited the US CEOs to his hotel suite, and we kicked off our shoes, had a drink, and hung out for a few hours. We chatted about everything, personal and professional. He was really one of us.

Of all the international trips I took, the most arresting for me was seven days in Africa in February 2018. Ten years earlier, I'd promised our Nigerian and Ugandan bottlers that I would visit if they achieved leadership shares in their markets, and, when they succeeded, I couldn't let them down. I had also long assured our South African team that I would come and see for myself how they'd built a wonderful snacks business.

This was my last big business trip as CEO, and I was drawn into the story and traditions of the continent in a broader way than I had been before. I really believe that Africa, with its rich mineral and agricultural resources and young population, could be an economic gem in the next three to four decades if

companies the world over properly invest in Africa, for Africa, and with Africa, including a keen sensitivity to individual country needs.

In Lagos and Kampala—busy, bustling cities—I witnessed how African women keep the economy going by operating small businesses. I met with women leaders, and our discussions were so familiar. They wanted education. They wanted economic and financial freedom for themselves and their daughters. They didn't want to be held back by men. They did not make me feel like a visitor at all: I was embraced as one of their own. We danced together under the midmorning sun; we laughed and chatted. There was a lot of love.

In South Africa, Sello Hatang, the CEO of the Nelson Mandela Foundation, took me on a personal tour of Robben Island, where Mandela was imprisoned for seventeen years. I felt the humiliation of oppressed people in the country when a random number generator picked me to walk through the "colored" line in the Apartheid Museum.

Our final evening still lives with me. At the Mandela Foundation, I met Graça Machel, Nelson Mandela's wife, and, at a public event she attended with me, we announced a five-year PepsiCo partnership to help address poverty, including supporting a program that distributes menstrual products so that girls never have to miss school because of their periods. The Soweto Gospel Choir, with colorful robes and spectacular voices, performed a wonderful repertoire of joyful music, including the antiapartheid song "Asimbonanga." That song—its tune, its sentiment—still haunts me.

I also met with a group of about twenty high school girls in a roundtable conversation. Each told a story—of growing up

without parents, being a parent to siblings, suffering tremendous physical and emotional abuse by people in power. Their courage, their determination, their resolve were breathtaking. At the end of our talk, I asked them all a simple question: "What can I give each of you as a gift for the time you spent with me?" No one hesitated. "Can we have a hug?" they asked. They lined up, and, one by one, I enveloped each girl in my arms. They just wanted a parental embrace. They were reluctant to let go. I was overcome with emotion.

So what about my personal life? Tara went off to college in New York City and Preetha graduated from Yale SOM and started a new job. Raj became an independent consultant helping large companies develop next-generation supply-chain solutions. I still headed home from the office almost every day with three bags of correspondence and other documents to read. Some people at work openly called me the "bag lady," and one executive jokingly remarked that I carried those canvas sacks for show. I recently got a letter from him, now the CEO of a major US company, telling me he was thinking about me as he headed home with his three bags of reading material!

I also had more reports and articles to review than ever because trends in technology and geopolitics were evolving so fast. There really was no choice. When I started at PepsiCo, I remember one senior leader telling people, "The distance between number one and number two is a constant." He meant that when a leader overperforms, the team comes along with him or her; when the leader underperforms, the same thing happens. I took that to heart. If I wanted PepsiCo to develop—to be an informed, curious organization—then I, as CEO,

had to always exhibit those qualities myself. I also loved the intellectual stimulation of all that reading and correspondence.

With Raj and I as empty nesters, I began to focus a bit more on myself. I started playing tennis at the Grand Slam Tennis Club, in Banksville, New York, twice a week at 7 a.m. My coach, Nesar Nayak, patiently accommodated my early start and many schedule changes.

I signed up for individual ballroom dancing lessons, just to learn something different from the Indian tradition I was brought up in and to enjoy the movement and music in a calm, private way. My instructor, John Campbell, a British dancer in his thirties, started out rather scared of me—the CEO who wanted to learn the waltz and the fox-trot. He was also very patient and, once we had worked together for a while, boldly told me as we danced together, "My job is to lead and yours is to follow. Sometimes if you learn to follow, you will be a better leader." I've taken this great advice to heart in many circumstances.

I added some daily exercise on PepsiCo's campus, too. I started walking on the roadway around the buildings, a 1.2-mile loop. And, finally, I took the time to explore the gardens and woods and to admire the sculptures. I got to know the Golden Path.

At some point in my CEO years, I also learned about the power of looking the part.

For a long time, I had paid little attention to my wardrobe. I worked with men, and they wore gray and blue suits with collared shirts. I did, too. I felt self-conscious about my legs, which I thought were too skinny, and chose long skirts to cover

them up. I didn't buy inexpensive clothes, and I appreciated fine fabrics. I shopped at Richards on Greenwich Avenue, an elegant store that began as an exclusive men's suit shop and then added a women's section. I usually chose a lovely wool suit with wide-leg trousers, and disregarding urges from Scott Mitchell, one of the partners at Richards, for me to update my style, had the tailor fashion the trousers into a skirt. I selected functional shoes, with small heels, but no colors, pointy toes, bows, or buckles.

Then, in a peculiar and wonderful episode, a young freelance consultant named Gordon Stewart asked permission to speak to me privately. We'd met briefly at a Gatorade new-product showcase. I didn't know him, but I agreed to a quick chat.

Gordon told me that I needed a sartorial makeover and that he had ideas to help me. He asked me to meet him at the Saks Fifth Avenue Club, a private shopping area in the Manhattan department store, on the following Saturday morning at eleven. I was not offended by his comments or offer of help. I was embarrassed, intrigued, and nervous. I accepted his invitation.

That weekend, I took the elevator to the fifth floor at Saks, where Gordon greeted me. He took me to a large dressing room, where dresses, skirts, jackets, shoes, bags, and jewelry for me to consider were arrayed on the walls. All exquisite, all coordinated, very professional. My first response was that I wouldn't try on the dresses and skirts because they were knee-length—too short.

But Gordon would not give up. He coaxed me to put them on, and, slowly, I came around to his point of view. It cost me quite a bit to give away the old and restock my wardrobe, but adding all this color and style gave me a newfound confidence,

which I carry with me even now. Occasionally, I go back and look at the "Look Book" that Gordon put together. His courage and attention to detail left an indelible mark.

To match all these new clothes, I also started to listen to my patient, longtime hairdresser, Anna Magnotta. I agreed to blow-dry my hair the way she wanted me to, and, boy, did this help my overall appearance.

Strangely, I got firsthand affirmation that changing my look made a difference in the boardroom, too. I started wearing nicely tailored dresses and jackets with pearls and maybe a scarf to work every day. At the end of one board meeting, one of our male directors wrote me that ever since I changed my clothing, he found me more intimidating.

I didn't quite know how to interpret that remark, except perhaps to infer that clothes might make a woman, too!

In 2016, I told the board that I thought we should start narrowing the list of who would become PepsiCo's next CEO. I think CEOs usually leave because they are tired, they want to do something else, or the board wants them out. I was starting to feel that exhaustion and was thinking about my future, but I also felt good about how the company was doing. And I knew we had built an amazing roster of senior executives who could take over.

Around that time, I moved four key candidates into expanded assignments to get to know new parts of the company. A year or so later, with the help of Ruth Fattori, then our head of HR, I gave our directors curated dossiers on each of the four, including detailed performance appraisals from the past five years and notes on their long and impressive careers. An

organizational psychologist provided a summary report on the arc of development for each candidate. I asked the board to meet each of them separately and to watch them in action in their businesses. Ruth and I would enable all this, I said, but I would not give my opinion on who should take over. That decision was up to the board. Led by the unflappable presiding director, Ian Cook, the board handled the job diligently, even hiring an external firm to conduct an independent assessment of each candidate. All four candidates were amazing in their own way.

In early August 2018, Ian told me that the board had picked Ramon Laguarta to be the new CEO. I met with Ramon in my office and informed him of the board's decision. I told him how proud I was of him and assured him of my ongoing support.

Telling the other three candidates was tougher: they were all highly sought-after executives, and I knew they'd be recruited away. Two left, a true loss for the company, and one stayed because of his loyalty to PepsiCo even though he had a CEO offer elsewhere.

A week later, PepsiCo announced I'd be retiring on October 2 and that I would remain chairman of the board until early 2019. I had been very clear that I wanted a short transition. PepsiCo's new leader had to start to put his own mark on the company as soon as possible.

Our employee town hall was an emotional event, with Raj, Preetha, and Tara on hand as they had been a dozen years earlier. I struggled to hold back tears as I reflected on my long and happy tenure, and assured everyone that PepsiCo would remain in my head and heart. Ramon would have my total support.

The next three months were hectic and somewhat liberating. I organized the move out of my office, although I still felt responsible for the company's results as chairman. I sent out my deeply felt farewell letter to our global employees with a few lessons learned—about vision, listening, and empowering the people you work with to succeed—and a final quote by the Sufi mystic Rūmī:

> *Goodbyes are only for those who love with their eyes.*
> *Because for those who love with heart and soul, there is no such thing as separation.*

When I departed 4/3 on a bright, sunny day, hundreds of my colleagues were waiting to bid me goodbye at an outdoor reception around our central fountain, the joyful *Girl with a Dolphin* sculpture by David Wynne. Ramon spoke, we drank prosecco and Sierra Mist from champagne flutes, and I posed for dozens of photos and selfies with the spirited, diverse team that now so defined the company.

I gave one last brief speech, got in the car, and left PepsiCo for home.

Part IV

Looking Ahead

11

The next day I was up, as usual, by about 4:30 a.m., drinking coffee and reading the news on my iPad. I reviewed my calendar to make sure I was ready for every meeting in the next month. There wasn't much. After a while, I pulled on a pair of jeans and a sweatshirt and drove the five minutes to work.

Raj and I had set up a lovely office in a Greenwich business park, an airy space with a conference room and a small kitchen. This was the setting for our next stage together, where we'd focus on what interested each of us and work just steps apart. I was excited to get on with it. That morning was also the first time I had ever headed to the office on a weekday in casual clothes. It felt weird. I remember hoping that no one would see me—totally forgetting that I was now a free bird.

In the three months since my PepsiCo exit was announced, offers had poured in for how I might spend my time: board seats, advisory roles, university teaching positions, writing requests, speaking engagements. I wasn't finished trying to

help the world, and I knew I'd be much less interesting as an ex-CEO if I stepped out altogether for a year or more. I had a few important decisions to make.

Still, my farewell letter to 270,000 employees at PepsiCo—sent just two days earlier—was also a blueprint of sorts for my own years ahead. In those two pages, written and rewritten over a few weeks with my gifted speechwriter, Adam Frankel, I advised my cherished associates to strive to be good listeners and lifelong learners. Then I wrote, "Finally, think hard about time. We have so little of it on this earth. Make the most of your days and make the space for the loved ones who matter most. Take it from me. I've been blessed with an amazing career, but if I'm being honest, there have been moments I wish I'd spent more time with my children and family. So, I encourage you: be mindful of your choices on the road ahead."

I had to heed my own counsel and to prioritize and learn to say no. Otherwise, I'd again have no time for myself. I was finally my own boss, and, after forty years of grueling, nonstop work, I deserved to relax a little and stick to what moved me. We might take more family trips, which had been few and far between, or Raj and I might do some hiking together, something which he really loves; I could break in the hiking boots he'd bought me several years ago. I could start to enjoy dinners with friends without constantly looking at my watch or phone. I could organize all of our closets and decrappify the girls' rooms. I could read more biographies and books on current events, and the Danielle Steel novels I found fun to fire through. I could go to more Yankees games. It was awesome—and a little daunting.

I got down to unpacking twenty-five years' worth of belongings that had been shipped over from PepsiCo. From

dozens of boxes, I pulled out signed books, awards, and gifts—sculptures, trophies, paperweights, and a giant blue glass football. I looked at all the baseballs and jerseys signed by the Yankees, and the photos of me with world leaders. I admired the candlesticks, decorative swords, Swiss cow bell, and Malaysian kite. I unloaded the oversized red-and-blue mosaic cricket bat in a plexiglass case created by PepsiCo's India team.

On our longest wall, Raj and I decided to hang eleven of my twenty or so guitars, including acoustics signed by the Chicks and Blake Shelton, and an electric guitar studded with red, silver, and Pepsi-blue rhinestones. Another electric guitar, painted with winged cherubs and daisies and the words "Yummy, Yummy, Yummy, I've Got Love in My Tummy," always brought a smile. It was a gift from the Frito-Lay marketing team, who'd told me they wanted to make sure I remembered them.

I was very proud of my work at PepsiCo. Total shareholder return in the twelve years between December 2006 and December 2018 totaled 149 percent, beating the Standard & Poor's 500 Index, which was up 128 percent. The company returned more than $79 billion in cash to shareholders, with dividends alone growing by 10 percent every year. Market capitalization rose by $57 billion in those twelve years, more than the gross domestic product of many countries. Net revenue jumped 80 percent to $64 billion in 2018. Twenty-two PepsiCo brands now topped $1 billion a year each in sales, up from seventeen brands when I took over, and we'd won incredible new food-service contracts, including New York's Madison Square Garden, which turned to Pepsi after 108 years with Coca-Cola.

But I was most gratified by PwP. It had transformed our products and environmental engagement. Good for You and Better for You offerings accounted for almost 50 percent of revenue, up from 38 percent in 2006. We had figured out how to make a bottle of Pepsi with fewer than 1.5 liters of water, down from 2.5 liters of water in 2007. We'd provided safe water access to eleven million people, working with Safe Water Network and Water.org. We'd converted a large portion of our fleet of trucks to hybrid, and now drew power from the sun in key manufacturing locations and sold back excess electricity to the utility grid. We'd reduced plastic usage in many of our bottles and developed a compostable bag for our snacks. PepsiCo's R&D was the envy of the food-and-beverage industry. The e-commerce business, started in 2015, had tripled its annual retail revenue to $1.4 billion. Our design department had won more than two hundred awards in 2018 alone and was helping drive our innovation.

We were on the Ethisphere Institute list of the most ethical companies for all twelve years I was CEO. In 2016, in the Kantar PoweRanking survey, where US retailers rank their suppliers' performances, we ranked number one—up from sixth place in 2010—and retained that position.

Our talent academy was the envy of American industry. In fact, nine senior executives were recruited away between 2014 and 2020 to become CEOs of other companies. But thanks to our systematic talent development processes, we had a strong bench of executives ready to step in.

I knew we could have done even more—or done it faster—if the financial crisis hadn't tossed us around like the rest of the global economy, but we'd handled that well, too. I had worked

as hard as I could and had truly loved the company with all my heart and soul.

I also had no regrets about leaving my job and was sure I wouldn't miss my role as PepsiCo's chairman either, when I stepped down in a few months. I was determined to be the best ex-CEO for Ramon, and that meant being discreet. I was around if necessary, but the company was now his to shape.

Really, during those slow October days, I was catching my breath, contemplating the past, thinking about the future, and brimming with gratitude. One afternoon, I read the entire *Fifty Years of Pep: A Storied Past, a Promising Future*, a 230-page book I had commissioned but never had the chance to open. Another day, I lingered over a beautiful scrapbook assembled by Jon Banner, our head of communications, detailing my twelve-year journey as CEO, with facts, photographs, and testimonials. It sure brought a lump to my throat. I looked at the hundreds of thank-you notes and goodbyes I'd received. I leafed through annual reports and reread each one of the shareholder letters I'd written on PepsiCo's progress. I had spent hours every year sweating over those letters. I was happy I did—together, they do an amazing job recounting the company's transformation. I also flipped through the many photo albums of my travels and thought about the people I'd met, the cultures I'd experienced, and the opportunities and challenges still ahead in so many countries.

None of these letters or books, of course, showed the frustrations and indignations of the job, but I reminisced about those, too. The activists, the quarterly earnings pressure, PepsiCo executives' resistance to change, the passive-aggressive

behavior directed at me, so many conflicting agendas. How did I cope with it? Indeed, the thousands of small decisions that PwP entailed, including both the victories and misfires, didn't happen without plenty of concern about whether we could do it all. But I had committed to this massive transformation, and, just as had happened when I arrived in Calcutta with the weight of my family's expectations on me, I had to stick with it no matter what.

I had heard of and seen male CEOs yell, throw things, and use four-letter words with great gusto, apparently a sign of their passion and commitment. But I was well aware that showing any of these emotions myself would set me back with the people around me.

So on days that I was mad that people, both inside and outside the company, didn't quite get what I was trying to do, I'd go into the little bathroom attached to my office, look at myself in the mirror, and just let it all out. And when the moment had passed, I'd wipe my tears, reapply a little makeup, square my shoulders, and walk back out into the fray, ready, again, to be "it."

Only one thing about leaving PepsiCo really nagged at me. So much discussion of my departure focused on how I didn't leave the company to another woman. A *New York Times* story was headlined: WHEN A FEMALE CEO LEAVES, THE GLASS CEILING IS RESTORED. Ugh. Of all those powerful men who retire every year, where were the articles about why their successor isn't a woman?

The number of female CEOs in the Fortune 500 rose from ten in 2006 to thirty-two in 2017 and then thirty-seven

in 2020. We've only moved from less than 2 percent women CEOs in the Fortune 500 to 7.5 percent over twenty-seven years. Progress on this issue, it seems to me, should not be about celebrating gains or lamenting losses when the number of women at the top of large companies is still abysmally low.

We need women in equal decision-making roles in this world because women are half the population. More female leaders will mean a healthier, wealthier, more egalitarian society. I also believe that we get the best decisions when people with different experiences come together to hash out the details and that true leadership requires learning from diverse teams. Like family, this is messy. There's no doubt that it's easier to run a company or a government when the people in the room come from the same social background, approach problems the same way, and reach consensus fairly smoothly. But easier doesn't mean better.

Writ large, half the companies out there—and 250 of the biggest 500—should be run by women. At the pace we are moving now, this will, absurdly, take more than 130 years.

My successor, Ramon Laguarta, joined PepsiCo in 1996, led the Wimm-Bill-Dann deal and integration in Russia, and served as CEO of PepsiCo in Europe and sub-Saharan Africa. He worked in five countries, and his wife and three sons moved around with him. In 2017, I promoted him to president of PepsiCo, and he moved to Purchase to get more exposure to how the whole company works.

The board selected Ramon after a rigorous process that prioritized PepsiCo's long-term vision. The fact that none of the final four people interviewed to follow me as CEO was a woman wasn't because we ignored the need for more female

CEOs. It's just that, despite years of effort, we weren't there yet.

This was particularly related to two heart-wrenching issues. First, several high-potential women whom I mentored, moved around for the right jobs, and introduced to the board over the years became chief executives and chief operating officers—but they left PepsiCo to do it. These executives, trained in our exceptional talent academy, drew the attention of recruiters and the boards of smaller companies. I was proud of them but upset that we'd lost them. Perhaps it was the right move; the competition to lead PepsiCo, such an enormous enterprise, was a long shot for anyone.

Second, I know some up-and-coming women moved on because of how they were managed in their midlevel jobs. One way I recognized this happening was when I listened to the performance appraisals of the top two hundred people in the company. I was in on them because we paid attention to rising leaders as part of the talent pillar of PwP, with a special focus on women and other diverse talent. I noticed that when a male manager was evaluated, the talk would go like this: "He did a good job, delivered on most of his objectives, *and* . . ." and then some details about this man's terrific potential. A woman's evaluation would get a different twist: "She did a great job, delivered on all of her objectives, *but* . . ." and then some details about some kind of issue or personality problem that might derail her future success. The and-but phenomenon bothered me tremendously. Many times, I stopped and asked managers pointed questions: "Did you give her timely feedback? Did you get her the right help to address these issues?" I often sent managers back and asked them to "make it work with female executive X."

This was not always a winning proposition. Sometimes these managers changed their views, but many stuck to their guns about the people working for them, men and women, and I can't say they were always wrong. At the same time, I know we lost smart, hardworking female executives at PepsiCo for reasons undoubtedly related to how men and women are perceived differently.

So many women in today's workplace have extraordinary skill, intelligence, ambition, creativity, determination, and good cheer. They are valedictorians and graduates with top grades from competitive schools. They have overcome adversity. They have sacrificed and worked incredibly hard. They are hungry to be financially self-sufficient. We no longer need to make the case for why women are so great as contributors to the bottom line. They just are.

There is no single reason why more women don't lead big companies. There is no list of ten items that simply need fixing. There are hundreds of issues—some tiny and difficult to pinpoint and some huge and structural—that add up to make it so. Despite all the progress we have made, the modern workplace is still replete with damaging customs and behaviors that hold women back.

This is gender bias—and it affects every woman's success. In some cases, women make the completely rational choice to move on or try something different to pay their bills. In other cases, this bias just grinds away at their confidence, which then affects their competence, and, at some point, attacks their performance. I think many people get caught in this doom loop.

Bias also presses many women with children—or even those thinking about having a family—to feel mightily conflicted about sticking with their jobs at all. A woman must contend with all that subtle prejudice in the workplace and, in the US at least, a largely ad hoc support structure for taking care of children until they are eligible to start public school at age five. Many women end up choosing, if they can afford it, to drop out of the paid labor force. Some hope to return one day but concede that they won't jump back onto a train to the very top.

Some call this a "leaky pipeline," although I think that kind of language downplays the problem. The pipeline is way beyond "leaky." It is broken. In any event, we still have relatively few women with the experience and fortitude to be considered for the position of CEO of a multibillion-dollar enterprise.

This is a real issue because we are just not enabling so many talented young women to achieve their full potential—a loss for the overall economy.

I was always aware that women in the corporate world were climbing a steeper, more slippery ladder than the men.

I think back to my days at BCG when one partner would never make eye contact with me. He spoke to me looking squarely at the men on our team. As a young consultant, I wondered what put him off: My wardrobe? My looks? Something else? Years later, a colleague casually told me that he behaved that way with all the women and people of color. Similarly, umpteen times over the years, I was addressed as "babe" and "sweetie" and "honey." I put up with it until I finally felt I had enough power in the job marketplace to take a stand with the new boss at ABB and just leave.

Even when I was on the very top rung, I was still on the women's ladder.

As PepsiCo's chairman for a dozen years, I led our board meetings sitting at the head of a large U-shaped conference table in a sunny corner room on 4/3. We were eight men and four women. The meetings would begin with friendly greetings and then get down to business. We analyzed performance, risks, strategy, talent, and what we saw across the world. I was lucky to work with a supportive board, but some of the comments in public and private by a board member or two were rude and patronizing, remarks I imagine they wouldn't dare make to a male leader. Additionally, I had put up with a couple of the men thinking it was OK to talk over me or interrupt me midsentence. I found this simply unacceptable and tried not to stew about it. Once, Sharon Rockefeller, who was a valuable board member for almost thirty years, had had enough: I watched her tell one of the men that his behavior of interrupting her constantly had to stop. She was direct, firm, and public. Everyone got the message. Every board needs a Sharon Rockefeller.

Another board member, early in my days as CEO, insisted on a one-on-one meeting with me every six weeks or so, almost always requiring me to travel to his home city to see him. He'd ask me questions, and my answers were always greeted with "I wouldn't say it that way." I'd then politely ask for his suggested response, hoping to learn something. He'd almost always repeat, verbatim, what I'd just said. I viewed this as a funny power game. He was a newly retired senior business executive who was struggling with giving up his position of power. He wanted to retain his influence through me. It drove me crazy—I viewed these dinners as a waste of my time.

When I was rising in PepsiCo, like many female senior executives, I was also the only woman in the room when our management team sat around debating tactics. I was always well prepared and offered good insight, and I know I was respected. But, quite often when I made suggestions, someone would jump in and say, "Oh no, Indra. That's too theoretical." A few minutes later, a man would suggest the exact same thing, using the same words, and be congratulated for his terrific, insightful idea. I once leaned over to a senior operating executive and loudly asked him to bring up a thought of mine. "Otherwise, it will be viewed as too theoretical," I quipped. That ended the "too theoretical" comments.

I really didn't think I could do all that much about how people treated me personally, but I always tried to support women in the organization. I made sure my corporate strategy team was as good as it could be, and it ended up 50 percent female. I held many women-only town halls to let female employees talk about anything on their minds. I quietly spoke with some about how they presented themselves, from how they sat in meetings to how they communicated their ideas. Most took my feedback and acted on it. A few thought I was too conservative and pushed back, although everyone accepted that I had their best interests at heart.

I also weighed in with a female perspective on marketing and advertising campaigns. One Diet Pepsi TV commercial in the 1990s sticks in my mind. The setting is a fancy wedding with the bridesmaids and guests waiting around. Something has gone wrong. One woman tells another that the bride's diamond is small, and then it becomes clear that the groom isn't showing up. The resplendent bride is crying. Her father gives her a Diet Pepsi. She sips. She peps up.

She looks at her dad and says, "This is diet?"

I saw this ad in an internal screening and told the creators that I didn't think it would encourage women to drink Diet Pepsi because it was insulting. None of the men agreed. And they were furious that I weighed in, noting that this wasn't my responsibility. The campaign went ahead. Later, a few of those guys actively avoided talking to me about the numbers when Diet Pepsi had a disappointing year.

I made one more memorable, very visible change. I had the beautiful French cobblestones on the walkway between our buildings ripped out in favor of an architecturally tasteful, flat surface. The cobblestones, installed in the late 1960s, were fine for men in business shoes but a menace for women wearing the heels expected of us in our professional wardrobes. The change infuriated Don Kendall, who had retired as CEO in 1986 but kept an office on 4/3. When he saw the construction, he fumed, "Who's messing up my walkway?" My male colleagues, who had long known those cobblestones were a hazard and seen people struggle and even trip and fall, pointed at me. Why they had never fixed them, I would never know. Don, surprisingly, never dared confront me about it.

My female colleagues, including Don's wife, Bim, thanked me for years for changing those stones.

The business world has improved immeasurably for women in the US since I was a sari-clad intern at Booz Allen Hamilton and was content to stay out of view. Much overt sexism has been quashed. Women no longer live and work in a legal landscape that is blatantly discriminatory or a cultural landscape that's bluntly demeaning. Job postings aren't listed as

male or female anymore. In the US, this is the legacy of decades of work by women like Ruth Bader Ginsburg, Gloria Steinem, and Shirley Chisholm, and by the feminist movement.

More recently, the #MeToo movement and Time's Up campaigns have had a profound impact on exposing the degree to which women are subjected to sexual violence and harassment. The movement and campaigns have created a necessary community for survivors.

I was never sexually assaulted. I did witness and hear about plenty of male behavior early in my days in the corporate world that offended my sense of decency and my values. I later made it a priority to shut down offensive behavior as soon as I saw it or it became known. After I became PepsiCo's president, I instructed our compliance department to address harassment complaints made to our anonymous Speak Up Line immediately; we were quick to fire confirmed harassers. The number of sexual harassment complaints fell, although I still worried about whether women held off calling the Speak Up Line for fear of retaliation.

When I crafted PwP, I knew the talent piece was the easiest to conceive and would be the hardest to execute. I wanted PepsiCo to be a phenomenal place to work. I wanted our associates to both make a living and have a life, and for everyone to be respected as individuals. At the same time, our talent-related actions had to be measurable and related to PepsiCo's business outcomes.

So here was my plan: We'd do the basics very well—hire the best without discriminating, give these people the right assignments, stretch them, mentor them, pay them fairly,

celebrate them, give them useful feedback, promote them when they showed great results, move them out if they didn't perform, and make sure they didn't confront conscious or unconscious bias along the way.

In addition—and this came from my own heart—we'd ask everyone to remember that employees are mothers, fathers, daughters, and sons. When we hired a person, we hired the family behind that person, too. Each employee had to be treated with an emotional connection, I said. There is no managerial formula that will do for everyone, but we also need universal support systems.

Needless to say, it was not easy!

I was lucky that Steve Reinemund had hauled diversity and inclusion into PepsiCo's executive suite when he became CEO in 2000. Companies at that time saw the dearth of women and people of color in their management ranks, but few did much about it. Steve thought our employee base should reflect our consumer base and insisted we recruit and promote diverse candidates at every level of management. He was convinced that we needed critical mass to truly change our culture and demonstrate the value of diversity. He created advisory boards to guide us on African American and Hispanic advancement and brought in actors to dramatize behavior in the workplace so that managers could realize what bias in action was all about. This was well before the ubiquitous bias training programs we see now. Steve also linked executive bonuses to diversity and inclusion metrics. He upset some senior managers, who felt they already had enough to do meeting their sales targets, but he stuck with it. We made good progress on representation between 2000 and 2006. The number of women in management positions rose from around 20 percent to almost 30 percent.

I needed to tie Steve's initiatives to PwP and take his effort further. We started examining HR processes to make sure every person was getting an equal chance for progress. We found, for example, that many employees weren't getting honest, properly documented performance appraisals in a timely way, so we added training programs on how to do this. I began to scrutinize end-of-the-year evaluations to ensure managers took the time to assess and document each person's contributions.

I also challenged our hiring processes when no women or minority candidates were considered for many jobs. One particular incident still makes me shake my head. We needed a new CFO for PepsiCo India, and the hiring managers were speaking to male candidates only. When I asked why they wouldn't be moving heaven and earth to look at the entire pool of candidates and maybe find a woman for the job, given that there were no women yet in the PepsiCo India C-suite, the answer was a stunner. "If it's a woman, she'll end up leaving if her husband gets moved," I was told. "We can't take that chance." Then I asked why the previous CFO had quit. "He is moving because his wife just got a big promotion."

We hired Kimsuka Narasimhan as CFO of PepsiCo India. She was an outstanding choice.

While I was CEO, I built on all the family-friendly policies in place. We increased paid maternity leave to up to twelve weeks and, wherever possible, added on-site or near-site childcare, on-site medical facilities, private space for breast-feeding, and a Healthy Pregnancy Program. We also created the company's first global flexible work arrangement. Employees were grateful that we didn't cut these programs

when we were looking for cost savings. Our organizational health scores improved a lot: 82 percent of PepsiCo employees answered that they were satisfied with the company as a place to work by the time I left, up from 74 percent when I took over.

Many PepsiCo employees cheered our talent initiatives. Others thought our associates' personal lives were their own business, and we shouldn't be quite so generous. I couldn't quibble with either response, but I didn't change my agenda. I was happy with our progress.

For me, personally, there was also a more painful criticism that came through when we asked for feedback: "She only cares about people like her"—that is, women and people of color.

I knew I had been referred to as a "quota hire" when I joined PepsiCo in 1994, implying that I was only hired because I was a woman of color. But I really thought I had pretty much proved myself. Now, when I stepped up to champion diversity and inclusion, my ethnicity and gender were front and center. Some incidents related to this sentiment galled me. If an Indian American was hired into PepsiCo North America in a management job, for instance, it got back to me that people said, "This must be Indra's contact." When a woman or person of color was promoted, it was common to hear "It must be her focus on diversity and inclusion."

Our IT department once outsourced work to an Indian company that was doing similar projects for many US clients, a tiny contract that I knew nothing about. Someone called the Speak Up Line to complain that the job went to my relatives.

Sometimes I felt like people assumed that everyone from India—all 1.3 billion people—were my cousins or somehow related to me. It was disheartening but amusing in its own disturbing way.

Diversity and inclusion are here to stay, and corporate leaders need to get used to the concept as a major business driver. Some senior managers talk about talent and then say they look forward to the day when they don't have to worry about diversity and inclusion because the problem is solved. I don't see this happening anytime soon. As long as we keep growing, competing, and moving toward the idea that the economy belongs to everyone, we will be working on this.

I do believe, however, that some of our ideas on how to address bias should evolve. I wonder, for instance, if appointing a diversity and inclusion vice president alone is the right approach. Diversity and inclusion cannot simply be delegated to one individual. That is a cop-out. It should be on the CEO's plate as a priority and central to the HR agenda, not something that ebbs and flows with the quality of a diversity and inclusion leader. Human resources, in turn, can't be shy about the challenges. Covering any of this up is building a house on a weak foundation. It doesn't work.

Further, the tone at the top of any division or work group is critical. We need training that says to a broad swath of leaders and managers: "How do you make sure the organization is welcoming to talented, qualified people of all kinds?" Along with the obvious goal of fairness, it just makes business sense: talent drives performance, and it takes so much time and money to hire people and train them. Why not do all we can do to hire the best from the whole population, include them, and help them succeed?

Leaders must then model the behavior themselves. There can be no tacit acceptance of stereotypically biased behavior, and, in my view, it needs to be called out when it happens.

When you see people talking over anyone, especially minority voices who face this regularly, stop it. When you see a woman being put down, stop it. I firmly believe this can be done artfully and effectively. And doing it sets the tone. We don't tolerate negative, discriminating behavior against our daughters or sisters or wives. Why do we allow it in the workplace, directed at women who are daughters and sisters themselves?

Companies should also rethink how to deliver bias training. In the early days, many companies insisted on across-the-board diversity training for all employees. We needed to create awareness in generations of employees who perhaps didn't grow up in very diverse environments. Now we have millennials and Gen Zers, who are far more accustomed to working in diverse groups when they walk in the door. Unconscious bias still needs attention but talking about it must be super relevant and tailored to the audience for us to move forward.

I also believe that boards of directors could play a more significant role in stamping out bias and creating an inclusive environment. First, boards must select CEOs based on their ability and desire to hire and get the best out of a diverse workforce. Then those directors should hold their CEOs accountable and, once a year, dedicate time to a comprehensive discussion on issues related to bias, inclusion, and sexual harassment in the company. Directors should also review organizational health surveys to ensure the right questions are being asked and to make sure all results are analyzed by gender and ethnicity.

Most important, boards must show genuine care for and intent about this topic. If it is viewed as yet another item on a long list of corporate governance changes, it will never result in meaningful progress.

I also believe CEOs and boards have to finally step up on pay parity. We all know that women, on average, are paid less for the same work as men. This is a travesty, and we need a far more precise effort to resolve the discrepancies. Some companies are now publicly revealing their pay disparities, putting their own feet to the fire. I admire this, but I am not sure it's needed. I absolutely believe, however, that directors should demand and review fully transparent compensation analysis and hold the CEO accountable for getting to pay parity. It's about time.

Each of these points is a matter of a company's integrity, but the markets are paying attention, too. Gender, diversity, and work-life matters belong in the environmental, social, and corporate governance goals that are increasingly used as screening standards for investors. The best run, most successful companies in the coming decades will be those that demonstrate the most foresight on people matters, and I think their stock performance will reflect this. This doesn't mean ever more generous HR programs. It means companies, as part of their purpose, must pursue the smartest combination of policies to let employees flourish at work and at home.

Related to all of this: who is on the board?

If the bosses of the CEO don't understand these issues at a deep level and nudge the company toward them, change won't happen. Unfortunately, women hold just 26 percent of US corporate board seats. In my view, companies should consider setting term limits on board members of fifteen years and a mandatory retirement age of seventy-two. Immediately, they could also expand their boards by one or two members to make room for qualified people who better understand the issues facing working women and young families.

Shortly after I took over PepsiCo, I invited female CEOs of large companies to my home for a dinner party. Some were friends with one another, and some did business together, but, as a group, we hadn't gathered this way before. I was hoping we could collectively make our voices heard for women in corporate America. I also thought we might forge some sort of kitchen cabinet, an informal network that we could rely on for advice or support as we ran our companies.

I was spurred to do this, in part, by a memorable visit to PepsiCo a few weeks earlier by Hillary Clinton, who was one of New York's US senators at the time. I'd never met her before. She was very friendly, and we first sat down in my office with a small group of senior executives to talk about PepsiCo's business and our role in New York State. Then we headed to our auditorium, packed with employees who wanted to see and interact with her, and she gave an incredible detailed and upbeat speech, incorporating every one of the statistics about PepsiCo she'd just heard. No notes. It was a master class in holding the crowd.

On her way out, Hillary and I walked alone for a few minutes. "I know you are taking over in a few weeks," she said. "I am giving you my number. And if you ever need to talk, call me. If you don't get me, call my staff and they will contact me. I am always available for you. These jobs are tough."

It certainly made sense for Senator Clinton to know the CEO of PepsiCo. But I felt much more from Hillary that afternoon, and, in my first week as CEO, the first note to arrive was from her. She wished me the best in my new job, and she wrote, "Good luck!"

The dinner at my house with the woman CEOs was a wonderful evening. Ellen Kullman of DuPont came from Wilmington, Delaware; Anne Mulcahy of Xerox came from Connecticut; Pat Woertz of Archer Daniels Midland and Irene Rosenfeld of Kraft (now Mondelēz) flew in from Chicago; Andrea Jung of Avon came from New York City. We shared stories of the little things that added up in our careers to define us, separate from the men. We found that our paths were distinct but familiar to one another. We talked about the markets, our industries, and the burdens of being the boss. We discussed the slow progress for women in leadership and the tough slog of convincing men in power that elevating women is worth their true attention.

As everyone put on their coats to leave, we vowed to meet regularly and to add to our group. Nine months later, I hosted again. Cherie Blair attended with her husband, Tony Blair, who had just stepped down as UK prime minister. She was working on women's initiatives and was eager to join forces. We talked more about what we might do to help women in the pipeline. Yet again, we vowed to meet soon. Someone else insisted they would host.

Then, nothing happened. This was no one's fault. The simple truth is that none of us had an extra ounce of time to create a strong support organization for female CEOs and our protégés.

If anyone is wondering, there is no club of the most senior women in corporate America.

Men in business operate in a system with centuries of history related to playing that role in society. Their clubs and

associations were established long ago, and they don't have to do anything extra to set them up. The men who went to war together had a camaraderie and emotional connection that extended well into their work lives. Despite our advances, women are still breaking into this world. We belong to every industry group and fill the seats on nonprofit boards, but men have the distinct advantage of having created the rules of the game, and we aren't invited everywhere. Even in the most obvious circumstances, integrating women into the customs of power and influence has proved strangely controversial. In 2012, the Augusta National Golf Club, in Augusta, Georgia, which hosts the annual Masters golf tournament, withheld the club membership it traditionally grants the CEO of IBM because Ginni Rometty is a woman. IBM is one of the Masters' biggest sponsors. To be sure, this was a tipping point. A year later, the club changed its eighty-year-old male-only policy and admitted its first two women members.

Golf-and-business stories may seem cliché, but connections forged over eighteen holes aren't incidental, and some of the most coveted places to play in the US still bar women. In 2007, Don Kendall pressed me to join Westchester County's Blind Brook Country Club, founded in 1915. It is adjacent to PepsiCo's Purchase campus. Some of our past CEOs and many more executives had used the club for years to entertain customers and friends. The catch for me was that this club only accepted male members. Don thought getting around that was easy: Raj could be the member. After all, he was the golfer in our family. I went home and asked Raj if he wanted to join Blind Brook and regularly play a course he so admired every time we drove down Anderson Hill Road. He looked at me in horror. "Why would we ever become members of

a country club that doesn't accept women?" he said. "Forget it." Don never understood why I turned his idea down.

Gender inequality is hardly an issue in the shadows.

Hundreds of organizations are working to create a more level playing field for women in business and industry. This has been true for decades. New York–based Catalyst, now funded by eight hundred companies, was founded in 1962. *Lean In*, the 2013 book by Sheryl Sandberg, encouraged women on the professional track to expect and ask for more, and millions of millennial women have benefited from that message. The Lean In Foundation's annual Women in the Workplace research, compiled with painstaking surveys, provides deep insight into what's holding women back in corporate America. Consulting firms, banks, and investment companies also report on what's wrong and the importance of understanding the problem. Academics, economists, governments, think tanks, and other nonprofits weigh in on the causes, too.

Women's progress—or lack thereof—is dissected every year at a plethora of women's conferences, from glamorous media-sponsored breakfasts with exclusive guest lists to giant industry meetings with technical sessions and recruiting booths. There's no lack of appetite for these get-togethers; some attract tens of thousands of women.

Over two decades, I received many invitations to speak at conferences to support and advance women. I accepted as many as I reasonably could. These events are important for keeping society's inequities in the spotlight and for supporting women as they maneuver in tough careers. But they do more than that. They build our sisterhood. Women share. We gain resolve

when we hear others' stories and meet people who sympathize with our struggles.

At the same time, we shouldn't confuse gatherings geared to empower women and build female networks with the conferences and summits that remain so popular with the most senior executives and global power brokers. Women's events, I fear, won't accomplish much systemic change because most of the world's most influential people—whether we like it or not—are still men.

It's true that some big events focused on business, finance, technology, and the economy now acknowledge gender inequality and diversity issues with special sessions presented by women and diverse people. (I tick two boxes—no wonder I'm approached as a star panelist!) But I find that these sessions are often poorly attended, or, worse, men in the audience are bored, fidgety, and ready to move on to topics focused on making more money. I'm disappointed that even major universities host global conferences where this scenario plays out.

We need to be more deliberate.

We must expand the future-of-work conversations that dwell on robotics and artificial intelligence to include another critical dimension of our success: how to shift our economies to better integrate work and family and ensure that women get equal pay and share power. Only then we will have proof positive that these issues have filtered into the mainstream power structure—and broken through our biggest barrier to change.

12

INSEAD is a storied business school in France with a main campus on the edge of the Fontainebleau Forest, about an hour's drive from Paris. The school assembles the most internationally diverse class among revered MBA programs, with students from more than eighty countries. INSEAD always intrigued me. All those years ago, when I was applying to Yale, I thought about applying to INSEAD, too, but it required I speak English, French, and German, and I didn't think I could pass the German test.

In 2016, I was invited by the Society for Progress, a group of academics studying how capitalism and social well-being come together, to give a speech about PwP in the school's large, sunny auditorium. I later began teaching a seminar every June with Subramanian Rangan, the society's founder, and Michael Fuerstein, a philosophy professor, called Integrating Performance and Progress. As Professor Rangan describes the course: "Students have to decide whether they want to make just a career or also a contribution." Our class fills very quickly. It's usually about 60 percent women.

When I look out at the students—the faces from Asia, Europe, the Middle East, Africa, the Americas—I see myself at Yale forty years ago. I see the future leaders of PepsiCo and other big multinational companies. I see scientists and entrepreneurs with global vision. And I see, in those women and men, my own daughters, who now both have graduate business degrees and grasp the world as a social and economic puzzle the way I do.

We end the two-day seminar with a relaxed, open conversation, in which the students can talk to me about anything. And, after lots of insightful global business questions, these young people, so full of promise, invariably ask me this: "How did you do it? How did you rise in your career and keep your family together?"

And, then, anxiously, they add: "How can we do it?"

I reply honestly. It wasn't easy. My life was a constant juggling act, with pain, guilt, and trade-offs. Running a global company was a tremendous privilege, but I have some regrets, too. Life is like that.

I have been asked some version of these questions hundreds of times—at Yale, West Point, and other schools; at PepsiCo factories; at roundtables in Latin America or the Middle East; at major women's events; after fireside chats with academics; and with young leaders of the World Economic Forum. I get dozens of emails and letters from friends, acquaintances, and strangers who want my advice about how to combine work and family.

Sometimes I feel like these people think I have some sort of secret recipe because I managed to pull it off. I don't. In many ways, I was just lucky—with my close-knit household, great

education, and parents who valued their daughters as much as their son. I married a man who shared my ideals, we supported each other, and we started out carefully and frugally. We've had our disagreements—that's true in every marriage—but Raj and I have steadfast love and commitment to each other and our children. I also had constant help from relatives and, later, could afford to hire people to help me both at work and at home. I met mentors at critical moments. And, as many have reminded me, I have the special genetics of not having to sleep more than five hours a night.

I had the good fortune, too, of landing at PepsiCo, a company with a youthful ethos that was male dominated when I joined in the 1990s but not so stuck in its ways that I didn't fit in. PepsiCo named me the CEO—and that made all the difference. I don't think many other US corporate boards at the time would have selected someone who looks like me to lead.

I don't mind repeating that doing well at work is, by definition, a full-time job. Being a mother, a wife, a daughter, and a daughter-in-law can also be full-time jobs. And, I found, being a CEO is at least three full-time jobs. So, while I devoted every drop of my talent and time to it all, my success was actually a bit like winning the lottery.

Somehow it worked out.

This is no model for achieving real progress on combining career and family in a world where society's explicit message to young family builders in recent decades has largely been this: If you want jobs and kids, it's your problem.

My story doesn't change the heartbreaking reality that we, as a society, haven't built robust, contemporary systems to truly

support anyone—male or female—who wants to both earn a good living and build a happy, healthy home life. In fact, the situation in the US is even tougher now than when Raj and I started out. Health care, childcare, education, and housing use up a far larger percentage of average incomes than in the early 1980s.

The stress surrounding work and family has many millennials, sadly, delaying marriage and childbirth or deciding not to have kids at all. In 2019, the US fertility rate fell to 1.7 births per woman of childbearing age, a record low. Meanwhile, some women are doing all they can to hang on to their chance to have a baby, including paying the enormous financial, physical, and emotional cost of freezing their eggs. A few corporate benefit plans now cover this procedure, an accommodation to those who may have spent so much time on their education and jobs that they haven't yet had the chance to take on pregnancy and motherhood, too. It's more evidence that our system puts the career clock and the female biological clock in direct conflict.

I am so excited to see how the millennial generation and the Gen Zers who follow them will drive our economy and improve the world. I have been witness, as a CEO deeply interested in people, to countless examples of their sincerity, imagination, and purpose in a shifting business world. But I believe that we also need these women and men to be parents and to let them actually enjoy that incomparable experience.

Not everyone has to want children, let alone the 2.1 babies that are the standard population replacement rate. But, broadly, I think we need to do more to value families having children and raising them to be educated, productive citizens.

Those children are also necessary. The demographic picture is clear: in the US, ten thousand baby boomers turn sixty-five

every day, a pattern that's expected to continue into the 2030s. These folks, and the ones who come after them, will live longer than any previous group. The number of older Americans is expected to double by 2060. We will need the stability of a strong economy and, over time, millions of new workers paying into the system to support the aging population. The US is not alone in this; a similar scenario is playing out in developed countries everywhere and, increasingly, in developing countries, too.

I'm not the first to say it, but it's also tragic to me that no matter how hard our young women and men work—in a school like INSEAD or in a family business in India or in a factory in Indiana—they're still dealing with so many rules and expectations from the past that don't reflect real life. Again, this is the most skilled, creative, and connected group in history—with so much potential.

We can't go on having them repeatedly stymied by "How can we do it?"

I was atop a Fortune 50 company for a long time, and it's second nature to me to calculate return on investment. With PwP, PepsiCo acknowledged that the line between business and society was blurring, and our challenge was not to deny the ambiguities but to accept them. We set the company on a course that delivers great results for shareholders, and PepsiCo is evolving, with some trial and error, to become a model of sustainable capitalism.

Now I have the same instinct about elevating work and family to much more prominent consideration in business and the economy. Once and for all, we must embrace the fact that both women and men work in jobs outside their homes; that

children need fantastic care; that our aging parents need tender attention; and that governments, companies, communities, and individuals need a common road map to address the massive, complex social issues involved in making life a little easier.

What better purpose could we have for this than to take care of our loved ones, advance gender equality, and—I am convinced—generate tremendous economic benefit?

The return, in the long haul, will be extraordinary.

Often when people approach me to talk about their struggle with work and family or to ask my advice, they begin with a story. Some women say they are torn between their career and the tug of a baby at home. Single parents say they are coping with a sick child and afraid they will lose their only source of income. Some people mention aging parents with dementia or adult children whose kids have landed on their doorstep. Others talk about cultural expectations to do more at home in a way that can't align with their paid work obligations. The issues, I find, are frequently a question of care. Care is a warm and fuzzy word, but they talk about it with so much pain. That has always moved me to somehow want to smooth their path.

Now, our collective experience with COVID-19—billions of people struggling to balance their livelihood with obligations at home when kids weren't in school, when family and friends were sick, or when they were isolated like never before—has added a new urgency to this work for me. As the global order responds to what we learned during the pandemic, we have arrived at a unique moment for change.

To begin, I think we must recognize that supporting families—and the role that women, in particular, play both in paid work and at home as mothers and caregivers—is essential for all of us. That's evident in every culture in the world, and I don't think we need to spend much time and energy reframing this message yet again.

The problem, in my view, is who is receiving the message—and who has the power and influence to respond to it in a meaningful way. This is where we should all be frustrated. With so few women in leadership positions—including in companies and government—we have to rely on men.

I know that men with real power in our society admire their mothers, wives, and daughters and that they have seen loads of evidence that helping women succeed in their organizations can help the bottom line. They also understand that the march to women's equality spells progress in the twenty-first century.

Still, many men—CEOs and others—perpetually linger on the sidelines of the work-family debate, in part because they are reluctant to break routines that are, ultimately, easy, comfortable, and lucrative for them. I've noticed that younger men—including husbands and dads who are just as stressed as their partners—also refrain from this discussion, perhaps fearful of hurting their own chances to move ahead.

I believe that men need to recognize how many women are held back or depart the workforce in the middle of their careers and how many women, often in the shadows of the economy, are working to hold up our entire system. They need to realize that this is their burden, too. Real change in the matter of integrating work and family isn't going to happen without men, especially those in power, helping drive the discussion and helping implement the solutions.

I think that a woman aiming to be CEO of a public company or anything close to it in terms of power, pay, and responsibility also needs to be realistic about how things will play out. I celebrate women's ambition to lead and have no doubt of the bias they encounter. Still, competing to reach the very top of an organizational pyramid is a brutal business no matter who you are, and once a woman or a man is within striking distance of the CEO's office—two or three levels away—the idea of balancing work with any kind of normal life outside work isn't practical. In my experience, the requirements for doing those jobs are boundless and can occupy almost every moment. This isn't to say that female CEOs shouldn't have children and happy families. Of course they should. I did. But, make no mistake, the required support systems and sacrifices to lead at the very top are enormous. Broad-based solutions that help most people find better work-family balance may not apply.

In 2019, as is my style when tackling a big idea, I began reading a load of books and research on integrating work and family, on women's roles in the economy, and on why some women advance to leadership positions when so many don't. I started speaking to scholars, advocates, and entrepreneurs, and looked at government and corporate interventions from around the world on these issues. One day, I even organized my thinking by creating equations, with "career woman + systemic bias + family + social pressure" on one side and a long list of possible offsets on the other side.

Through it all, I thought often of my own story. I was happy I finally had some time, post-PepsiCo, to better understand the interplay of bias, gender, families, employers, and the global

power structure. I also thought about the great diversity of the US—how this country welcomed me and, despite some early bumps in the road, let me flourish and make a name for myself. I wouldn't have risen to these heights in any other country in the world. Despite our continuing struggle with how to evolve as a nation founded on the idea of equal opportunity to everyone, I am proud of how far we've come and where we can go next. This is a very personal road.

My conclusion is that our society can leap ahead on the work-family conundrum by focusing on three interconnected areas: paid leave, flexibility and predictability, and care.

We must recognize that these three elements of how we look after one another function together and must evolve together. I believe that collective action on each of them will lay the foundation to transform our economy and communities because, finally, the next generation of families will have the reasonable, systemic foundation they need to prosper.

First, paid maternity and paternity leave must be mandated by the US government as soon as possible. Maternal and child health are compromised every day when women return to work too soon after having a baby because they can't afford to be off without pay. The US is the only developed country in the world where paid leave for a new baby is only now making its way into law because some state governments have taken it up. This isn't enough; we need this to be true across the nation, including for all federal government employees.

Some may rail against the cost to governments and business of this basic social provision. That's entirely outdated thinking because we know the long list of physical and mental benefits to

both infant and parent when they bond and heal in the weeks after birth. Paid maternity and paternity leave are a necessary link in the chain of creating healthy lives and, in the long run, a successful, robust country.

In fact, this is not spending; it's investment. Women who take paid leave are 93 percent more likely to be in the workforce twelve months after a child's birth than women who take no leave. And fathers who take leave are more likely to share childcare and household responsibilities equitably with their female partners over the long term and to have greater empathy for family demands. This is a no-brainer.

I would start with twelve weeks of paid time off for the mother or the primary caregiver of a new baby and eight weeks for the father or secondary caregiver. Some will argue for more or less time, although this baseline is a good start and, I believe, could be accommodated by a wide swath of employers. It's very true that small businesses will have a tough time when integral employees are away for a few months. But I also think this is an area where we can think more creatively about solving the problem. What about a corps of retirees who can step in to help, funded by a community's pooled resources? What private, public, or philanthropic resources should we use? Where does technology fit in? This pressure point is fixable if we put our minds to it.

The US paid-leave debate includes extending the benefit to those caring for sick family members or employees recovering from illness. These are very important provisions. I would not have become the CEO of PepsiCo without taking advantage of all three types of paid leave during my early career: BCG paid me both when my father was sick and when I was recovering

from my car accident, and I received paid maternity leave twice, through both BCG and ABB.

However, while we debate the cost and parameters of how to expand this benefit within a broader care economy, I see no reason why paid leave related to all newborn babies in the country should not be implemented immediately.

Of course, parents returning to work after their maternity or paternity leave still have a very young child. And we know that the long-standing constraint of absolutely set times and places for work are no longer required in many jobs.

I support work flexibility as the norm. In addition to its advantages across the whole economy, flexibility is an integral part of giving families some breathing room. It obviously helps both women and men look after kids and aging parents and deal with the other strains of modern life. Plus, we learned fast during the COVID crisis that our economy is fully equipped, across many roles and industries, for people to work remotely.

To be sure, I also think offices are here to stay. We crave the creativity that bubbles up when people are working together in the same space and can talk face-to-face and share human connection. But, in general, I believe our workdays should be organized around productivity, not time and place.

At a minimum, we should give workers whose jobs mostly happen at a desk the choice to work from wherever they want—at home, in a coworking space, or in a central office. Evaluations should be adjusted so that people who spend less time physically in the office aren't judged differently from those who spend more time there. We don't want to create different

classes of workers, again casting people with family obligations in a negative light.

Shift workers who must physically be in a space to do their jobs, from a factory floor to a retail shop, have a different set of struggles. Work flexibility is very limited in these jobs, but we need to make sure these employees have schedule predictability at least two weeks out. This is paramount and a matter of respect. The lack of predictable hours for many workers, especially those with care responsibilities, is extremely difficult to manage. Meanwhile, shift workers who have predictable schedules have proved to be both more productive and committed to their employers. Today, every company has access to sophisticated scheduling technology. Why not use it to make life easier for the workers who need it most?

Early in my career, my lack of work flexibility—and the feeling that I could never simply schedule my time in a way that made sense for me—were among the most stressful aspects of my life. The only way I got through this when Preetha and Tara were small was that I had Gerhard as a boss at both Motorola and ABB. He knew my family and was very understanding. At PepsiCo, I was senior enough to allocate my hours however I wanted to but, given all that was going on at the company, I allocated almost all of them to PepsiCo.

Not long ago, I was driving near my home one afternoon and saw a couple of school buses dropping children off on a street corner with their parents waiting to greet them. Moms and dads, working from home, were able to take a quick break to pick up their kids from the bus. I looked longingly at this scene, again reminded that I missed that experience because of the era in which I had my career. As work flexibility becomes

more typical—supercharged by our experience during the pandemic—I'm glad that more parents may be able to take a little time to welcome their kids after school.

I also believe in taking the idea of flexibility one step further. Workers should be able to pause their careers for the sake of their home lives for longer periods without suffering the social and economic penalties that are still common. This doesn't oblige employers to keep a job open for years or pay people for the extra months they are away, but we should encourage many more options to let people come in and out of paid work. Some companies have introduced programs that acquaint returning employees with new job requirements and new organizational priorities. For those who build this into their business model, there are clear advantages: returnees, with institutional knowledge and networks, can be very valuable hires. Why not take advantage of their expertise? This could very well be the future of work.

Finally, we must address care. This is the most important.

I believe that the biggest investment we can make in the future of our population is to build a reliable, high-quality, safe, and affordable care infrastructure, focused on childcare from birth to age five, and to expand our thinking to include the whole cycle of life.

The COVID crisis exposed the beleaguered state of the US care economy. One consequence of this mess was that hundreds of thousands of women who had been managing jobs and kids felt they had to quit their paid work. We were also reminded that so many of our essential workers, including caregivers to both children and the old, don't earn enough money to live on.

It's about time that care attracts moonshot thinking in the US. Fixing this issue will remove barriers to work for women and young families and help many women achieve financial independence. This is a commitment to future generations that will lay the foundation for a healthier, more prosperous population.

I believe, though, that focusing on care will do even more. As a businessperson who successfully ran a large American company for a dozen years, I can attest that this will be a competitive advantage for every company, community, and state where we make it happen.

Let's start with children. Regardless of paid-leave duration or a parent's time flexibility, babies and young children need care when their moms and dads are working. Right now, for many parents, finding good day care in a center that is either close to home or close to their job is near impossible because there simply aren't enough spots or they are just too expensive. And that problem doesn't take into account care for children whose parents work at night or need backup help.

A different plan might be hiring an individual nanny to look after the child, an approach that is usually more expensive and presents more questions again: Whom to hire? How much to pay? How to supervise? What are the boundaries?

Many parents still end up with the kind of makeshift care arrangement that Raj and I relied on in Chicago when Preetha was a baby thirty-five years ago. We met someone in a social environment and left our precious child with her. Vasantha was wonderful and had brought up four kids of her own. But she was an acquaintance, not a trained childcare worker. The fact that she worked out well as Preetha's babysitter for us that winter

was really just luck. If we hadn't liked her, we would have spent a lot of time and energy looking for someone else, draining our momentum at work. That's the scene that played out for us in Connecticut a few years later, even when we spent the extra money on a nanny agency. Nothing much has changed.

We need the federal and state governments, the private sector, and experts in early childhood education and community building to come together to create a full-scale, creatively designed childcare system that eliminates so-called childcare deserts. I laud the people who have been working on this issue for decades, as well as programs such as Head Start and other pre-K initiatives that do tremendous work to prepare children for their school years ahead. But I am suggesting we go much further. We need to expand programs that exist today, network them with in-home care options, and link them with community organizations that have buildings—from religious institutions to libraries—to create a new generation of terrific options.

We also need comprehensive licensing and training programs for childcare owners and staff. And we need to pay caregivers wages that reflect their awesome responsibility. Early childhood education, so critical for every baby's lifelong well-being, is a growing field. Why not create incentives to get young people into these jobs?

It is heartening to see the Biden administration taking on care as critical infrastructure for the country, and I cheered on Janet Yellen, the treasury secretary, when she recently declared that "our policymaking has not accounted for the fact that people's work lives and their personal lives are inextricably linked, and if one suffers, so does the other." But the follow-through for any

White House initiative will be paramount. Giving block grants to states to address care is a good start, for instance, but it's important that the template for great care networks is specified upfront and that details of the spending are monitored. This issue deserves a historic commitment that should extend for decades to come.

While the government sets out how best to implement this moonshot, large companies and other employers should step up. Where possible, companies should add on-site or near-site childcare for their employees. If the number of children doesn't sustain that investment, companies should work with others to pool childcare services either near offices or in residential clusters. At PepsiCo headquarters, the total cost of retrofitting one floor of our headquarters into a childcare facility, an amount that I insisted we spend even with skeptics all around me, was about $2 million. We hired Bright Horizons, a childcare pioneer, to staff and operate this center and paid for insurance and maintenance. The expenditure offered incredible return in terms of loyalty and peace of mind for our current employees. It saved them commuting time, and they were close by if their child had an emergency. It was also a terrific recruiting tool. The service wasn't free to employees: they paid for their children to be there. But, within a year, PepStart was oversubscribed.

Smaller companies or those with a more flexible workforce should consider creating consortia to run joint childcare centers or work in partnership with existing community networks. In an economy with more parents working from home or using neighborhood workspaces, childcare attached to coworking locations should be a given.

I call this a moonshot, but we are not betting on the unknown here. Those countries with comprehensive childcare networks do keep mothers working. In France, where national childcare begins when a baby is two-and-a-half months old, working women who become pregnant have the peace of mind of knowing they have a care option. In Quebec, Canada, a heavily subsidized care system for all children under five proved, over the last twenty years, to bring more women back to work and increased economic growth in that province.

We must also include elder care in our discussions and recommendations. The caring responsibilities of families do not end when the youngest child leaves home. That is not just because the emotional work of a parent is never done. It's because more people than ever will require help well into their eighties, and the majority will rely on unpaid care from family and friends. Many of these unpaid caregivers, who are mostly women, are in the "sandwich generation" and have both children and older relatives to support. Redesigning the structure and location of senior care centers may be part of this effort, too, as we contemplate a world with a growing senior population.

One complement to senior care centers is multigenerational living. I grew up with three generations of family and have no doubt that this brought great benefits to my sister, my brother, and me, not least the presence in our home of our wise thatha. Aging populations all over the world are reviving the idea of the multigenerational family as more people become great-grandparents and even great-great-grandparents every day. This is often written about as a growing problem, a demographic time bomb where pensions are becoming unaffordable and health services overburdened. We need to turn this on its head. A large aging population could be a blessing.

The older generation is a great support system for families. Millions of grandparents in the US provide childcare. But, again, we haven't adjusted to make it easier for these vital family structures to work. For instance, many US planning and zoning laws, stuck in the last century, prevent houses with separate kitchens or entrances and prohibit multifamily dwellings. This presents another path for change: we need to get local, assess these laws, and gather the steam to change them. While we are at it, let's embrace our common spaces—parks, walkways, benches, playgrounds—and forge community design that truly harnesses our human instinct to care for one another.

After I left PepsiCo, I joined the board of Amazon and now have a front-row seat to the thinking of one of the most innovative, customer-centric companies I've ever encountered. I also recently became a director of Philips, the Dutch company that is changing the face of health care. This board seat, along with my memberships on the boards of the Memorial Sloan-Kettering Cancer Center and the executive committee of MIT, give me a window into the technologies of the future, broadly, and, more specifically, how health care will be transformed in the next few years.

I also accepted an invitation to serve as the Class of 1951 Chair for the Study of Leadership at the US Military Academy at West Point, where I spend a few weeks a year sharing my knowledge with the faculty and cadets. I am moved and inspired by the selflessness of everyone I meet at West Point, especially the young men and women who are so committed to contributing to our country and who will be deployed to guard our freedoms.

And I continue to serve on the board of the International Cricket Council, where I am the only female member of the governing body of cricket. It's been quite a journey from that day in 1973 when I walked onto the field in Madras in my whites!

In February 2019, at the request of Ned Lamont, my Yale classmate who had been elected governor of Connecticut, I agreed to cochair AdvanceCT, an organization that works closely with the state government on economic issues. When COVID-19 struck, I stepped up to cochair Connecticut's advisory committee on how to reopen the state post-pandemic, working with Dr. Albert Ko of the Yale School of Public Health. We had to carefully balance lives and livelihoods, and the work was intense. But Connecticut is our home, and we wanted to help our governor get to the right decisions during an unprecedented crisis. I am very committed to giving back to the state that has given so much to my family over the years.

During this time, Raj and I were at home with both girls and my mother. Preetha had come from Brooklyn as the coronavirus raged in New York City, the first time she was living in our house for some years. It didn't take long for her to see that I was working eighteen hours a day. "I thought you retired," she exclaimed one morning. "We are supposed to be playing board games and bonding!" But she also knew that duty called and that nothing much had changed with her mom. Interestingly, Preetha soon started working with 4-CT, a state organization supporting first responders, food banks, and others providing frontline COVID-19 relief.

One day, after I worked through all my meetings on Zoom and then spent a few hours reading and writing, I turned my attention to a few household tasks. Amma approached me.

"You know," she said, "you are someone who wants to help the world and not many people are like you. I don't think you should worry about the house so much. You have to give back as much as you can. Keep on."

She surprised me.

I know that I am driven by purpose, and that this comes from a place deep in my heart. This sentiment has guided me throughout my life—from working on my badges as a Girl Scout to envisioning how Stayfree pads would help women in India. I sought purpose in every one of my consulting jobs and, at Motorola, saw great value in helping people communicate without wires. I am still so honored, and a little staggered, that I was entrusted to lead PepsiCo through a change we called "performance with purpose." Somehow, this is in me.

I am also motivated, at this point in my life, by gratitude, especially to my schools and teachers, to my communities, and to the two countries where I have lived. I am never far, in my heart, from Holy Angels and MCC. A few years ago, I had the science labs in both schools completely rebuilt and a new women's lounge created at MCC. I hope more girls like me at these schools, interested in science, have the chance to soar because they now have the equipment and encouragement to pursue their passion.

My connection with Yale remains profound. In 2002, I was invited to join the Yale Corporation, the committee of sixteen trustees who oversee the university. The meetings take place around a big dark-wood conference table with the patina, to me, of centuries of American history. Yale was founded in 1701. The first time I walked into that conference room I

immediately noticed a brass plaque engraved with my name on the back of one of the heavy brown leather chairs at the table. And when I sat in that chair for the first time, I was overcome with emotion. I was taken back to my first days at Yale, in awe of the majesty of the institution. Now, my education at Yale had helped bring me to the highest levels of the university. It was surreal.

Raj and I take great pride in being able to give time and resources to all of the institutions and communities that have educated and supported us and our children. And, in June 2021, Raj agreed to serve as the interim CEO of Plan International, a global human rights group that supports the world's most vulnerable children, especially girls. He was on Plan India's board several years ago and was the first person they asked to assume this role. I know Raj will give his all to helping improve the plight of young girls—he cares so deeply about this issue.

The next act in my life—fueled by my great sense of purpose—is to do all I can to elevate and support those people and organizations who have long recognized care as fundamental to our common good and have been working tirelessly to develop great ideas and move them to real life and implementation. I am convinced this will relieve the stress on young people around building families and will help women advance, including rising to run our companies.

In early November 2020, Raj's mother, age ninety and living with his brother, fell down in their kitchen and broke her leg in two places. I looked at the photo on Raj's iPhone of my dear mother-in-law in the hospital, a small woman amid stark white sheets and pillows in a large bed with metal railings and a few

machines in the room. She was OK. But she looked a little lonely, a little frightened.

Raj immediately went into overdrive to have her moved to Bangalore, closer to her sisters and other relatives, where he could go and care for her while she recovered. He figured out how to get to India from Connecticut amid all the pandemic-related global travel restrictions, and, two weeks later, he left.

While he was away, for three months, I stayed home in Greenwich taking care of my mother. Now Raj and I were each our parents' primary caregiver. Amma, in her late eighties, is still physically independent and perfectly sharp. She is extremely disciplined, insisting that her meals are made a certain way and delivered at exactly the same time every day. And she likes to know where I am all the time. If I'm fifteen minutes later than I thought I'd be, she calls me. She worries. I know I have it easy, but it's still not easy. The woman who took care of us in our big house in Madras and showed me, by example, how to look after my elders, is now in need herself. My siblings and I, regardless of any of our accomplishments or other commitments, regard this as a primary obligation.

As I spend time with my mother and my adult children—and I sit in the middle of them—I reflect often about the care cycle that I've been part of all my life. I've told Preetha and Tara that when they marry and have children, I will be right there to help, a devoted grandmother and teacher to our next generation, and a backstop and fierce supporter of my daughters as they seek their own paths in the world. And I will also do all I can to help us build the future of care for all the families that don't have this kind of support.

This is my promise.

EPILOGUE

I departed India forty-three years ago, but India has never left me. I am still a vegetarian; I don't smoke or drink alcohol beyond a few sips of wine; I have a puja alcove in my home where I light my lamp every day – and, as much as I love the New York Yankees and American TV shows, I can't resist watching IPL cricket, *Kaun Banega Crorepati*, Indian movies and *Indian Idol*. They all bring me home to my wonderful upbringing in Madras, and to the energy and rhythms that are so familiar and precious to me.

I also find that these shows are a window into how India has changed since I was a teenager who dared play "These Boots are Made for Walkin'" in a rock 'n' roll band. So much of today's popular media features characters and performers who are strong, educated, determined women making their way in the world. These shows help young girls understand how they, too, have a voice and can dream of forging an independent life. At the same time, I still see plenty of women playing traditional roles that were the norm many decades ago, both on TV and in real life. They are deferential, attentive, taking care of everyone,

engaged in unpaid labour. I'm reminded that, when it comes to women, India has one foot in the future and one foot in the past.

Over the years, I have tended to see the country in this way too, perhaps letting my nostalgia get in the way of reality. Several years ago, I sent my daughter Preetha to Madras for a holiday with a suitcase full of loose-fitting T-shirts, modest jeans and salwar-kameez sets, convinced that girls in India remained perfectly content in the conservative styles of my youth. I soon got a panicked phone call from her telling me that everyone her age was dressed in the same tank tops and shorts that she wore in the US. "Mom! I need different clothes," she exclaimed. She was right. I had to move with the times.

Now, I believe it's imperative that we all move with the times. Girls and women need to be allowed to flourish, and that means breaking traditional patterns that some see as necessary, but that, in fact, hold us all back. By embracing change, we have everything to gain and little to lose. We must support the next generation of smart, driven young people, and help them combine their livelihoods with their lives, including the multifaceted roles they play in their extended families.

I have often said how proud I am to have grown up in the world's largest democracy. As I traced my journey while writing this book, I was in awe of how India has passed so many intelligent laws to protect its citizens, and how many of these focus on women, from maternity benefits to equal remuneration to anti-discrimination provisions, and rules against domestic violence, child marriage and sexual harassment in the workplace. I was heartened to see how the stage is set for progress.

But then I ran into a few more facts: Women account for only 20 percent of the paid labour force in India, a figure that has fallen by 30 percent in the last twenty years. Women do almost ten times more unpaid domestic work than men. Although girls are increasingly outperforming boys in school and women now make almost half of college graduates, they fill far fewer entry-level professional jobs. Those that do have jobs outside the home still face incredible bias in the workplace. In the World Economic Forum's 2021 Global Gender Gap Index, which measures gender equality in 156 countries, India ranks number 140. In the subset measuring economic participation and opportunity, the country falls to number 151—an embarrassing position.

I believe that all women deserve the power to earn money, for their own sake, and for the sake of their children, their communities, and the good of the whole society. But these unfortunate statistics reveal the gap between the law and reality. The needle will only move if leadership at all levels commits to improving the situation for all women, including timely justice for those who have often been left behind in rural India and in unorganized sectors of the economy.

I am the first to recognize the incredible role that women play in families, and I think *My Life in Full* explains how I maintain that core faith. But I believe that India, perhaps more than any other place because the country has 1.3 billion people to care for, needs to tap the brilliance of all its citizens in order to grow and thrive. According to a 2018 McKinsey Global Institute report, increasing women's participation in the economy to the same level as the best in the Asia Pacific region would boost India's GDP by 18 percent a year, an enormous payoff. This

requires that we remove the barriers to Indian women engaging in paid work, that we recognize their value and right to be equal in society, and that they live free of harassment and violence, at work and at home.

As India emerges from the devastating impact of Covid-19, the country must rethink some of its economic priorities under the umbrella of Atmanirbhar Bharat. I hope whole new ecosystems around next-generation industries emerge, and new investments in core infrastructure, including roads, the railways, water and sanitation, and health care. I also hope to see a more predictable framework in support of foreign direct investment, and a massive commitment to improving education for all—from kindergarten to grade twelve and beyond—so that the country has all the talent in place to realize its terrific ambitions.

While this goes on, I also believe it's time to unleash the superb abilities and ingenuity of women across the country, in every strata of society. Corporations, governments and nongovernmental organizations working in the country must come together on this. And, most importantly, men and women must join forces to create a more inclusive, more productive, more caring nation. Only then will India be truly on the road to sustainable prosperity.

ACKNOWLEDGMENTS

Writing this book has been a new experience for me—a journey, a labor of love, a different kind of hard work. I didn't intend to write my own story in such detail when I started out. I thought that I would write a few articles filled with facts and figures on how we must support women, young family builders, and our collective well-being, and I was sure I would find an audience.

But Bob Barnett, a greatly respected legal mind and wizard of book publishing, convinced me otherwise. He was the driving force behind this book, and has participated actively in its development over the past two years. He is a gem of a person who cares deeply about his clients. I feel it every day. Thank you, Bob.

This book was shaped and written by Lisa Kassenaar, a most gifted writer. She took all of my stories, facts, anecdotes, and pages of edits and wove them into beautiful chapters, each with core lessons. She is a real treasure, and I am in awe of her skills. Every author needs a Lisa to bring their ideas to life.

Adrian Zackheim and Niki Papadopoulos—thank you for your wisdom and for being captivated by these ideas from the start, and, along with Tara Gilbride, Kimberly Meilun, Mary Kate Skehan, and the whole team at Portfolio, for your expertise

in bringing *My Life in Full* to reality. Thanks also to Thomas Abraham and Poulomi Chatterjee at Hachette India, and to Zoe Bohm at Piatkus, and your teams, for the enthusiasm and care you gave this book.

It was a privilege to be photographed by the incredible Annie Leibovitz. The book is better for her vision. Thank you, Annie, and to your dedicated team. It was a pleasure working with all of you. Thanks also to Anna Wintour, for your friendship and for introducing me to Annie; and thanks to Stefano Porcini and Yesenia Rivera for helping with the cover layout and design.

I'm so grateful, too, for my trusted PR and digital partners: Juleanna Glover—simply the best at what she does; and Preeti Wali—whose quiet approach always endears me. I so appreciate how you made this book your particular project and cheered it on. The work you do to support me is world-class. And to those who support you—Jane Caldwell, Isabelle King, Ali McQueen, Kaiulani Sakaguchi—many thanks. Thank you, too, to Don Walker, Emily Trievel, and Elizabeth Platt at Harry Walker Agency, who so efficiently handle my external speaking engagements.

Several researchers also supported this effort and I truly value their insight and dedication—the brilliant Phil Collins, my thought partner for over a decade; Allison Kimmich, who early on realized I needed a writing partner and brought Lisa into my life; Martha Lein, Kate O'Brian, Ruth Fattori, and Molly O'Rourke. I know this book is personal to each of you.

I'm also grateful to those who gave me so much of their time and attention by reading the manuscript and offering detailed, thoughtful comments: Prisca Bae, Amanda Bennett, Phil Collins, Adam Frankel, Ted Hampton, Brad Jakeman, A. J. Kassenaar, Allison Kimmich, Linda Lorimer, Antonio

Lucio, Rich Martinelli, Erica Matthews, Emma O'Brian, Kate O'Brian, Mauro Porcini, Roopa Purushotaman, Rangan Subramanian, and Anna Wintour. And to Swati Adarkar and Ann O'Leary, thank you for your excellent input on the policy chapter.

Thanks to our wonderful administrative assistant, Brenda Magnotta, who joined us after a long career at PepsiCo and keeps our office in Greenwich together and my life organized. Thanks to Srilekha, my assistant in India, who provided information needed to recount the early years of my life and so meticulously worked on several items related to the book launch. To Rahul Bhatia, Sebastian Rozo, Simi Shah, and Joe Vericker, thanks for your behind-the-scenes help in pulling this book together.

To my close friends, without whom I couldn't remain centered: Alan and Jane Batkin—you top the list. For more than twenty years, you have been there for me, listening to me, counseling me. I treasure our close connection tremendously.

Nimmi John, Soni Singh, Chitra Talwar, Sujata Kibe, Jenny Storms, Ofra Strauss, Annie Young-Scrivner, Cathy Tai, Neil Freeman, Prakash, and Pradeep Stephanos—know that I value our friendship enormously.

Brad Jakeman—I am so glad you came into my life. Thanks for looking out for me at every opportunity and for handling so many of the activities around the book. You are a true member of our family. Likewise Mauro Porcini, for your wisdom on many aspects of the book's design. Mehmood Khan, without whom I could not have made Performance with Purpose a reality. Larry Thompson, for your wise and quiet counsel over the years.

To John Studzinski, Tom Healy, and Fred Hochberg, thank you for your steadfast support and wise counsel.

Bim Kendall and Jan Calloway—thanks for your friendship over the years.

I am also deeply grateful to the incredible mentors who lifted me—Norman Wade, S. L. Rao, Larry Isaacson, Carl Stern, Gerhard Schulmeyer, Wayne Calloway, Roger Enrico, Steven Reinemund, Don Kendall, and Bob Dettmer.

To Henry Kissinger, who, beyond teaching me about geopolitics, explicitly endorsed me in public meetings, boosted my credibility, and picked me up when I tripped. I will never forget your kindness.

To Jacques Attali, my advisor, friend, and counselor, and to Jeff Sonnenfeld, available at any hour as a valuable sounding board, thank you both for being in my life.

Thanks also to Hillary Rodham Clinton—a mentor, a great supporter, a wise advisor, and a connector. Everyone knows you as US Secretary of State, First Lady of the United States, Senator from New York. I know you as one of the most brilliant people I have ever met.

To the Boston Consulting Group, thank you for teaching me all about strategy consulting and, most important, by example, what honest, ethical consulting is all about.

To members of the PepsiCo board of directors between 2006 and 2019, thank you for the steadfast support that enabled the company to effect our transformation and implement PwP. To Cesar Conde, Ian Cook, Dina Dublon, Alberto Ibarguen, Bob Pohlad, Sharon Percy Rockefeller, Darren Walker—our connection has evolved beyond the boardroom. It's a pleasure to call you dear friends.

To all the men and women who were my direct reports at PepsiCo and contributed so much to the success of our company

over many years. Thank you. You made all the hard work fun; you stepped up to the challenge.

To the young executives who supported me in the CEO's office and still stay in touch with me—John Sigalos, Adam Carr, Adam Frankel, Erica Matthews, and Rich Martinelli. Thank you for your dedication and hard work. I miss you all so much.

To Rob Baldwin, Pat Cunningham, Richard DeMaria, Jeanie Friscia, Monty Kelly, Neal Robinson, Chuck Smolka, Joe Ursone, Joe Walonoski, and all the others in PepsiCo aviation, and to Dominick Carelli, Frank Servedio, Robert Sinnott—you made my office in the air and on the road comfortable and welcoming. The many trips we took together were less tiring because of you. My gratitude.

To Colonel Everett Spain, chair of the Behavioral Sciences and Leadership department at the USMA and all the faculty in the department—thank you for welcoming me and treating me as one of you. I am in awe of what you do for the country.

To Albert Ko, department chair, Yale School of Public Health and all members of the Reopen CT Task Force—it was a pleasure working with you to advise Connecticut during the pandemic. I learned so much from all of you.

And to the many others who helped me in the early days, including the Shankar family for welcoming me into your home and helping me settle down in New Haven, and Holly Hayes, my Yale classmate, whose hospitality and friendship Raj and I will never forget.

To Mike Tusiani of the New York Yankees, who helps keep me connected with my favorite sports team. Thank you.

To the people who departed this world prematurely and left a void in my heart—my dearest friend Jassi Singh, I'll never

forget your love and friendship. I was lucky to have you in my life. Saad Abdul Latif, your loyalty and warmth will stay with me forever.

To my parents, Shanta and Krishnamurthy, and to my thatha, Narayana Sarma—you gave me the foundation, the confidence, and the wings to fly. To my mother-in-law, Leela, and father-in-law, N. S. Rao, thank you for treating me as your daughter and for your incredible support. And to all the other members of my extended family—my sister, Chandrika, and her husband, Ranjan; my brother, Nandu, and his wife, Ramya; my brother-in-law, Shekar, and his wife, Shalini; and all of my nieces, nephews, aunts, and uncles—thank you for keeping me grounded.

And finally, and most important, thank you to my husband, Raj—my rock, my biggest supporter, my soul mate. I love you dearly. And to my children, Preetha and Tara—you taught me what love from the deepest part of one's heart really is all about. I love you more than anything in the world. You three make me whole.

NOTES

70. **In fact, working women's kids:** Rachel Dunifon et al., "The Effect of Maternal Employment on Children's Academic Performance" (working paper, National Bureau of Economic Research, Cambridge, MA, August 2013), https://www.nber.org/system/files/working_papers/w19364/w19364.pdf.

70. **see their mothers as valuable role models:** Kathleen L. McGinn, Mayra Ruiz Castro, and Elizabeth Long Lingo, "Learning from Mum: Cross-National Evidence Linking Maternal Employment and Adult Children's Outcomes," *Work, Employment and Society* 33, no. 3 (June 2019): 374–400, https://journals.sagepub.com/eprint/DQzHJAJMUYWQevh577wr/full.

70. **More women in the workforce makes:** Jonathan Davis Ostry et al., "Economic Gains from Gender Inclusion: New Mechanism, New Evidence" (International Monetary Fund, October 2018), https://www.imf.org/en/Publications/Staff-Discussion-Notes/Issues/2018/10/09/Economic-Gains-From-Gender-Inclusion-New-Mechanisms-New-Evidence-45543.

118. **cultures where multigenerational living is common:** Peter Muennig, Boshen Joao, Elizabeth Singer, "Living with Parents or Grandparents Increases Social Capital and Survival: 2014 General Social Survey-National Death Index," *SSM Population Health* (April 2018), https://www.ncbi.nlm.nih.gov/pmc/articles/PMC5769098/.

134. **"Pepsi-Cola hits the spot":** chris1948, "Pepsi Cola 1940's," March 10, 2012, YouTube video, 0:21, https://www.youtube.com/watch?v=-PU1qeKGVmo.

135. **"A typical investor looks us over":** WorthPoint, "1994 PepsiCo Annual Report Cindy Crawford," https://www.worthpoint.com/worthopedia/1994-pepsico-annual-report-cindy-504948360.

167. **"make big changes to big things":** Patricia Sellers, Suzanne Barlyn, Kimberly Seals McDonald, "PepsiCo's New Generation Roger Enrico, PepsiCo's New CEO, Has Traveled a Career Path as Curious as They Come. But Then, He Says, 'I Think "Career Path" Are the Two Worst Words Invented.'" CNN Business, April 1, 1996. https://money.cnn.com/magazines/fortune/fortune_archive/1996/04/01/210991/index.htm.

175. **We know that, on the whole, women's median:** Thomas B. Foster et al., "An Evaluation of the Gender Wage Gap Using Linked Survey and Administrative Data" (working paper, Center for Economic Studies, November 2020), https:/www.census.gov/library/working-papers/2020/adrm/CES-WP-20-34.html.

197. **We were an "odd couple":** Nanette Byrnes, "The Power of Two at Pepsi," Bloomberg.com, January 29, 2001, https://www.bloomberg.com/news/articles/2001-01-28/the-power-of-two-at-pepsi.

197. **"feisty candor":** Melanie Wells, *Forbes*, "Pepsi's New Challenge," January 20, 2003, https://www.forbes.com/forbes/2003/0120/068.html?sh=2f4c09a72f41.

213. **Twelve years after I laid out PwP:** Business Roundtable, Statement on the Purpose of a Corporation, August 2019, https://system.businessroundtable.org/app/uploads/sites/5/2021/02/BRT-Statement-on-the-Purpose-of-a-Corporation-Feburary-2021-compressed.pdf.

218. **We committed to remove at least 1.5 trillion:** Shu Wen Ng, Meghan M. Slining, and Barry M. Popkin, "The Healthy Weight Commitment Foundation Pledge, Calories Sold from U.S. Consumer Packaged Goods, 2007-2012," *American Journal of Preventive Medicine* (May 2014), https://www.ajpmonline.org/article/S0749-3797(14)00248-7/fulltext.

261. **Net revenue jumped 80 percent:** PepsiCo, 2018 Annual Report, 2018, https://www.pepsico.com/investors/financial-information/annual-reports-and-proxy-information.

264. **The number of female CEOs in the Fortune 500:** Catalyst, Historical List of Women CEOs of the Fortune Lists: 1972–2020, May 2020,

https://www.catalyst.org/wp-content/uploads/2019/06/Catalyst_Women_Fortune_CEOs_1972-2020_Historical_List_5.28.2020.pdf.

265. **more than 130 years:** World Economic Forum, "Global Gender Gap Report 2021: Insight Report," March 2021, http://www3.weforum.org/docs/WEF_GGGR_2021.pdf.

287. **In 2019, the US fertility rate:** Brady E. Hamilton, Joyce A. Martin, Michelle J. K. Osterman, Births: Provisional Data for 2019 (Division of Vital Statistics, National Center for Health Statistics, May 2020), https://www.cdc.gov/nchs/data/vsrr/vsrr-8-508.pdf .

287. **The demographic picture is clear:** America Counts Staff, "2020 Census Will Help Policymakers Prepare for the Incoming Wave of Aging Boomers," United States Census Bureau, December 10, 2019, https://www.census.gov/library/stories/2019/12/by-2030-all-baby-boomers-will-be-age-65-or-older.html.

293. **Women who take paid leave are 93 percent:** Linda Houser and Thomas P. Vartanian, "Pay Matters: The Positive Economic Impacts of Paid Family Leave for Families, Businesses and the Public" (New Brunswick, NJ: Rutgers Center for Women and Work, January 2012), https://www.nationalpartnership.org/our-work/resources/economic-justice/other/pay-matters.pdf.

295. **Meanwhile, shift workers who have:** Joan C. Williams et al., "Stable Scheduling Increases Productivity and Sales" (San Francisco: University of California Hasting College of the Law; Chicago: University of Chicago; Chapel Hill: University of North Carolina Kenan-Flagler Business School, March 2018), https://worklifelaw.org/publications/Stable-Scheduling-Study-Report.pdf.

300. **In Quebec, Canada, a heavily subsidized:** Pierre Fortin, Luc Godbout, Suzie St-Cerny, "Impact of Quebec's Universal Low-Fee Childcare Program on Female Labor Force Participation, Domestic Income, and Government Budgets" (Quebec City: Université du Québec, 2008), https://www.oise.utoronto.ca/atkinson/UserFiles/File/News/Fortin-Godbout-St_Cerny_eng.pdf.

308. **women account for only 20 percent:** Singh, P., and Pattanaik, F., "Unfolding Unpaid Domestic Work in India: Women's Constraints, Choices, and Career," *Palgrave Communications* 6, 111, 2020, https://doi.org/10.1057/s41599-020-0488-2.

308. **a figure that has fallen by 30 percent:** Singh, P., and Pattanaik, F., "Unfolding Unpaid Domestic Work in India: Women's Constraints, Choices, and Career," *Palgrave Communications* 6, 111, 2020, https://doi.org/10.1057/s41599-020-0488-2.

308. **almost ten times more unpaid domestic work:** Singh, P., and Pattanaik, F., "Unfolding Unpaid Domestic Work in India: Women's Constraints, Choices, and Career," *Palgrave Communications* 6, 111, 2020, https://doi.org/10.1057/s41599-020-0488-2.

308. **girls are increasingly outperforming boys in school:** Saswathi Natta, Sonalde B. Desai and Reeve Vanneman (University of Maryland, College Park), "Gender and Educational Attainment in India: Girls Outperforming Boys," P9-38, Population Association of America Annual Meeting, 2017.

308. **World Economic Forum's 2021 Global Gender Gap Index:** World Economic Forum, "Global Gender Gap Report 2021: Insight Report," March 2021, http://www3.weforum.org/docs/WEF_GGGR_2021.pdf.

308. **boost India's GDP by 18 percent a year, an enormous payoff:** Jonathan Woetzel et al., "The Power of Parity: Advancing Women's Equality in Asia Pacific," McKinsey Global Institute, 2017, https://www.mckinsey.com/featured-insights/gender-equality/the-power-of-parity-advancing-womens-equality-in-asia-pacific.

QUESTIONS FOR DISCUSSION

Part I: Growing Up

1) Why do you think that Indra Nooyi chose to start her book with so many details of her childhood home and upbringing?

How did this lay the foundation for her life's journey? What elements from her early days do you think helped her succeed?

Indra writes that "family comes in every form." Do you think that our communities—including schools, transportation, workplaces, and available services—are set up well to accommodate different types of families?

What works? What could be improved as we adjust to a world where a nuclear family, with two parents and a few children, is not the case for many people?

How should we create social infrastructure—outside of the traditional family structure—to support the next generations?

2) Indra writes that her family in the 1960s was particularly progressive when it came to education—and that both girls and boys were treated the same way. Why do you think she calls this idea "progressive"? Has this attitude changed compared to when Indra was a child?

Do you know anyone who didn't have access to education because they were a girl or because their family didn't have the resources to let them study? How did that affect their life?

About sixty million girls in the world still don't have access to education. How do you think educating more girls will allow our societies to prosper?

Do girls and boys where you live have the same opportunities in the classroom, sports or after-school programs, or job opportunities upon graduation?

3) Indra came from a middle-class household in the south of India and rose to lead a famous American company. She writes that she could not have had the same career anywhere in the world but the US, where she could work her way up in a meritocracy.

Do you agree with her? In what ways is the US still revered as a place for immigrants to arrive and build successful economic and family lives? Why is this important to the history and future of the US?

Which immigrant story has affected your life? Do you relate to Indra's experience? What do you think are the common threads for immigrants around the world?

Part II: Finding My Footing

4) Throughout her work life, Indra was supported by critical bosses and mentors. Why do you think these people chose to support her? Do you have sponsors in your work life? Are you a mentor or sponsor to someone? Why are these relationships important? What are the characteristics of a great mentor?

Indra's boss at BCG, Carl Stern, gave her six months of paid leave when her father was sick with cancer. This helped Indra, but was this the right decision for the company?

What are the advantages for employers of shouldering the expense of paid leave, either for childbirth, illness, or caretaking family members? What are the advantages or disadvantages for families or for individuals who never take maternity or paternity leave?

5) Indra and Raj struggled to find childcare when their oldest daughter was a toddler. This is quite common in the US, where the childcare system is unable to keep up with the demand and many working parents rely on ad hoc arrangements until their children start preschool or kindergarten.

Have you had difficulty finding childcare so you could go to work? Have you considered giving up your job because you could not find adequate care or the cost of childcare was too high?

How should the US childcare system be improved? Do employers or governments have a role to play or do you think families should look after care arrangements outside of work or the public sphere?

6) Indra's husband quit his promising career at Hewlett Packard, bucking all convention for men like him, so that she could take a promotion in another state. After they moved to Connecticut, her mother, his parents, and their aunts and uncles helped the working couple care for their kids and the household.

How did their families pave the way for rising female leaders? Have you felt supported in your career by family members or

others in your community? Have you chosen to step back so another can soar? What were the reasons?

Are employers doing enough to create on-ramps for people who want to return to the workforce after a break of a year or more? What would smoothen the path for people to more effectively move in and out of paid work over the course of their lives?

Are men more willing to see women's careers as equal to their own now than they were thirty years ago, when Raj made his decision to follow Indra? What has changed? What has stayed the same?

Part III: The PepsiCo Years

7) PepsiCo has more than 250,000 employees around the world and more than $65 billion in annual revenue. What do you think are the biggest challenges of leading a company of this size?

Indra set out to transform the company with Performance with Purpose (PwP). Where are the pitfalls of trying to change an established business? What is your view of PwP as a strategy for PepsiCo?

What is the role of large companies in your community? Do you have a relationship with a company like PepsiCo as an employee or supplier? How do these large entities influence our society?

8) Many companies now embrace diversity and inclusion as business imperatives, recognizing that the workplace should be free of bias and unequal treatment of employees.

Do you think our workplaces are improving on this score? Are we succeeding in shedding the "ideal worker" model that favored men with wives who were taking care of the home?

How do new generations of employees approach diversity in different ways? How do you feel about diversity programs in companies? Do you think such programs address unconscious bias work? Are we moving fast enough to address diversity and inclusion?

How do you think companies should address the issue of pay discrepancies between men and women doing work of equal value?

Part IV: Looking Ahead

9) Women earn the majority of university degrees and are an exceptional talent pool. They also drop out of the workforce at a higher rate than men do, citing unequal treatment, harassment, or the pressures of juggling work and family life with little systemic support. Meanwhile, many millennials are choosing not to have children or delaying pregnancy because of their jobs.

What are the biggest barriers to women achieving equal footing to men in the workplace? Why do you think more women don't rise to lead companies?

What are the implications for our society that more women don't head companies or governments?

How have these trends affected you or those around you?

10) Some women say they aren't always helped by other women, either at work or in their communities. Many women

also say they feel guilty about not doing enough at home or at work.

What's your opinion of whether women as a group work together to support each other? Would more support help alleviate this guilt?

Do professional clubs and associations for women help? Do you think women should carve out their own spaces in the business world or move into established spheres still dominated by men?

How do younger generations of female workers approach these dynamics differently from older generations?

11) In *My Life in Full*, Indra describes how she noticed that global business, academic, and government leaders rarely talked about "family" in conversations about "the future of work." These groups are still largely male.

How do we bring more men to the table to talk about issues related to work, women's experience, and the work-and-family juggling act?

How do you think the pandemic has changed how we think about work? What are your ideas for integrating work and family, and connecting this conversation with how our companies and communities function?

How would you and your family benefit if the care ecosystem was elevated in how we talk about business, the economy, and the future?

ALSO AVAILABLE

ISBN: 9789391028503

ISBN: 9789350098875

ISBN: 9789351950615

ISBN: 9788194657798

ISBN: 9781444792492

ISBN: 9780349140438

ISBN: 9781473621640

ISBN: 9781913068219

"When a history of modern India is being written, women like Indra Nooyi will be the icons we look up to as role models. She is an inspiration for generations of women in India and across the world. In her book, Nooyi recounts beautifully the story of an immigrant and of a woman functioning at the apex of her abilities. Her achievements make her a beacon to the millions of girls who aspire to do more, be more—and in that her accomplishments belong not to her alone but to all women. Through this book she has effectively laid down a template of how it is done, and done right."—**Jaya Bachchan**, award-winning actor and member of Parliament

"Indra Nooyi's life story is one of absolute merit, grit and determination. Way before upskilling was a trend, she set the example of being a true life-long learner. Her journey from her Thatha's room to the PepsiCo chair has been marked by constant curiosity and innovation, and reflects deep values that transcend all cultures. I am glad that she decided to share her incredible journey with us, for rarely are we invited to learn from not just the achievements but also the regrets of a brilliant and immensely successful business leader." —**Roshni Nadar Malhotra**, Chairperson, HCL Technologies

"Gritty, joyous, and visionary, Nooyi tells the story of an everyday person living an extraordinary life, leading beautifully and confidently from the front. A must-read for all." —**Ursula M. Burns**, former chair and CEO of Xerox, author of *Where You Are Is Not Who You Are*

"'CEO' and 'care' do not usually go together, but for Indra Nooyi, they always have. Rather than offering us a list of policy prescriptions, she shows us what is possible when businesses care about family and families have time to care for one another."—**Anne-Marie Slaughter**, CEO of New America, author of *Unfinished Business*

"We have so much to learn from Nooyi's remarkable story and wisdom on lifting up girls and women in the decades to come. She shares a great road map for anyone who aspires to merge social change with leading a large organization."—**Matt Damon**, actor, screenwriter, and producer

"Nooyi's honesty, integrity, and humor shine through at every turn. Truly inspiring."—**Mindy Kaling**, actor, writer, producer, and director

"An extraordinary window into the life, career, and family of a brilliant business strategist. A terrific addition to the story of American business." —**Brian Cornell**, CEO of Target Corp.

"An amazing read, filled with lessons, optimism, warmth, and heart, about an extraordinary woman who rose to be a fantastic role model for all women." —**Sofia Vergara**, actor

Praise for *My Life in Full*

"With candor and good humor, Nooyi has written a wonderful book that brings her story to life, from her early years in India, surrounded by love and high expectations, to her determined efforts to succeed in the corporate world, all the while questioning the tradeoffs she had to make. She reveals just how our society continues to sacrifice talent instead of changing how we organize work to maximize everyone's potential to live full and productive lives. A must-read for working women and the men who work with us, love us, and support us."—**Hillary Rodham Clinton**

"A fascinating narrative of an intrepid woman who broke the barrier of gender and race to emerge as an iconic business leader of the twenty-first century. Indra Nooyi's leadership legacy is her trailblazing philosophy of Performance with Purpose, whose time has only just arrived!"—**Kiran Mazumdar Shaw**, Executive Chairperson, Biocon Limited

"*My Life in Full* is just what it says it is: a vibrant account of a full life, lived wisely and well. It is the authentic, transparent, honest journey of a young Indian girl who made it to the top of corporate America—vivid with struggles, triumphs, and thoughtful decisions. Along the way, we get a glimpse of the extraordinary capacities that helped shape Indra Nooyi's distinctive leadership style, and her great ability to define a mission and bring people together to achieve it."—**N. Chandrasekaran**, Chairman, Tata Group

"*My Life in Full* is an engrossing account of the life of an extraordinary woman, from her early days in India to the pinnacle of one of the world's iconic corporations, breaking many glass ceilings on the way. Writing from the heart, Indra Nooyi shares her authentic story of finding great business success and balancing a close-knit family. Inspirational and a must-read!" —**Nandan Nilekani**, Chairman and co-founder, Infosys, and Founding Chairman, UIDAI (Aadhaar)

"Indra Nooyi's life and career have been nothing less than inspirational. The passion with which she has approached every aspect of her life—her family, her role as a global business leader and even as a cricket enthusiast—shines through in her memoir, *My Life in Full*. Every reader will find in this book something that will stay with them—whether they are aspiring professionals or simply looking for wisdom gathered from a life well lived." —**Sachin Tendulkar**, former captain of the Indian national cricket team and member of the ICC World Cup 2011 winning team